'Essential reading. This is an accessible, coherent and up-to-date non-technical introduction to the fast-paced jargon-laden world of cryptocurrency. Comprehensive in scope, it provides lucid insights into the philosophy of money, the evolution of the major crypto-currencies, token economics, state-issued cryptocurrencies, regulation and much more.'
Professor William Knottenbelt, Director, Centre for Cryptocurrency Research and Engineering, Imperial College London

'A recommended read to understand how blockchain technology shapes the future of finance. Rhian Lewis tells an exciting story about the rise of cryptocurrencies while also explaining complex concepts behind them.'
Quynh Tran-Thanh, Chief Product Officer, CryptoCompare

'*The Cryptocurrency Revolution* is essential reading for anyone who wants to gain a clear understanding of digital currencies and blockchain-enabled economies and the way these rapidly evolving technologies are set to change our world.'
Jamie Burke, Founder, Outlier Ventures

'This book is an excellent overview, with topics including Bitcoin, other cryptoassets, as well as money in general and its regulation. It is not purely technical, but goes exactly as deep as needed to under-stand this inspiring and highly dynamic blockchain ecosystem.'
Professor Dr Philipp Sandner, Head of Frankfurt School Blockchain Center, Frankfurt School of Finance and Management

The Cryptocurrency Revolution

*Finance in the age of Bitcoin, blockchains
and tokens*

Rhian Lewis

KoganPage

First published in Great Britain and the United States in 2021 by Kogan Page Limited

2nd Floor, 45 Gee Street
London
EC1V 3RS
United Kingdom
www.koganpage.com

122 W 27th St, 10th Floor
New York, NY 10001
USA

4737/23 Ansari Road
Daryaganj
New Delhi 110002
India

Kogan Page books are printed on paper from sustainable forests.

ISBNs

Hardback   978 1 78966 570 3
Paperback   978 1 78966 568 0
Ebook   978 1 78966 569 7

British Library Cataloguing-in-Publication Data

A CIP record for this book is available from the British Library.

Library of Congress Catalogue Number

2020033333

Typeset by Hong Kong FIVE Workshop, Hong Kong
Print production managed by Jellyfish
Printed and bound by CPI Group (UK) Ltd, Croydon CR0 4YY

For Andrew and my parents, Colin and Diana

CONTENTS

ACKNOWLEDGEMENTS

So many conversations have inspired the writing of this book that it is impossible to list everyone here. However, I'd like to extend particular thanks to my interviewees, Teana Baker-Taylor, Citlali Mora Catlett, Richard Crook, Eden Dhaliwal, Helen Disney, Damien Ducourty, Ian Grigg, Barney Mannerings and Colin Platt for their time and insight. Thanks to Danny Weston, Raiomond Mirza and Martin Jee for conversations and feedback that informed some of the themes in this book.

The world of Bitcoin and cryptocurrency has introduced me to literally hundreds of amazing people whom I would not otherwise have met, many of whom have become friends. So thanks go to all Bitcoiners I have met in Berlin and London (and on Twitter!), especially Anna Kurth, Chris Davis, Magda, Neha M, Nind, Ali, Su, Michele, Ksenya and the Proof of Work tribe. Thanks to my CountMyCrypto co-conspirator Bruce Thomas, to YoperSouls Enrico Mariotti, Massimiliano Gerardi and Gianluigi Davassi for our adventures with Yope and Mamoru, and to my amazing colleagues at B9lab.

Thank you to Amy Minshull, Heather Wood and their colleagues at Kogan Page for believing in the book and helping me at every step. And a heartfelt thanks to all my friends who do not necessarily share my obsession with these topics but kindly indulged me and listened to me all the same, especially Clare Hyam and Amelia Harris.

Finally, I would like to thank the mysterious Satoshi Nakamoto, for giving me the reason to write this book.

Introduction

If you're reading this book, you want to know more about virtual currencies, perhaps because you want to know how your business can take advantage of this new technology, or because you want to understand the wider financial implications of cryptocurrencies and other blockchain-based payments.

If you are under the impression that Bitcoin is a niche payment mechanism used primarily for ransomware, it may surprise you to learn that in the 10 years of its existence, this original cryptocurrency has become so mainstream that you can pay your taxes with it or include it in your pension in some countries, buy it from a ticket machine at a Swiss railway station or buy a coffee with it.

Banks and financial institutions are investigating the use of Bitcoin's underlying blockchain technology to develop new asset classes as well as introduce streamlining and greater efficiency in their processes. Meanwhile, tech behemoths such as Facebook are introducing their own virtual currencies, while governments around the world are vying to be the first to introduce a truly effective national blockchain-based digital currency.

With cryptocurrencies and other forms of digital money moving firmly into the mainstream, it has become more and more important for individuals in all walks of life to understand the revolution that is currently taking place in payments and economics.

This book will help you understand why the current wave of virtual currencies is beginning to gain traction when similar innovations that were launched decades ago died a quick death. It will also demonstrate why those who claim that it is a fad will be proved very wrong indeed as this revolution in payments changes everything about the way we live and transact with each other.

Blockchain-based money also poses new challenges for individuals, corporations and governments, such as the ability of individuals to choose methods of payment other than national currencies such as the pound, euro, yen, yuan or dollar, and the extra powers that companies such as Facebook will gain if they become issuers of a type of virtual currency.

All this reminds us that the most notable feature of the digital currency revolution over the last 10 years has been the pace of change. Cryptocurrency years are like dog years, and the eye-watering speed of innovation in this sector means that ideas that sounded new 18 months ago have been quickly discarded in favour of new theories. Small startups with their flexibility and 'fail fast' approach have been well placed to take advantage of these exciting new technologies because larger businesses tend to have more layers of management, shareholders to keep happy and a greater desire to work with – rather than challenge – regulators.

In this book, you will be introduced to concepts such as tokenization, the differences between private and public blockchains, and some of the financial use cases for blockchains that do not explicitly have a currency attached to them.

People tend to talk about 'blockchain' or 'cryptocurrency' as though it is some kind of magic, monolithic entity, but in fact these terms encompass a whole lot of overlapping innovations that share certain attributes.

This book focuses mainly on digital currencies and payments, rather than the general application of blockchains for uses such as supply chains or voting. Payments are important because the internet has changed the way people pay for goods and services, and the fintech sector has become one of the most exciting and profitable areas of business innovation the world over. Besides, it would take a book many times the size of this one to cover the many different areas in which people and businesses are innovating with the help of blockchain technology.

If you are a programmer or IT professional who wants to take a deep dive into the nuts and bolts of how Bitcoin actually works, then this is probably not the book for you. People who are interested in Austrian economics and why Bitcoin works as 'hard money' will not read a better book than *The Bitcoin Standard* by Saifedean Ammous. And *Mastering Bitcoin* by Andreas Antonopoulos is in a league of its own for readers who want to understand at a deeper technical level how the Bitcoin network functions.

Neither will this book teach you to trade cryptocurrencies or lure you into buying the latest cryptotoken with a fancy name and the promise of becoming rich. If that is what you want to do, then that is fine. This book should help you see through some of the wilder claims made by some token startups, and help you focus on the things that matter.

However, for many people, the ideas behind this technology are the exciting part. I hope I can help you understand why ideas such as decentralization and tokenization are so important and fundamentally different from our current systems. And you will – I hope – gain an understanding of the potential impacts (many beneficial, others perhaps less so) for individuals, businesses and indeed society itself that may come about with the adoption of these new technologies.

References

Ammous, S (2018) *The Bitcoin Standard: The decentralized alternative to central banking*, John Wiley & Sons

Antonopoulos, A M (2017) *Mastering Bitcoin: Programming the open blockchain*, O'Reilly

1

What is money?

Cryptocurrencies like Bitcoin are a medium of exchange that is secured by cryptography. 'Medium of exchange' is simply a fancy way of saying 'money'. So before we can understand what cryptocurrencies are, and how they are used in business and in our daily lives, we need to think about what money is at its deepest philosophical level.

This may seem a completely ridiculous thing to say. We use money every day. As individuals, we store it in our bank accounts, we give corporations money in exchange for food, shelter, clothing and services, and we pass it around among ourselves, as gifts or loans. Businesses exchange billions of dollars' worth of money every day. But what is it, really?

Money is an abstraction of reality: a manifestation of the value of a physical item or unit of labour that is represented by something that does not have to have intrinsic value. You cannot eat a pound coin or a dollar bill. It will not keep you warm or give you shelter, but you are able to exchange it for food, warmth and shelter.

In the 21st century, we are so used to this abstraction that even an animal can begin to grasp the idea. One of my favourite YouTube videos features a dog in Colombia who had been adopted by a university. Over time, he watched the students go into the campus cafe and hand over notes in exchange for food. One day, the cafe owner was amazed when the dog trotted in, having collected a large leaf, and presented it, expecting a snack. Of course, he was rewarded with a treat, and has continued to 'pay' for his food with leaves.

We might chuckle at this cute behaviour, but the dog is behaving no differently from our ancestors. Over millennia, many different things have been used to store the fruits of our labour, from giant boulders, to shells, beads, banknotes and coins, and finally the digital representation of money that we use today. When we tap our debit or credit card on a contactless point of sale machine, we are performing exactly the same function as someone in 1000 BC who handed over a rare cowrie shell in exchange for grain and produce to feed his family.

The first forms of money

The concept of money has been around for so long that it is difficult to imagine what a money-free society would look like. If you cannot buy the products that you need, you need to grow, make, catch and process every single thing you need – or find someone who happens to want something you have so that you can swap it for something you want. And you need to grow, make, catch and process what you need exactly when you need it, as many things are perishable and cannot be stored indefinitely.

Even in the simplest hunter-gatherer or early agrarian economy, one person – or one family – could not produce every single thing they needed. One person might be fast and a particularly good hunter, while another might happen to have discovered a particularly pro-ductive source of wild fruits. As far as we know, the earliest human societies survived by sharing food in some informal sense. Some academics contend that as humans evolved into a less nomadic life-style and settled into an agrarian way of life, this informal sharing eventually evolved into a barter structure, where individuals would swap plants and livestock with some notion of equivalent value.

We know that people were using such barter mechanisms as far back as 9000 BC, but such an economy would have been unwieldy and inconvenient. Cattle are not easily divisible – at least while they are alive. And without some complicated tables to equate heads of cauliflower against chicken feet or bushels of barley, keeping track of who owed what to whom would have been impossible.

It is more likely that instead of evolving as a unit for measuring the utility (and hence value) of bartered goods, money developed as a medium for saving the value of one's labour so it could be accessed at a future date: a way of transferring value through time. If someone owes you something, this IOU is a form of saving for the future, or of insuring yourself against shortages or ill fortune. You work now to grow or collect food, and by exchanging some of it, you will also have food in the future. It is not overstating the importance of money to say that without it we would still be living in small communities, forced to grow and produce everything we needed.

Metal has been a popular choice for currency for thousands of years, as it is one of the most durable substances. As far back as 5000 BC, small metal objects were exchanged for agricultural produce, but it was not until around 1000 BC in China that this turned into a formal tradition. This so-called 'tool money' or 'spade money' is particularly interesting as it appears to represent the link between barter and symbolic money. Agricultural tools such as small shovels had been used for barter purposes, and at some point, they began circulating purely for symbolic purposes, eventually losing their original function. We can see this in the tool construction: some are sturdy enough to be used in the fields, while the later ones are small, lightweight and clearly designed to be used as currency rather than for agricultural work.

The Chinese were not the only civilization to use a form of money that represented real-life assets. As far back as 7500 BC, the Sumerians (in the area we now know as southern Iraq) used a book-keeping system based on clay tokens. In many cases, the tokens were made in a shape that accorded with the item they represented – an oval for a jar of oil, for example. Intriguingly, the Sumerians also produced a uniform token that represented a standard day of work.

Shell money

It is fascinating to see the different trajectories of these early currency systems, developing independently of each other. Yet there was one form of currency that appears to have been used in many different countries: shell money.

Shells, whether exchanged individually or worked into jewellery, were such a well-established currency that in some parts of western Africa, they remained legal tender until well into the 19th century. Similarly, cowrie shells were used as currency in some parts of India until the practice was abolished by the East India Company in the very early 19th century. And like the spade tools, the Chinese also made representations of cowrie shells that were used as currency. As humans spread across the globe and began to make contact and trade with each other, having some kind of universally accepted payment system was very useful, and shells fulfilled this function, at least for a while.

We often hear that money was 'invented' by the Lydians around 700 BC (in modern-day Turkey), but as we can see from the above examples, money was already being used all over the world in various different forms. However, the achievement of the Lydians was to develop the idea of minted coins – standardized circular metal tokens, stamped with lions or bulls to prove their authenticity, which had a set value. These coins were formally issued by the king, and thus we see the beginnings of currency supplies that are created and backed by a nation state.

Unsurprisingly, these coins became popular for trade across the Mediterranean. The fact that a specified value could be attributed to them was important for frictionless transactions. The practice of issuing coinage quickly spread, and by 400 BC, more than half the 2,000 or so independent city states in Ancient Greece were minting their own coinage, which was frequently used to pay soldiers as well as circulating among the population at large.

The supply of these coins extended far beyond Greece. The weight of silver or gold specified for each coin meant that the coins had an intrinsic value and could thus be trusted. Each city state minted their own coins with a different stamp, usually their city emblem, such as a particular flower or a bee. The certainty of being able to set aside one's wealth for future use brought about a fundamental change in society, encouraging mercantilism and wealth accumulation – and not everyone was happy with this. For example, the Spartans famously banned coinage and ruled that iron ingots were the only acceptable means of exchange.

Metal coinage was so overwhelmingly popular as a means of exchange because it fulfilled the five key properties of money: portability, durability, divisibility, fungibility and limited supply. It was portable (to a degree – large quantities of gold or silver coins are quite heavy), durable, divisible (smaller denominations of coins were introduced over time, so ordinary citizens could use them for small purchases) and uniform (fungible) – or as uniform as hand-punched coins could possibly be. And the supply was limited, not only by the authority of the issuing state, but also by the constraint of using precious metals such as gold and silver, which had to be mined.

Of course, there were also elements of trust involved in this process. Merchants who accepted the coins had to believe that they were not counterfeit – created out of a lesser metal, and punched to look exactly like their gold and silver equivalents. But it was not necessary to trust the issuing authority above and beyond this. Even if the state that issued the coinage ceased to exist for some reason, the underlying value of the gold or silver meant that the coin was intrinsically valuable.

Today, our money in the bank is represented by bytes. Even if we withdraw it from the bank, we do so in the form of paper notes and coins that are not gold or silver, and which have at best a notional value. So, how do we trust that these notes or coins are worth what their face value states, and how do we know that we will be able to spend them in future and that they will retain their value? The movement away from precious metals and towards trust-based currency (fiat money) is almost a more dramatic development than the invention of money itself, and has been the subject of great debates over centuries and even millennia.

Promissory notes and the beginnings of paper cash

The Chinese had been officially using standardized copper coins since around 200 BC. But at some point over the next few centuries, it became apparent that their use for large purchases was inefficient

– even strung together, they were bulky and heavy to transport and exchange. So merchants began to deposit them with trusted individuals, who issued them with a promissory note: a promise to pay the bearer. These promissory notes in turn became exchangeable and informally circulated among the mercantile community.

By around 1100 AD, the ruling dynasty, having noticed the economic advantages of printed paper money, decided to issue their own banknotes. Marco Polo noted this development with fascination, and wrote a detailed account in *The Travels of Marco Polo*. In mediaeval times, promissory notes were circulating widely among the merchants and banks of Italy, but it was not until 1661 that the first government-issued banknotes were printed. Interestingly, this happened in Sweden, rather than one of the Italian states, although this turned out to be a short-lived experiment. We will discuss this in more detail in Chapter 12, which deals with government-issued currencies. The conceptual leap, from a means of exchange with an intrinsic value (a gold or silver coin) to a piece of paper where you have to trust the issuing authority, cannot be overstated.

The stones of Yap

An interesting experiment in trust happened on the island of Yap, in Micronesia. Although Yap now uses modern, government-issued currencies, there is a parallel value system based around large limestone boulders, carved into discs, with a hole in the middle. Some of these are huge, weighing more than a car. There is no gold or silver on Yap – and there are no limestone boulders either. But hundreds of years ago, explorers from the island found these big rocks on another island. They began to transport them back to Yap, which was a painstaking and dangerous process. And here they were used as currency.

The reason economists love talking about Yap and its historic currency system is that while the boulders have a very limited supply, they often are too heavy to move physically. So the person who owns one of them may receive some goods, or a wedding dowry, or whatever, from someone else, and the ownership of the rock will change, despite the fact that it has not physically been moved. All such payment records are kept in the oral history of the islanders – and even rocks that cannot be seen are part of this trust-based currency system.

Local history has it that at some point, one of the canoes that was bringing one of the Yap stones back to the island sank to the bottom of the sea, along with the stone. Luckily, the islanders who were transporting it survived to tell the tale. The people keeping the oral records of stone ownership collectively decided that although they could not see or touch the stone, it definitely existed. And so the stone became part of the circulating currency supply, and could be used for payment in exactly the same way as the stones that stood outside houses in the island's villages.

The story of Yap is interesting because it tells us much about the human ability to extrapolate and to trust. While using boulders as money is ultimately a dead end in financial evolution as they do not fulfil most of the other criteria (they are durable, but not portable, uniform or divisible), the story shows us that people are able to accept the idea of value locked into something that they cannot always see or touch, and that such an item can be used for payment. Once we grasp this, then we can begin to understand the conundrum of the modern financial system. Most of us do not think at all about money, beyond whether we have enough of it, or whether we should be saving it.

And if politicians talk about it at all, it is often in the most simplistic terms, such as the 'pound in your pocket' phrase made famous by the late British Prime Minister Harold Wilson in 1967. Many people, even today, believe that national currencies are backed by gold, and that a banknote or a coin is a promise to pay the bearer the equivalent in precious metals.

Fiat currencies and the gold standard

Over the past few centuries, we have therefore moved from a system where the money itself had a value (gold or silver coins), known as commodity money, through a system of promissory notes that could be redeemed for gold or silver, known as representative money, to the fiat money system we have today, which is backed by nothing except the trust we have in our governments. Fiat money – 'money by decree', according to the Latin – does not always have to be issued by governments and can in fact be anything that is agreed as legal tender by consenting parties, but in practice it normally means the currencies that are issued by governments.

Different countries moved off the gold standard at different times. While the UK abandoned the gold standard in 1931, the United States stayed on it until 1971. There are attractions for governments in moving away from an economy that is backed by gold: economists such as John Maynard Keynes argued strongly for a centrally managed approach, in which the ability to print money in order to boost economic activity and thus to mitigate the severity of recessions were important weapons.

FIGURE 1.1   Milestones in the history of money

Sumerian clay tokens	7500 BC
Chinese spade money	5000
Lydians mint metal coins	700
Metal coinage widespread	400
Metal coinage in China	200
Use of promissory notes in China	1000 AD
Tally sticks used in UK	1100
First European banknotes	1661
UK leaves gold standard	1931
US leaves gold standard	1971
Bitcoin genesis block	2009

While the idea of printing unlimited money to spend on socially useful schemes or to prevent recessions might sound like a fantastic idea, there are many problems associated with this approach. Unless the supply of real-world goods and services matches the supply of money that people are using to buy these goods and services, a country may end up with too much money chasing the limited real-world assets. This means that the price gets bid up, and eventually you end up with inflation, where goods end up costing more and more over time. This makes people unhappy because their wage packets are fixed and they can buy less and less with the money they have. So they begin to demand higher wages, which in turn pushes up the price of the goods and services they produce. And thus a vicious circle is started, which is made possible by governments giving into the temptation to expand the money supply. There have been some extreme examples of hyperinflation in recent history, such as Zimbabwe, where in November 2008 the inflation rate hit 89.7 sextillion (10^{21}) per cent (Hanke, 2017), and a loaf of bread cost around 10,000,000,000 Zimbabwean dollars.

Hyperinflation in Germany

But probably the hyperinflation episode that is best known is the series of economic events that occurred during the Weimar Republic era in Germany – a textbook example of the way life can spiral out of control with alarming speed when governments decide to print money with a disregard for the underlying value of the economy the money represents. Anyone wanting to read more about the crisis in detail should read Adam Fergusson's excellent book, *When Money Dies: The nightmare of deficit spending* (Fergusson, 2010).

Germany's public spending to finance the First World War was completely unsustainable. There was an assumption that victory would enable them to pay off the public debt, but when they were defeated and had punitive war reparations forced upon them, this plan failed. After the war ended and the wave of patriotic support for the government had died down, it became apparent that the country was short of goods and awash with printed money. The government had managed (by closing the stock exchanges and banning the publication of exchange rates during the war) to disguise the complete imbalance between the circulating money supply and the value of the economy. Additionally, the weakening mark, whose value had fallen dramatically, was pushing up the price of imported goods. The worst affected were working people, who found that prices were increasing on a weekly or even daily basis, as more and more money chased fewer goods.

The falling exchange rate catastrophically increased the cost of the war reparation instalments, which were denominated in gold. The mark had fallen from around four to the dollar before the war to 330 just after it. But this was nothing compared with what was to come. In order to buy the hard currency they needed for the war reparations, the government decided to print more and more marks. This in turn devalued the mark even more, to the extent that by 1923 the exchange rate was running at 4.2 trillion to the dollar (Jung, 2009).

This was not simply a theoretical problem. The price of staple foods rose by 30–40 times between the beginning and the end of the war, with wages rising at a much slower rate. When products appeared on the shelves, they would promptly be bought as people feared they would be even more expensive in the following week. While the inflation was temporarily slowed down for a while, it returned with a vengeance between 1922 and 1923, when the price of feeding an average family of four rose from 370 marks to 2,600 in nine months. Iconic photographs of people taking a wheelbarrow of notes to buy a loaf of bread circulated, and at the height of the crisis, a trillion-mark note was issued. Although the currency crisis was eventually brought under control, it had caused social unrest, brought about political assassinations and sown the seeds of discontent that would sweep the National Socialists to power.

With the same monetary process having been repeated over and over since then in countries such as Argentina, Zimbabwe and Venezuela, it seems that governments have still not learnt the lesson that reckless money-printing is not just an accounting technicality, but can bring about unimaginable human misery.

Banks and systemic risk

It is not the money supply alone that has the potential to wreak havoc. In modern economies, imbalances of power have great power to destabilize the financial system, as well as stirring up anger towards those favoured by particular policies. Let us look at the banks in particular. In the UK, following the deregulation of the City of London in the 1980s, the financial sector boomed. Banks were freed from the constraints of a staid era when their prime purpose was to be the custodians of ordinary people's money, and instead they focused on the growth of departments that traded securities and commodities. They also hired teams of mathematicians and computer scientists to develop new financial instruments that were used to bet huge sums of money on predicting price movements – sums of money that were many multiples of the price of the original object they were betting on.

Generally, people who believe in the free market see deregulation as a good thing. And in many ways, it is. But these large banks were operating in something that was far from a free market because as long as the same institutions were holding people's money and also gambling billions in separate divisions of the same company, they were safe in the knowledge that however much they gambled, there was a safety net. And that safety net was the government.

The words 'too big to fail' entered the national vocabulary in the UK after the failure of Northern Rock. This was a hugely symbolic failure, as this particular bank had its roots in a small building society, which was a kind of cooperative venture founded to allow working-class people to save for deposits for their houses. However, as the bank's aggressive strategies grew, so did its vulnerability, and there was nothing homely or cooperative about Northern Rock by the time rumours began circulating in late summer 2007 that the bank was in financial trouble. Savers began to panic and formed long queues to withdraw their money. The British television news was full of images showing the police being called in to manage long queues, and as the bank's shares tumbled, £1 billion was withdrawn on Friday 14 September alone (Wallop, 2007), followed by nearly another £1 billion the following Monday. At this point, the British government was clearly worried that the panic would spread beyond Northern Rock. Savers in the UK – along with others in the European Union – are protected by a guarantee of some €85,000 or the sterling equivalent. But some savers had far more than that in the bank – for example, people who were in the middle of buying and selling houses.

Origins of the modern banking system

Modern banks work under a principle of fractional reserve banking, which means that for every sum deposited by a customer, only a very small percentage is retained by the bank, while the rest can be given to other customers as a loan. This effectively creates money and increases liquidity in the general economy, as from the original saver's point of view, their bank statement shows the original amount they deposited, while the borrower has access to almost the same amount (minus the small percentage the bank is obliged to retain as a reserve). Naturally, the bank makes money from these activities and they are also able to raise funds from elsewhere to lend to their retail customers, as happened in the Northern Rock case. So everyone is happy: the bank makes money and its shares go up, pleasing the management and shareholders. The saver may gain a small amount of interest on their deposit. And in return for paying some interest, the borrower has access to an increased pool of money which allows them to pay for a house or a car with wealth that they have not yet earned.

This commonly accepted state of affairs means that most people and most businesses are happy to transact via banks, using currencies issued by governments. Banks in the 21st century do a lot more than simply let customers make payments with their debit cards. Most are multinational concerns that make their money from trading a dizzying array of complicated financial products with each other. So, how did banks originate?

While archaeologists have found tokens used for such record-keeping in Mesopotamia and the Near East, which date back thousands of years BC, banks in their modern sense did not come into being until the Middle Ages. In mediaeval times, northern Italy was the world's epicentre of merchant activity, and it was mainly merchants rather than peasants or nobles who needed the services of a bank. These banks would not simply lend farmers money to be redeemed later in the year against a successful harvest, but would also provide the facility for merchants to trade with their peers in other cities or in other countries by issuing what were known as promissory notes. Previously, if merchants wanted to make money by shipping a product to a customer in a distant place, they would have to trust that the payment (in gold, silver or other precious metal) would be paid and transported back to them. Naturally, the temptation for the person shipping the product would be to steal some of this payment for themselves. So the valuable function provided by these early merchant banks was to provide liquidity by issuing a note known as a promise to pay. This was important as it introduced the idea of storing value for the future, as well as providing a mechanism for trust. The merchant who was selling the goods could trust the good name of the bank and be assured that the payment would, in due course, be redeemed.

Although our world is very different, modern retail banking works in exactly the same way. When we use our debit card or our credit card to buy our weekly groceries, the name of the bank on the card, and the validation mechanism of the point-of-sale machine proves that our bank is willing to transfer a particular sum of money to the shop on our behalf. In effect, the supermarket does not have to trust us. It just has to trust our bank.

Anyone who was old enough to have a bank account in the 1990s or earlier will remember a time when most store transactions were carried out with cash. If you wanted to go shopping, you visited the bank and either withdrew notes from the ATM or over the counter. But whether you are withdrawing money directly as notes and coins or are paying someone for their goods or services, the process is the same. The bank maintains a ledger – a record of the value that is attributed to your account – and when you make a payment to someone else or withdraw cash to spend, that value is subtracted from your balance.

The balances of all the bank's customers' accounts are stored in a database in a specialist data centre that has safeguards against outages and attacks. What is a database? It is simply a collection of data, stored in a structured way. The 'structured' part of this is important because if we know in advance that the information is stored in a particular order, it makes it easy to write computer software to retrieve this information. In the past, when ledgers were written on paper, there were all kinds of rules around who could access them and make changes to customers' balances. These rules and checks existed so that bank staff or potential fraudsters could not make alterations to customers' accounts and credit their own accounts instead. Various physical mechanisms existed that made it difficult to fake a ledger like this. Generally, transactions would be countersigned by other staff and in the early days of banking, wax seals were used so that records could not be retrospectively altered. To go back in time and completely falsify a ledger of this kind was not impossible, but it was a deterrent to all but the most determined thieves.

Now, imagine this record held in digital form. The easiest way to visualize it is in the form of a spreadsheet on your own laptop or desktop computer. Think about how easy it is to change a number or a character, with just one click of a key. Of course, records that are held by retail banks are not like a simple spreadsheet where one person can go in and delete data. To begin with, additions and subtractions to customers' balances are not done manually. Instead, other computer programs are permitted to interact with the ledger, making demands for payments to stores or for bill payments. And, to ensure that an unforeseen event such as a fire or an earthquake cannot wipe out the records of customers' accounts, the information is backed up to various data centres in multiple locations.

A complex system of authentication and protection exists to limit the people or the programs who can access particular data. Every country has its own regulations dictating how individuals' accounts are secured, to ensure that financial institutions such as banks cannot take risks with their customers' money. Additionally, there are over-arching international bodies that oversee payments made from one bank to another to prevent such activities as money laundering. Banks have internal compliance teams to make sure the rules are being followed, and are also visited by external auditors so that the general public has confidence in the banking system.

I am emphasizing the regulatory framework around retail banking to show that with a traditional technological model, where the data is entered into tables that are stored by the bank that owns that information, layers of high security are paramount – whether these secure layers are bomb-proof, flood-proof data centres with backup generators and backup generators for the backup generators, or detailed regulations specifying who can read or write to the data store.

Such regulation means that when you or your customers go into the supermarket and pay for your shopping and the exact sum is debited from your account, your bank has the responsibility of ensuring that this is done correctly and that the records are up to date. We choose a bank on the basis that we can trust them to do this, and in turn, we place trust in our governments and in the legal framework of the country we live in to ensure that our bank adheres to the rules.

We looked earlier at the chaos that can ensue when hyperinflation sets in. But it is tacitly acknowledged by governments that the optimum situation is not in fact a fixed money supply, but one that inflates, albeit in a controlled manner. While the general public might complain that their groceries are becoming more expensive, as long as the change is gradual enough not to provoke social unrest, inflation is good for governments as it allows them to borrow money denominated in their own national currency and then repay the same face value some years later – which is, of course, worth much less in real terms.

Gradual inflation can also be a vote-winner in property-owning democracies such as the UK, as house price increases have traditionally been seen to be a good thing. When house prices rise, consumers who own homes feel rich, even if they have only a very small amount of equity in the property, and the rest is held by the bank on a 30-year mortgage. Banks and mortgage providers are then able to encourage people to withdraw more and more of this equity to spend on other consumer goods, which in turn stimulates the economy.

The Northern Rock story, to no one's surprise, did not end with the bank collapsing and thousands of ordinary Britons losing their life savings. The prospect of retail bank contagion, where the majority of the population lost faith in the idea of fractional reserve banking and the queues outside Northern Rock were replicated outside more and more banks was just too catastrophic for them to contemplate. The future of the entire financial system would take years to reset if a public relations disaster of this nature happened.

So a decision was taken to underwrite the savings of retail investors. The bank was taken into state ownership and everyone's money was guaranteed. Gradually, confidence was restored and things went back to more or less normal. Of course, this was not the end of the Northern Rock story. Eventually, after much unnecessary government expenditure, what remained of the bank's retail arm was sold to Richard Branson's Virgin Money.

Private money and legal tender

What does all this have to do with cryptocurrency? I have talked about the fiat economy, the fractional reserve banking system and a British bank run at some length because it is important to understand the backdrop against which Bitcoin was invented, and also because it is important to understand the role played by trust in modern economies. It also raises the important subject of legal tender. As we saw with the stones of Yap, anything that is commonly accepted by people in lieu of goods and services can be classed as 'money'. But modern jurisdictions have a principle of legal tender, which defines what money must be accepted to settle financial obligations. As an example, imagine walking into a supermarket in a provincial town in the UK and trying to pay for your groceries with Polish zloty, US dollars or a gold necklace. The store would refuse to serve you – and they would be legally entitled to do so, as the only legal tender in the UK is the pound sterling.

Of course, people could accept other currencies on an entirely voluntary basis, as long as they could agree between themselves what constituted an acceptable exchange rate. But when a potential buyer offers a potential seller the specified price in legal tender, the seller is bound by law to accept it. Thus, if one individual offers to pay another using Bitcoin or other cryptocurrency, the recipient can choose to accept it and there is nothing illegal about this.

The legal tender in most countries is the national currency, although there are exceptions. The European countries which are in the eurozone accept the euro (which has a common value across all the participating nations) as their legal tender. And some countries who have an unstable national currency accept the US dollar instead of their own currency, or alongside it. For example, Panama accepts the dollar in addition to the Panamanian balboa, while some other countries have simply abandoned the idea of having their own currency. Ecuador and El Salvador are among a handful of countries who have adopted the dollar as legal tender, while some small countries bordering the eurozone have adopted the euro instead of their own currency. These include Monaco, Montenegro and Kosovo.

As we've seen from the countries where both the national currency and the US dollar are legal tender, it is perfectly permissible and workable to denominate more than one legal means of exchange. In fact, after Zimbabwe abandoned its own currency in 2009, it adopted no fewer than eight different currencies as legal tender, including the US dollar, British pound, Japanese yen and the national currencies of several bordering states.

So if you cannot compel someone to accept a currency that is not legal tender, what about the case where two people or two businesses voluntarily offer to use a different accounting unit? This is what is known as private money, and a couple of hundred years ago, such currencies were very popular. While there was a brief craze in the United States between the 1830s and 1860s for money issuance by private companies, the most common variant of non-state money was company scrip. Scrip is a catch-all term for a type of credit note. It can be issued by companies for any purpose, but its most common use is for payment – or part-payment – of employees.

In the 19th century, scrip and the practice of forcing employees to accept it, had a bad reputation because it was seen as another way for companies to exploit their workers. A typical use case would be a mine or a logging company, far away from the nearest town, where the workers would be issued with a paper note that could be exchanged for food and other goods at an on-site shop owned by the same company. Unscrupulous employers, with a local monopoly because workers could not buy food and drink anywhere else, would often seize the opportunity to charge extortionate prices and make even more money out of their already underpaid staff. Or religiously inclined entrepreneurs would use the chance to inflict some well-meaning paternalism on their workers and issue them in scrip that could only be used at a company shop that did not sell alcohol. For whatever reasons, the compulsion and/or exploitation gave the use of scrip a bad name and it was banned or restricted in many countries. Although as recently as 2008, Walmart workers in Mexico campaigned against receiving part of their wages in Walmart vouchers (Reuters, 2008).

Different countries have very different attitudes to private money. While banknotes issued by private banks in Hong Kong are available from ATMs, private money has been restricted in the United States since the National Banking Act of 1863 established a national currency. Shortly before this law was passed, there had been as many as 8,000 different currencies, all competing with each other. With little in the way of governance, there was nothing to stop a bank or a currency issuing notes to people and then closing down and skipping town, making the notes totally worthless.

But, just like in Hong Kong, the idea of currencies that are not issued by the state is a fascinating idea that refuses to die. Ultimately, it is all down to whether the money is usable – in other words, whether people are prepared to accept it as payment. Even in the heavily regulated UK, there are some local currencies that circulate within communities. The idea is that an accounting unit that is accepted only in a certain area will help keep money flowing around the community, rather than putting it straight into the hands of multi-national corporations. Among British local currencies, the now defunct Totnes pound and the Brixton pound are perhaps the best known. It is important to understand that such currencies are pegged to the national one, something that can also happen with cryptocur-rencies. We will look at so-called 'stablecoins' in later chapters.

But something doesn't have to look or feel like cash to be money. As we saw in the examples of the shell money and the Yap stones, anything that is exchangeable for goods and services can be counted as something that is currency, even if it is not legal tender. This looser definition means that there are hundreds of different private payment methods circulating today, even in heavily regulated economies like the United States and the UK, for example: reward point schemes, Air Miles, taxi meter tokens, iTunes or Play Store vouchers, or gift cards for different stores. All these are – in a sense – money, and if you doubt that people think of them in this way, consider the situation of some content creators who prefer not to receive payment through their bank account and instead opt for Amazon gift vouchers, or even for a public wishlist from which donors can buy items. Some even look like traditional money! Dishoom, the upmarket chain of Indian restaurants, mints its own 'coins', each of which can be used to pay £10 towards the bill for your meal.

FIGURE 1.2   Dishoom coins, issued by the restaurant chain

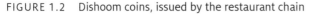

Modern examples of private money

Computer games often have their own currencies. Second Life Linden Dollars or Clash of Clans Gold are used within the game as closed-loop tender within the virtual confines of the game, and governments have been slow to legislate these currencies, even though economic activity from popular games leaks into the real world all the time. But computer games apart, probably the most commonly used 'alternative currency' today is reward points. These have been around for many decades, pre-dating the digital age. In the UK, the popularity of Green Shield stamps reached its height in the 1970s. In Japan, which in many ways lags behind the rest of Asia in embracing new fintech ideas, there is an entire culture built around the reward schemes tied to different convenience stores.

While most reward points, such as Air Miles, are issued in return for the customer purchasing something, some schemes offer other ways to earn them. Think of medical insurance schemes where walking a certain number of steps each day earns you cinema tickets or free drinks or healthy snacks. Effectively, the user is being paid in a unit of account that is denominated in points rather than in the national currency. If a coffee is worth ten points rather than five dollars, then it can be argued that the reward scheme points are operating as money.

Gift cards certainly operate as cash equivalents, as police in America's opioid-affected areas know. Stealing gift cards to pay for drugs is an unfortunate side-effect of the drugs epidemic that has ravaged lives, but it shows that in particular areas and communities, for specific purposes, anything can be used as cash.

When Bitcoin first started hitting the headlines, most people were bemused by the idea that something that was purely digital and which lacked any kind of backing by physical goods could have value. In the next chapter, we will examine exactly why this happens, but it is important to point out here that Bitcoin was not the first time that a currency that existed solely in cyberspace – 'magic internet money' – had been used for transactions. Multiplayer games such as Second Life or World of Warcraft sometimes had their own currencies, as mentioned above, which were used to purchase assets in the game, and which occasionally bled through into the physical world, blurring the boundaries between digital and physical worlds.

About 10 years ago, there was a spate of articles in the mainstream press, most of whose staff were not gamers, describing the sophisticated in-game economy of Second Life, where gamers could buy and develop land and businesses within the game. The idea that people could speculate in a virtual world and earn a currency that could then be exchanged for fiat cash was a difficult one for many people to comprehend. Just as would later happen with Bitcoin, analysts and commentators asked the rhetorical question: are such payments legal? The fact is that paying with any currency or object you choose is perfectly legal – as long as the recipient agrees to accept it, and as long as it is not designed to launder ill-gotten gains or evade tax. The fact is that transactions with cryptocurrencies, precious metals or gaming currencies do not require special legislation to make them legal, because they were never illegal in the first place.

However, Linden Dollars, or Clash of Clans Gold or any of the other virtual currencies used by gamers were as far from cryptocurrencies such as Bitcoin as the latter is from shells or stones. Not only were these tokens issued by a central authority, in this case the game manufacturer, just like a state-backed fiat currency, but their supply could be increased at a whim. Just like the in-game assets they purchased, they remained the property of the game creators, and reams of small print specified exactly what you could or could not do with them. Ultimately, if you broke the rules, or if the game manufacturers simply decided to issue another currency, you lost your money.

Along with virtual currencies used in games, another trend that has emerged in the last 10 years is the rise of the challenger banks and new payment methods introduced by technology companies. The West was slow to embrace new developments, bound by the glacial pace of change of its legacy banking system. In contrast, Chinese consumers were well served by innovations such as mobile payments, for example Alipay (launched 2009) and WeChat Pay, launched five years later. These services profited from lenient regulations and a large customer base, and WeChat Pay had 100 million customers within just one month of its 2014 launch. In contrast, mobile payments did not really start to take off in the UK, the United States and continental Europe until 2016–2017, with the result that for some people, their first experience of mobile payments was with Bitcoin, rather than with their bank's mobile app.

In this chapter, we have seen how money and our attitudes towards it have changed over the centuries. It is against this backdrop that we will consider in the next chapter the evolution of Bitcoin, the world's first and most important cryptocurrency.

References

Fergusson, A (2010) *When Money Dies: Germany in the 1920s, and the nightmare of deficit spending, devaluation, and hyper-inflation*, PublicAffairs

Hanke, S (2017) Zimbabwe hyperinflates again, *Forbes*, 28 October. Available from: https://www.forbes.com/sites/stevehanke/2017/10/28/zimbabwe-hyperinflates-again-entering-the-record-books-for-a-second-time-in-less-than-a-decade/#64d126093eed (archived at https://perma.cc/TE9B-R2GB)

Jung, A (2009) Germany in the era of hyperinflation, *Der Spiegel*, 14 August. Available from: https://www.spiegel.de/international/germany/millions-billions-trillions-germany-in-the-era-of-hyperinflation-a-641758.html (archived at https://perma.cc/295H-7JCW)

Reuters (2008) Court outlaws Wal-Mart de Mexico worker vouchers, 5 September. Available from: https://www.reuters.com/article/mexico-walmex/court-outlaws-wal-mart-de-mexico-worker-vouchers-idUSN0546591320080905 (archived at https://perma.cc/JS6Z-G98B)

Wallop, H (2007) Northern Rock customers withdraw £1bn, The Telegraph, 14 September. Available from: https://www.telegraph.co.uk/finance/2815806/Northern-Rock-customers-withdraw-1bn.html (archived at https://perma.cc/4MWJ-WM9Z)

2

The first 10 years of Bitcoin

On 31 October 2008, something happened that was noticed by probably no more than a few hundred people, but which was unique in its significance. An unknown person – or team of people – working under the pseudonym of Satoshi Nakamoto released a white paper with a technical proposal for a digital money system. It was of little interest to anyone outside a very small community of cryptography enthusiasts and computer scientists.

While many of these may have been excited by its potential, perhaps few would have predicted the headlines, wild rumours, hysteria, admiration and hatred that this idea has precipitated in the intervening years.

Donald Trump has made it clear he is not in favour of Bitcoin. Warren Buffett once described it as 'probably rat poison squared'. Jamie Dimon of JP Morgan once famously stated that he would fire any traders he discovered were trading Bitcoin (while JP Morgan was quietly developing its own virtual coin). As we will see in Chapter 11, India talked openly about banning all cryptocurrencies and make trading or mining them a criminal offence. In contrast, former British Chancellor George Osborne had a publicity photo taken buying £20 worth of bitcoin at a (Bitcoin) ATM (Griffith, 2014), and Portugal became one of the more recent countries to make a public pronouncement on their position on cryptocurrencies, promising a regime of low – or even no – taxes.

So what is this innovation that has polarized public opinion to this extent? Bitcoin is nothing more than software, publicly and freely available. When an individual downloads the software and begins running it, they are able to join a peer-to-peer network that allows payments to be sent around the world without the participants having to trust a bank or other financial service company. Billions of dollars' worth of value is kept in this network, and people all around the world use it to store and transfer millions of dollars every day. Yet no one owns this network, and no one promises to keep your money safe or restore it if it is lost. As the meme states, there is no CEO of Bitcoin!

It is notable because these lines of code – developed on a voluntary basis by a handful of unpaid programmers – allow money to be transmitted around the world as securely as a banking network that takes hundreds of thousands of people to develop and maintain.

Think about all the huge companies, with their data centres, their teams of security specialists and the millions of dollars they spend guarding their customers' and their own data. And yet, still people are hacked, forfeiting their money, their livelihoods, their reputations, their identities – sometimes even their lives. Think back over the last five years to the Equifax hack, the Facebook hack, the Marriott hack, the British Airways hack, the OPM hack, the Ashley Madison hack, the Bangladesh Bank hack, which cost that country's central bank more than $80 million. And then consider Bitcoin. No one has sat in a meeting room and decided to spend millions of dollars protecting Bitcoin from hackers. No one has gone out and hired brilliant security engineers to ring-fence precious data and hide it from view. No one has hidden away the source code from prying eyes and restricted the reading of the code repositories to only the developers working on it.

And in more than 10 years, no one has ever hacked Bitcoin – barring an early incident in 2010, in the very early days of the network, in which the network underwent an emergency hard fork (separated into two separate networks, more on this in Chapter 8) following a code fix. This may sound like sorcery, but it is not. Bitcoin is not secured by organizations, by legislation, by secret data centres or firewalls. Bitcoin is secured by its own code and has no need of anything else. There are many reasons why this is possible, but we will look at three of them in turn: transparency, distribution and mathematics.

Let's first talk about transparency. As I mentioned in the preceding paragraphs, in the past, companies hid away their source code. The reasoning went that the more a hacker knew about how the system worked, the more able they would be to hack it. This is obviously true in many ways. But it means that customers and regulators have to trust the expertise of a tiny subset of engineers who happen to be working on the bank's software. Bitcoin – and other open-source cryptocurrencies – turn this logic on its head. If everyone can see all the transactions that happen on the network in real time, and can also inspect the code and even contribute to the code themselves, then the network can be constantly monitored by everyone in the whole world who is interested, not just a tiny subset of engineers working for one company.

Distribution – or decentralization – is a crucial element of the Bitcoin network. In a traditional system such as a bank, remember that the information is stored in a centralized place, albeit with secure backups. This makes sense in a situation where you have to protect this data, keeping it away from prying eyes. But now imagine a situation where the data is copied over and over again so that it exists in multiple places and anyone can keep a copy of it. I often use the example of a Google spreadsheet to illustrate this. Of course, it is an imperfect analogy, as Google spreadsheets are kept in one centralized place (in Google's cloud infrastructure) and can be changed at any time by anyone who has access, so obviously there are fundamental differences between Google spreadsheets and Bitcoin. But there are some parts of the analogy that are helpful.

Imagine you belong to a community group in your town or village where everyone contributes some money each week. The traditional way to do this used to be for a treasurer to collect the cash and keep the records in either a paper ledger or a spreadsheet. But then imagine that the same community group decides to use a Google spreadsheet instead. Everyone in the group can see the changes that are made, and it is no longer necessary to trust that one person will do the right thing. Of course, if the treasurer wanted, he or she could still defraud the other members by removing the cash from the bank account or from the envelope under their mattress. But the record-keeping would at least be transparent, showing who had contributed what amount and on what date, so that restitution could be easily made in the case of a fraud.

A public blockchain such as Bitcoin shares these same principles of transparency and distribution, meaning that any transaction that is made on the public network can be viewed by anyone, anywhere in the world, who either has a copy of the blockchain or who accesses a type of website showing a block explorer tool (more on that later). Just like our hypothetical Google spreadsheet, the Bitcoin blockchain lists the value transactions that come into or go out of a particular address on the network. These are not quite analogous to a bank account, as one person may have many addresses. But it can be useful to think of them in terms of a bank account or a wallet. Keeping the ledger up to date shows the value that is associated with each address, and tells the network whether value can be sent from this address to another address, or if there are insufficient funds.

Resilience and high availability

Decentralization offers many more benefits than simply allowing people to view the data that has been generated. A network that is spread across many different computers, owned by many different types of people and which is located in many different locations in the world has high resilience and high availability, compared with a data centre in one or two places.

So, what do these expressions 'resilience' and 'availability' mean? As we all know, computers can go wrong. Hardware can fail, or there can be a problem with the software that can either cause the computer to go offline or stop the software performing as it should. A particular company may find it is targeted either by serious hackers or by teenage mischief-makers who want to disrupt its operations, steal data or take it offline. Or natural disasters such as earthquakes, lightning strikes or floods can damage physical infrastructure, such as the buildings where data centres are located.

Sometimes availability outages are planned, to allow software upgrades to take place. I'm sure you have seen warnings from time to time on your banking apps and banking websites warning you that services may not be available between particular times because of the need to do maintenance. Occasionally, these outages are longer than planned. In the UK in 2018, a data migration by engineers at the TSB bank did not go as expected and customers were locked out of their accounts for a week (Monaghan, 2018). This is the opposite of resilience and high availability.

To visualize this more clearly, imagine one computer and how vulnerable it is to attack. Now imagine 10 computers, in 10 different countries. And a hundred, and a thousand, and so on. The number of computers running Bitcoin software fluctuates as people decide to join or leave the network, but it is usually around 10,000. Various websites exist where anyone can view the location of the computers running the network.

This probably sounds like a recipe for total chaos: thousands of computers running the same software and keeping the same records. How on earth do they manage to agree with each other? And what is there to prevent bad actors from simply falsifying the records, making fake transactions and ensuring that they end up with lots of money in their accounts that does not belong to them? Mathematics is the answer. In the same way that an old-fashioned clerk's office might have their clients sign documents, place them in envelopes and then bundle them together into a bigger envelope, which was sealed with a wax seal to prevent tampering, every transaction in the Bitcoin network becomes bound to the previous transactions in such a way that it requires a lot of computing power to alter it. A group of trans-actions is packed into a block, which is then linked to the block before it in a chain of blocks, right back to the first block in the chain, on the day when the particular blockchain was begun. To perform the calculations that allow the blocks to be bound together in this way takes a great deal of computing power, but it is this mechanism that allows us to have confidence that the balance in a certain person's account is really there and has not already been spent.

Expending this amount of computing power (and by extension, electricity) is expensive. Very few people would do this unless there was something in it for them (although there are some altruistic people or organizations who feel that having a global, censorship-proof currency is so important that they support it at their own expense). So, public networks normally have some kind of reward that is given in compensation for this record-keeping process. And this is called 'mining'.

The single source of truth

Before Bitcoin, people who wanted to use electronic cash had to use banks, because this was the only way they could make sure that the money that was being sent to them had not already been sent to someone else. If you receive a dollar bill, a pound or euro coin or even a gold sovereign, you know that it has a certain value attached to it and that (as long as it is not counterfeit) no one else can have the same note or coin that you own.

This is known as the 'double spend' problem. In other words, if Alice sends Bob a digital coin that represents a certain value, how does Bob know that Alice has not already spent this by sending it to someone else? Bitcoin solves this problem by ensuring that all of the thousands of computers on the network have an up-to-date record of all the credits and debits that have been applied to the address from which Alice is trying to send money. You notice that I do not say 'Alice's address' because Bitcoin addresses are not like a bank account, where there is a one-to-one relationship.

We refer to this commonly held record, which is shared between all the computers on the network, as a 'single source of truth'. Imagine the chaos that would ensue if one month or one year later, the data record of all payments that had been made were suddenly to be rewritten or to disappear. We need to know that this will not happen. Thus we cannot accept the word of just one or two computers in the network that a transaction has happened. When a payment has been made from one Bitcoin address to another, this transaction is broadcast on the network.

Rather like when we go to the supermarket and make a payment on our debit card, this transaction is sent over the internet. But unlike a bank payment, where the destination is our own bank's network, a Bitcoin transaction is sent out on to the Bitcoin network where it goes into a pool of unconfirmed transactions, and other computers on the network will retrieve it from there and attempt to include it in a block and add it to their own version of the network's history. But before it can be added to the unbroken chain that makes up the history of Bitcoin transactions, right back to the beginning of time, each node on the network will check the transaction to see if it is valid. Once the transaction is in a mined block and a sufficient number of miners have validated this block and mined on top of it for a number of times, one can reasonably safely presume that it will be permanent.

The need for multiple confirmations before a transaction is verified may seem clunky and nerve-racking for people who are used to a traditional banking scenario where the bank can tell a retailer immediately whether a person has enough money in their account for the transaction to be valid. But it is also a necessary trade-off that keeps the network secure. If multiple different, unrelated entities can confirm that a transaction conforms to the shared history of the network, then it must indeed be a valid transaction.

Bitcoin fees versus banking fees

So, how much do we expect to pay to use this highly secure, global network? Bear in mind that it is possible to send Bitcoin to anyone in the world, even if they do not have a bank account. The simple answer is that, unlike your bank, where you may pay a flat fee to run your account, or where you may have free transactions in your own country but must pay to transfer money to people in other countries, there is no fixed fee for a Bitcoin transaction. Instead of paying your bank to keep the records of your account safe and send money to other people on your behalf, you need to pay a small amount to the Bitcoin miners who keep the records of the network up to date.

How small is a 'small' amount? The first interesting thing to note is that the transaction fee is not directly linked to the value of the transaction; the fee is simply a payment for your transaction's position in the queue of transactions waiting to be included in a block and mined. Bitcoin mining software picks up a transaction from the pool of unconfirmed transactions based on various criteria – and one of these is the potential fee that can be earned by including it in a block. So it makes sense that the higher the fee, the more attractive your transaction is. End users typically use wallet software – either on a laptop or a phone – to send transactions, and wallets will calculate the current default transaction fee that will result in your transaction being confirmed in a reasonable amount of time. If you need a payment to go through urgently, it can be worth manually adjusting the fee upwards.

Although there have been spikes in Bitcoin fees in the past, a quick glance at a transaction fee calculator at the time of writing shows fees may be as low as a few cents. There is no upper limit on the size of a Bitcoin transaction, and no limit on fees. In early September 2019, one transaction was recorded for just under $1 billion. The sender paid a fee of just $690. At times of high demand, you may need to pay more to get your transaction through, but the interesting thing to remember is that the fee is related to the size of the transaction (in bytes), not the value of the transaction.

Hence you could send several million dollars from the UK to someone in the countryside in Botswana or Indonesia, far away from the nearest bank, for a few cents (although sometimes if there is suddenly a lot of demand on the network, it can clog up, and fees can rise to many dollars). When one considers that the alternative for many people who do not have bank accounts is to pay Western Union or similar remittance companies up to 30 per cent of the value of the transaction, one begins to see the attraction of a public blockchain network like Bitcoin.

What protects the balance of our Bitcoin address? The equivalent of writing a signature in blockchain terms is using a private key. You can think of this as being a very special type of password. A private key does not exist in isolation. It is always paired with a public key. This is not a new idea. People who work in technology have been using this system to verify their identity and gain access to systems for decades. A private key is a long sequence of seemingly random letters and numbers, like this: L5bUo3o6djwoC9hmk6toc8hJnjzq1aecJHQsBpffjKD3QrXTTYzA. This is a real Bitcoin private key, but it has not been used.

You can safely give other people the public key so they can send funds to it or make you the beneficiary of some other transaction. But what they cannot do is derive your private key from this sequence of characters, in the same way that providing someone in the real world with your mailing address does not give them the power to let themselves into your house (unless they are Amazon, in which case it is a different story…). Of course, if you are using a mobile app or a website or something else that interfaces with a blockchain, this process of key storage and signatures happens without you being aware of it. We will learn more about key pairs later in this chapter.

Cypherpunks and their vision

Now we have begun to gain a basic understanding of how blockchains work, and what some of the advantages are, let's look at cryptocurrencies in more detail. There is so much mythology around Bitcoin that sometimes it is hard to separate fact from fiction. As with the invention of the internet and any other transformative technology, there have been people who saw the potential of particular inventions before the tools and frameworks were in place to make this possible.

As far back as the 1980s, there were people looking ahead to a networked future and imagining what an internet-enabled world would look like. One only has to read the science fiction of the time – books like William Gibson's *Neuromancer* trilogy – to see the vision of the future that was circulating in people's minds. The ideas were there: we just had to wait for the technology to catch up. This was a time when computers could still fill a room, and when punchcards were still used for data processing. Mobile phones had yet to be invented and while universities had access to dial-up modems, the latter did not start appearing in homes until the 1990s. Computers were many times less powerful than today's machines: for example, the computers on board the Apollo spacecraft that took men into space and then to the moon had less processing power than a smartphone that you would find in the average person's pocket today. The first bank ATMs only began to appear at the end of the 1960s, and even in the 1980s it was common to go into a bank and withdraw cash over the counter, and to use cash or cheques for any day-to-day payments, so envisaging a world where electronic payments were universal was a revolutionary idea.

In the early 1980s, a pioneering computer scientist called David Chaum wrote an academic paper that suggested a mechanism for secure electronic payments, using a new type of digital signature (Chaum, 1983). He later founded a company called DigiCash to further these ideas and turn them into commercial reality, but left the company before his vision could be realized. Chaum's breakthrough was to solve the so-called double-spend problem. His paper was the first indication that an electronic form of money could be invented that could be used just like cash for private purchases, but would provide the assurance that it really belonged to the person who was offering it.

His system was designed to work very much as a secure alternative to cash, but as something that was complementary to the existing banking system. While it was groundbreaking work, it needed the participation of banks and regulators to incorporate it into the financial system, but differences of opinion with the central bank in the Netherlands meant that this never happened (Grigg, 2014). It has been theorized that perhaps governments were not keen to put powerful, privacy-enhancing cryptographic tools into the hands of normal citizens.

But this idea of taking back control of one's digital identity and privacy through cryptography was something that one group of people felt very strongly should be a priority. The people who advocated this were known as cypherpunks, and the technical roots of the idea that had first been espoused by Chaum gradually turned into a movement, with the cypherpunk mailing list starting up in 1992. Cypherpunks were a loose association of individuals who foresaw our current problems with data privacy decades before anyone else. You can read a copy of their manifesto here: https://www.activism.net/cypherpunk/manifesto.html (archived at https://perma.cc/BW4B-38BZ).

A useful analogy for encryption, which is used so widely that it has been part of the common syntax that is used to talk about it, is the idea of physical keys and locks. A piece of information, rather than being locked in a physical safe box, is transformed in some way that means it cannot be read or understood. Only the person who has the key to the puzzle can undo this transformation – 'decrypt' – and restore it to its readable state. It is rather like a message sent in invisible ink where only one person has the solution that can be poured over the page to reveal the words underneath.

Many types of encryption work on a system of key pairs – one public and one private. This is not something new that came along with Bitcoin: computer scientists have been using systems like this since Phil Zimmerman invented PGP (Pretty Good Privacy) in 1991. Key pairs work on the basis of asymmetric encryption. Each pair consists of a private key and a public key. It is safe to show someone the public key and they will not be able to gain access to your private key because they cannot guess your private key from knowing the other one. It is rather like baking a cake and trying to extract the original eggs that went into the recipe, unbroken.

Figure 2.1 shows an example of a key pair, which can be used for all sorts of things, including by programmers to access and some-times change repositories of code.

Developers can safely hand over the public key so they can be given permissions to the code without disclosing their private key, which lives on their own computer. When they access the repository where the code is kept, instead of entering a password, the public key that they have entered is matched with the private key that is securely stored on their computer. Because of our tendency to be lazy and not always follow the best practices when choosing passwords, using keys is regarded as far more secure than using usernames and passwords.

FIGURE 2.1   Example of an SSH key pair

Private Key

```
-----BEGIN RSA PRIVATE KEY-----
MIICWwIBAAKBgGBB8EMGiSJgvkznlm86C/1Cr2QS+v3CJIfNcKkZLS82n62TBo7I
naKmDGH4/JYyQI31gwncjPDuR8j19n6bZoHMyfgocpA3Rwh0n2YMe375XHgj63a0
w+/nKaHQ2R3HgU6h/dJXnnNcYJjYbQ1byRYCsF7ZHAqkXmkEZQiek0MIAgMBAAEC
gYAGKhLd5/w+RF3LhQVASEJeTLf4u7JxL86xF7oASkl3fZMKRaEk4boeoW2nlI9w
evV/GOr0Zbhs8YWNXBsWDpOo5f92P3AU98bLNMCM7PkDt5R+NqfOxBpeTPta9VO6
JdybEdLP1j431z04grTecuuIVcbxIVfAddKxzyns90LLPQJBALeDyLWhYHhGKusR
oNRXyOJqmRMfUqQBl8zg+/3oD6ut1mIzNEY1W2Idtm5GOPqOo4x6CwW/5sFs76VV
j6IKAMsCQQCGRxXWGTKuu2RdtmnQwUhh9P6nB3bXqRfmNtcwaBcZpS2QX9WSK2vw
7NWcJSxZSwW9viOQbUrEUFhhk9NunP3PAkAqvS9eVaIhAL54FpftPDCVwpu5316g
wX8z9OXbIVOc+RRntGMIQsHwnNji38nfWJ7wVXABu8qjG5rIV5/m7gt3AkBcsx6E
HAk9T+IOOOx8TbNmzPgw35pP8FCrghi1NmccMUhvb3nF22w9e4NMtO0VCBICmC6g
epMvTDh3xNImfwNJAkEAtu8/JbowPYEnr0QKXfNO2DWM1FNLtruRJ8UR1t3CbqNe
/QAZds8InJE085CpiNoBW4wftiCYpkVpcatqJNK1rg==
-----END RSA PRIVATE KEY-----
```

Public Key

```
-----BEGIN PUBLIC KEY-----
MIGeMA0GCSqGSIb3DQEBAQUAA4GMADCBiAKBgGBB8EMGiSJgvkznlm86C/1Cr2QS
+v3CJIfNcKkZLS82n62TBo7InaKmDGH4/JYyQI31gwncjPDuR8j19n6bZoHMyfgo
cpA3Rwh0n2YMe375XHgj63a0w+/nKaHQ2R3HgU6h/dJXnnNcYJjYbQ1byRYCsF7Z
HAqkXmkEZQiek0MIAgMBAAE=
-----END PUBLIC KEY-----
```

Double-entry and triple-entry accounting

Encryption, of course, allows us to do more than access repositories of computer code or simply verify our identity. It can also be used to verify and timestamp records, via a system known as triple-entry accounting. Let's first return to the 15th-century merchants we described in Chapter 1. When we talk about innovations that have changed the world, we tend to think about things we can see in the physical world, such as steam engines, monoplanes or spacecraft. But there was an invention that evolved during the 1400s – it was recorded by Franciscan friar and mathematician Luca Pacioli in 1494 but not actually created by him – that enabled capitalism to spread beyond the mediaeval city states of Northern Italy and brought about the world of modern commerce that we know today. That invention was double-entry accounting, where every credit and debit must be entered in two places in a ledger, offset against each other so that the sum of all credits equals the sum of all debits.

Financial cryptographer Ian Grigg explains its significance thus:

> Double-entry accounting created a method whereby you could trace transactions and separate out errors and frauds. With single-entry accounting, you can't tell the difference between an error and a fraud. So what happens is that you end up getting robbed by your accountants... which basically means in a world of single entry a firm can only be as big as a family because you need your family to run the accounts. With double-entry accounting you can employ professional accountants, and because of the traceability of errors and fraud within them they can do their job properly.
>
> Double-entry accounting is thought to have caused the rise of the great trading houses in the Italian city states in the 1400s. It made possible the growth of those trading networks because accounting was essential for managing the business as it grew beyond a certain size.

Grigg is known for inventing Ricardian contracts in the mid-1990s – human-readable documents that are cryptographically signed so that legal commitments can have their intent locked into each transaction they touch, and then reflected by software to the user – and for his work on triple-entry accounting, a system in which all accounting entries involving outside parties are cryptographically sealed by a third entry. While triple entry was built into the original Ricardo system developed by Grigg and Gary Howland, it was 2004 before Grigg realized the true significance of it – 'I was having a long think in bed about the nature and impact of the cryptographically sealed entries, and the fact that the record was the transaction, and I had a Eureka moment' – and in 2005 he published his paper, 'Triple Entry Accounting' (Grigg, 2005). He explains:

> Triple entry is basically the ability to take one of those entries and cryptographically seal it as the transaction you have conducted with your counterparty.
>
> You want some honest player to also have another entry so you can resolve disputes. You have the same entry, cryptographically sealed

between yourself, your counterparty and some third party. The magic of triple-entry is that at the micro level we can say 'I know that what you see, I see', as Richard Gendal Brown would say.

So we now have a very accurate record, and we also have the ability to start sharing transactions between firms. That means we can now do transactions which are much more solid between firms, and this means our accounting can actually become self-auditing. So this level of proof between firms means that you've now got this ability to do more trustworthy activity with firms because the numbers cannot lie: they are the same numbers that the other firm has, and therefore there's this defence against rewriting history.

The Bitcoin white paper

The Bitcoin white paper written under the pseudonym of Satoshi Nakamoto (Nakamoto, 2008) has been much analysed and republished, and it is notable for its brevity and elegance, as well as the lack of breathless bravado and overhyped claims that would tarnish the reputation of the cryptocurrency ecosystem in years to come. In the white paper, Nakamoto proposed an entirely new monetary system, out of the control of nation states or banks. The vision was a grand one: the record of all financial transactions made on the network would be duplicated on all the different computers that participated in it and anyone with a computer could take part. The code would be published publicly so that anyone could analyse it, look for security weaknesses and run it. Nobody would own the code.

Nakamoto's idea would not have worked without some kind of incentive. No one but a small handful of enthusiasts would have downloaded and run the software without expecting some kind of reward. And if the network had been maintained by only a small group of enthusiasts, then that would be a centralized system, like a small-scale version of a typical bank. The original vision of Bitcoin was that the network would be run and sustained by those who wanted to send money using it. Not only would the users be responsible for keeping access to their balances secure (by keeping their private keys away from prying eyes), but they would also be responsible for keeping their own copy of the transactions that make up the Bitcoin blockchain, and for validating new transactions. And for that work, they would be rewarded by earning tokens, the native currency of the network. Nakamoto called these tokens Bitcoins.

Understandably, the publication of the white paper caused something of a stir in the cryptography community – and also, presumably, among the government operatives whose job it is to monitor these conversations. Some have even theorized that perhaps Bitcoin itself is an invention of a shadowy government agency, and that it has been a Trojan horse all along.

The conversation continued among the mysterious Nakamoto and various other contributors and collaborators, until an announcement was made on 3 January 2009 that the network was live. The first Bitcoin block had been mined! Although we still do not know the identity of Bitcoin's mysterious creator, it seems that Nakamoto wanted to be clear about at least one of the objectives behind the new currency. Encrypted in the genesis block was a newspaper headline from British newspaper *The Times*. The headline read: 'Chancellor on brink of second bailout for banks'.

Not only was this headline embedded in the very first block of transactions that were validated by the very first node on the live Bitcoin blockchain, it sent a message to the world that unlike the banking system, which had come so close to catastrophic failure in 2008, here was a type of money which could be used and maintained independently of this system.

Of course, the message that Satoshi Nakamoto sent in the genesis block was not one that was immediately picked up by the world at large. It was not until 11 January that block 78 became the first to be mined by a known individual other than Satoshi, the late Hal Finney. No one knows for sure how many people were following developments at this point, but we can assume the number was in the hundreds rather than the thousands.

The rewards that are generated for discovering a block of transactions during the 'mining' process are set to halve automatically at predetermined intervals. At Bitcoin's inception, the rewards for

FIGURE 2.2   Bitcoin issuance schedule

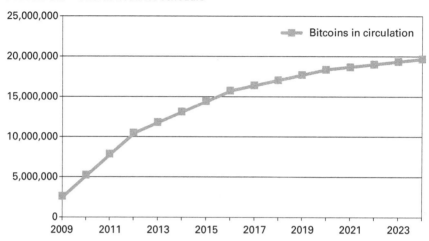

mining a block and solving the complicated mathematical puzzle that proved your computer had expended the power required to validate the transactions in the block, stood at a huge 50 bitcoins per block – less than one US cent's worth at the time – or $1 million at 2017 prices.

In a later chapter we will examine tokenomics: the balance of incentives and penalties, combined with token numbers and issuance schedule, which can signal the appropriate exchange value of cryptoassets. In the case of Bitcoin, it is sufficient to know that the total number of Bitcoins that will ever exist is just 21 million, and the number mined is set to decline dramatically over time. The last Bitcoin will be mined some time in 2140, yet already more than two-thirds of the tokens that will ever be produced are in existence. Figure 2.2 gives an idea of this schedule.

In the very early days, with so few participants and little or no demand for the tokens, it was so easy to mine Bitcoin that anyone with an ordinary computer was able to mine and be rewarded, thus reinforcing the trope that these miners were nerds sitting in their parents' basements, playing with imaginary money.

Throughout 2009 and 2010, little changed. More people heard about Bitcoin, and whether they were all genuinely enthusiastic about the freedom- and privacy-focused principles of an independent currency network or simply curious participants who had heard by word of mouth about this magic internet money, the network slowly grew. Even then, the majority of network participants were either technologists of some description, or particularly determined non-techies who had the patience to plough through web pages of instructions and who were determined to master the command line.

Bitcoin pizza – and the mystery of Satoshi Nakamoto

Slowly, growth began to snowball. The first forums aimed solely at discussing Bitcoin sprang up, with Bitcointalk.org becoming the most popular. *Bitcoin Magazine* was founded in 2012. And – perhaps most importantly – people began to trade Bitcoin, and to use it to pay for goods and services. In January 2009, when the first bitcoins were mined, their monetary value was as close to zero as it is possible to be. By October of that year, their first 'official' price was quoted: 1,309.03 BTC to the US dollar.

By May 2010, when programmer Laszlo Hanyecz famously bought two Papa John's pizzas for the princely sum of 10,000 bitcoin (or $95 million at 2020 prices), each coin was valued at 0.0025 cents each. We do not know who Satoshi Nakamoto is or was, or even if 'he' was a collective of many people, but that must have been a truly thrilling moment, seeing their invention used exactly as they had intended. In less than two years, a new currency had been created and people trusted it enough to use it to swap for assets that had cost real dollars.

Anyone can choose to become a miner and join the network, or conversely, to leave the network. If the core development team makes a change to the codebase that is seen as non-viable in some way, the miners are entirely free to decide whether they download the new code or stick with the old. In other words, it is a voting mechanism in which people or organizations vote with their feet. No one can compel a miner to upgrade their software, and the decision to upgrade or not is frequently one that is riven with debate and argument over the possible consequences. But ultimately, mathematics wins out and it is Bitcoin's inbuilt incentive mechanism that determines who joins and who leaves the network. Miners may often take decisions that seem principled or altruistic. But goodwill often masks hard business logic, and if a mining operative sees that a particular upgrade is proving contentious among normal users and that they will suffer economically because of the bad feelings and negative reputation that will be generated, they will often back off what seems to be the most immediately profitable option in favour of playing the longer game. We have been talking a lot about miners, but in the last 10 years, one of the most notable things that has happened to Bitcoin is the concentration of its production among massive, power-hungry mining farms run by companies and away from the individual or hobbyist.

One has to be careful about making pronouncements based on suppositions about what a certain person thinks when they are not around to clarify their intentions. This is very much the case with Satoshi Nakamoto, to whom Bitcoin enthusiasts and analysts tend to ascribe whatever political or commercial motivation most closely matches their own. It is remarkable that Nakamoto has managed to conceal their identity for so long, particularly as those inhabiting their domain are known for their technical and analytical skills.

What we do know is that since 12 December 2010, Satoshi Nakamoto effectively ceased to exist. It is as though this person, or people, dropped off the face of the earth, leaving no clue or trace of their presence. The 700,000 or so bitcoins that they are thought to have mined remain untouched to this day. There have been many theories about their identity. Nick Szabo and the late Hal Finney have both been named as individuals with the technical ability and motivation to have been Nakamoto. In later times, an Australian computer science professor called Craig Wright has on various occasions claimed to be Satoshi Nakamoto, and won the backing of some major figures within the Bitcoin scene, but his attempts to 'prove' that he was indeed Bitcoin's creator have been so far little other than stage-managed publicity stunts that ended up not proving anything.

Presumably, Satoshi Nakamoto was prescient enough to foresee that if they revealed their identity, simply saying that they were stepping back from development or involvement would not be sufficient.

Every utterance would be analysed for hidden meanings. With the market cap reaching $326.5 billion at its December 2017 peak – more than the GDP of some small countries – there is a lot at stake, and there would be commercial pressure from powerful entities to make decisions that benefited them.

Two of these decisions are particularly controversial: scalability and difficulty. Scalability essentially means the ability of the network to transition from a small platform processing thousands of transactions to a processing network that can verify thousands of millions of transactions. To use a concrete example, the current capacity of the Bitcoin blockchain is fewer than 10 TPS (transactions per second), while the Visa payments network can process 15,000 in that time. This is a statistic that people who are sceptical about cryptocurrencies often quote, yet as we shall see in later chapters, this is an oversimplification of the issue.

The emergence of Bitcoin exchanges

Tales emerged years later of ordinary people who had made – and often lost – fortunes during these early months and years. As the price trajectory in the early days was so shallow, some people mined for a while and then gave up, bored when it ceased to be a novelty. Some lost their private keys and others lost entire computers. In late 2017, the story of James Howells hit the news when his local council in Wales turned down a request to search a landfill site where the hard drive of his old computer was dumped, containing more than 7,500 bitcoins (Kobie, 2017). Others became excited when the price hit $10 and spent their earnings on gaming gear. Every early Bitcoiner has some kind of story like this.

As more and more people became interested in mining, the difficulty of generating bitcoins increased beyond the point where the CPU (central processing unit) in a normal home computer could mine efficiently without costing more in electricity than it was earning in Bitcoins. By 2010, people had begun to mine with GPUs. Graphics processors have far greater computational power than CPUs, and thus began the arms race in hardware and power consumption that would change the face of Bitcoin mining. At first the change was subtle. The activity was still mainly carried out by individuals, in their own homes – or sometimes at their workplaces or universities, without the knowledge of these third parties.

As time went on, the difficulty increased beyond the point where most home computers could process the transactions, and the business of validating transactions and generating new bitcoins was taken over by companies who were able to set up large factories of specially cooled racks of purpose-built computers. The excess heat that was produced meant that it was more cost-effective to set up in cooler environments – and some wacky ideas circulated, such as the radiator that would allow home users to mine bitcoins while enjoying the by-product of free heating. By now, exchanges had begun to spring up, providing a service for miners who did not want to hold on to their bitcoins but preferred to exchange them for fiat currencies. Unregulated and often run by enthusiasts who did not necessarily have the technical expertise to hold other people's assets, Bitcoin exchanges were a risky place to store your cryptocurrency.

One of the sorriest sagas in Bitcoin's chequered history started in February 2014, when a Tokyo-based exchange called Mt Gox suspended trading. It was later announced that 850,000 Bitcoins had gone missing, and proceedings dragged on until March 2019, when the former head of Mt Gox, Mark Karpeles, was given a suspended sentence for falsifying data, but found not guilty of embezzlement (Dooley, 2019). It served as a salutary lesson for Bitcoiners to trust themselves rather than third parties, and the maxim 'Not your keys, not your bitcoin' was frequently quoted. Unsurprisingly, further thefts and hacks have continued to plague the ecosystem, but despite such exchange hacks, the Bitcoin blockchain itself has never successfully been tampered with.

Some miners chose not to cash out into fiat currency and preferred to spend their coins directly. At first these sales were arranged privately, between miners and other people who wanted to acquire some bitcoin and had something to offer in exchange, but did not want to get involved themselves in mining. Bitcoin ownership was

FIGURE 2.3   2010 advert from the Bitcointalk forum

◇ **Re: Looking to Buy a 4GiB Flash Drive**
  June 24, 2010, 06:39:22 AM

Flash Pen Kingston Data Traveler 101, 4GB Cyan = 2200 BTC (shipment not included)

http://www.amazon.com/Kingston-DataTraveler-101-DT101Y-Yellow/dp/B001C9P5T4
(in the picture is the yellow one. also, it's brand new, never used)

SOURCE www.bitcointalk.org (archived at https://perma.cc/J5TN-Z9JE)

now spreading beyond those who maintained the network. Early advertisements for gaming goods sold for Bitcoin looked like the example in Figure 2.3.

Not everyone was able to see the potential when they were offered payment in Bitcoin. The singer Lily Allen was once offered 'hundreds of thousands of bitcoins' to perform a gig in Second Life and turned it down. Although she is not exactly poverty-stricken, she remarked wryly that she had missed her chance to be a billionaire and followed up by tagging her tweet about it with the hashtag #idiot.

The revolution gathers pace

Transaction volumes were also rising. Interest had now spread far beyond those with sufficient technical interest and enthusiasm to mine. Cryptoanarchists, libertarians and others who lacked a label but felt sufficiently disaffected by the creeping surveillance in modern society had become energized and excited about this new technology and found a new cause to rally around. Meetups began in cities all around the world and enthusiasts made videos, which they put on YouTube to show new Bitcoiners how to safely store and spend their newly acquired digital currency. The World Crypto Network released videos that attracted thousands of views. The LocalBitcoins website matched buyers and sellers, using a reputation system to guard against scammers and keep their users safe. This provided a crucial on-ramp for new users in the early days of Bitcoin and hastened adoption by making acquisition accessible for casual observers.

Individuals and companies began working on ways that would make Bitcoin usage simpler and more appealing for non-technical people. As ever, there were disagreements over this, as ease of use was rightly seen as a compromise that would inevitably lead to greater centralization and the need to trust someone or something. What is meant by this? In simple terms, the necessity to keep a copy of the entire Bitcoin blockchain, verify your transactions yourself and keep your private key offline or otherwise stored in such a way that it could not be compromised is something that is not an easy undertaking. You do not have to be overly technical: just capable of following instructions and understanding details. But in an instant-gratification society, it was becoming apparent that this initial cost of time and effort was proving a barrier to adoption.

Some companies went ahead and created successful businesses by obscuring the difficult stuff that goes on under the hood of Bitcoin. Some companies effectively became Bitcoin banks, providing their users with a website and/or mobile app through which they could buy and spend Bitcoin without having to go through the technical steps of running the software on a computer. Other wallet developers went down a route that was closer to (presumably) Satoshi Nakamoto's original vision, providing Bitcoiners with an easily navigable user interface while educating them at all steps of the process about what was happening, and providing a mechanism for them to hold their own private key. The best of these made their code open-source, providing a checksum that people could verify before downloading and opening the wallet application. (A checksum is the output value of a particular hashing algorithm. So the developer would run this algorithm against the contents of their program and when the end user does the same thing, the values should match.) Not only is this an ethical move; just like Bitcoin's code itself, it is a way of crowdsourcing security.

Phone wallets were popular with new users, and a common sight at meetups in 2013–2014 was the sight of people helping would-be Bitcoiners to acquire and spend their new coins. Mobile wallet functionality such as built-in converters between fiat and bitcoins, and the ability to scan a QR code instead of copy-pasting or typing out a long key were all popular user features, which made the whole process feel more accessible.

Transacting face to face: the growth of Bitcoin meetups

Still, the hardest part in those early days was getting hold of bitcoin if you did not have the motivation to mine. And mining – now the difficulty was rising – had started to become concentrated in the hands of commercial companies with the resources to hire or buy acres of warehouse space in locations where power was cheap and temperatures cold, in order to mine on an industrial scale. Iceland was popular, as were some of the less populated northern states of the US – and China, of course.

Mindful of possible new regulations specifically targeting Bitcoin, exchanges excluded customers in many locations from buying or selling the cryptocurrency in exchange for fiat. Some early enthusiasts had begun to take jobs or sell services where they were paid using Bitcoin, but their main problem was how to subsist in a world where fiat currency was king. The few businesses and places that accepted Bitcoin were a lifeline, and they were rewarded by the enthusiasm of early adopters.

Room 77, a bar in Berlin's hip Kreuzberg district run by long-time freedom advocate and cypherpunk Joerg Platzer was one of these, hosting monthly Bitcoin meetups, which later became wildly popular, attracting many more enthusiasts than the bar could hold. Room 77 holds a particular place in the rich folklore of Bitcoin's history because it was the first place in the world where you could walk into a bricks-and-mortar premises and use cryptocurrency to pay in person for a physical good. Soon Room 77 was joined by other bars and restaurants in Kreuzberg in accepting Bitcoin, thanks to Platzer's evangelical efforts.

The trend was an international one, and Twitter soon filled up with photographs of Bitcoiners in New York, San Francisco, London and any other major city you could care to mention, brandishing glasses of beer or other drinks paid for with their mobile Bitcoin wallet. Bear in mind that while China had mobile phone payments at this point, most Western countries did not, so for many people, the sheer novelty of being able to pay for anything with your phone was a heady feeling.

If you didn't earn bitcoin in some way, getting your hands on it was still an issue, unless you were lucky enough to know someone who would sell to you in person (those lucky people who had the foresight to add their public key to their social media profile in 2013 and earned tips ended up doing well for themselves). This was more common than it sounds, and in fact some of the early meetups were oriented towards people buying and selling for whatever they considered a fair price to be. In these early days, there were so few people interested in what most considered to be a wacky craze, that people got into the spirit of things, and much fun was had. The BXB meetup (Bitcoin Exchange Berlin) was, for example, renowned for its boards advertising the Bitcoin price, and its dealers in bowler hats. Meetups in other cities in other countries may have lacked the bowler hats and boards, but still offered the chance to buy bitcoins in person.

But many newcomers' first bitcoin came out of a machine like the one in Figure 2.4.

In October 2013, the world's first Bitcoin ATM, a Robocoin, was installed in a coffee shop in Vancouver and many others swiftly followed. Today there are more than 5,000 all over the world. Bitcoin ATMs – or correctly, Bitcoin vending machines, as some countries required them to be called – tended to cluster first in areas populated with tech-savvy Millennials: Shoreditch in London had a handful of machines before the south west of England and Wales had even one. And in huge countries like the United States, most people would not have had access to them without taking a flight. Sometimes the people who set them up were not particularly Bitcoin enthusiasts; just people who saw a good business opportunity. People often complained about the high commission rates, but running an ATM was not particularly easy money: they tended to go offline and needed to be rebooted manually, or the wallets ran out of bitcoin and needed to be reloaded. The latter, at least, could be done remotely. And most importantly, they provided an easy target for thieves, as they had cash

FIGURE 2.4   SatoshiPoint Bitcoin ATM

SOURCE Nind

inside, so they had to be situated inside existing premises, such as a
cafe, bar or shop. The premises owner would have to be persuaded
that a constant footfall of people seeking magic internet money was
good for business.

A single bitcoin was not worth a few cents any more. In 2013, the
price had briefly hit the heady heights of over $1100, and – drunk on
the possibilities of this new paradigm – Bitcoiners everywhere were

persuading family and friends to buy into this miracle that would not only presage a brave new world where government and corporate corruption were no more, but which also promised riches beyond their wildest dreams.

What could possibly go wrong? In late 2013, the price crashed to less than $200, where it hovered before cautiously edging its way back up to the $600 mark. Of course, while the technology itself is the most interesting thing about Bitcoin, it is the price that makes the headlines. In 2017, the excitement was palpable as the price accelerated upwards and upwards, smashing through $10,000 (and causing many enthusiasts to throw $10k parties around the world) right up to the giddy heights of close to $20,000.

The price began sliding soon afterwards, but a Rubicon had been crossed. Bitcoin was nowhere near a household name, but it was functioning as a means of payment and a store of wealth. Added to this, people had begun to see other possibilities in blockchain technology, the data structure that underlay Bitcoin.

If you wanted to buy cryptocurrency before 2011, Bitcoin was your only choice, but all that was to be transformed beyond recognition. As with every other advance in the cryptosphere, things were changing on a daily basis. As we will see in later chapters, the pendulum has since swung back to the idea of Bitcoin as the one network to rule them all, but six or seven years ago, many people truly believed they could build a 'better Bitcoin'. The next chapter will take a look at these efforts, and at the beginnings of the new cryptoeconomy that would coalesce around them.

References

Chaum, D (1983) Blind signatures for untraceable payments, *Advances in Cryptology Proceedings*. Available from: http://www.hit.bme.hu/~buttyan/ courses/BMEVIHIM219/2009/Chaum.BlindSigForPayment.1982.PDF (archived at https://perma.cc/F2M2-ML89)

Dooley, B (2019) Bitcoin tycoon who oversaw Mt. Gox implosion gets suspended sentence, *New York Times*, 15 March. Available from: https://www.nytimes.com/2019/03/15/business/bitcoin-mt-gox-mark-karpeles-sentence.html (archived at https://perma.cc/8ATN-JFRD)

Griffith, G (2014) George Osborne makes a quick buck on £20 Bitcoin buy at Level 39, *CityA.M*, 6 August. Available from: https://www.cityam.com/george-makes-quick-buck-20-bitcoin-buy/ (archived at https://perma.cc/TF3D-PLCH)

Grigg, I (2005) Triple-entry accounting. Available from: https://iang.org/papers/triple_entry.html (archived at https://perma.cc/2Q9Y-Z2T6)

Grigg, I (2014) A very fast history of cryptocurrencies BBTC – before Bitcoin, *Financial Cryptography*, 8 April. Available from: http://www.financialcryptography.com/mt/archives/cat_metafc.html (archived at https://perma.cc/WTD5-3CCG)

Kobie, N (2017) This man's lost Bitcoin are now worth $75m – and under 200,000 tonnes of garbage, *Wired*, 1 December. Available from: https://www.wired.co.uk/article/bitcoin-lost-newport-landfill (archived at https://perma.cc/Q5D5-3F4F)

Monaghan, A (2018) Timeline of trouble: how the TSB IT meltdown unfolded, *Guardian*, 6 June. Available from: https://www.theguardian.com/business/2018/jun/06/timeline-of-trouble-how-the-tsb-it-meltdown-unfolded (archived at https://perma.cc/Z8L6-HCV4)

Nakamoto, S (2008) Bitcoin: a peer-to-peer electronic cash system, 31 October. Available from: https://bitcoin.org/bitcoin.pdf (archived at https://perma.cc/T5YS-KJB4)

3

Litecoin, Ethereum and a tidal wave of altcoins

To anyone working in the traditional financial sphere, the subculture that surrounds cryptocurrency can be a surprising, entertaining – and sometimes alarming – space. Social media has been a crucial element in spreading the word and stimulating debate around the technology, politics and ethics that intertwine around the subject. Twitter, Reddit, Telegram, YouTube and, to a lesser extent, Facebook all have their own communities, and the feeds of user comments on crypto exchanges (popularly known as the 'trollbox') and crypto-focused online publications such as CoinDesk, Cointelegraph, Decrypt Media and The Block provide opportunities for cryptocurrency developers and marketers to promote their ideas and their coins.

Tribalism between supporters of different cryptocurrencies is a huge element of the grass-roots cryptocurrency scene, as distinct from the venture capital firms and fintech companies who now make up a large part of the ecosystem. So, where did this maelstrom of memes, rivalries and wild rumours originate? The first focal point, other than the developer IRC (internet relay chat) channels, was the BitcoinTalk message board founded by none other than Satoshi Nakamoto in 2009. Since the last known post by Nakamoto in December 2010, this forum has been run by other moderators, many of them anonymous. BitcoinTalk began as primarily a technical resource, where people could discuss cryptography and mining practicalities. However, as time went on, more and more users joined who were not necessarily techies, and sections devoted to economics and other less technically focused topics began to spring up.

The idea of alternate cryptocurrencies – or 'altcoins', as they were swiftly tagged – was already the subject of experimentation immediately after the birth of Bitcoin. Many of these first attempts were scams destined to live for just a few weeks before being consigned to rest among the thousands of others listed on cryptocurrency graveyard sites, but some were serious attempts, inspired by Bitcoin, to create interesting decentralized technologies that could be used for global payments and potentially support other features. In this chapter, we will look at some of the major players of the time. Note that there are literally thousands of coins that this chapter does not have space to cover.

Litecoin: silver to Bitcoin's gold

In October 2011, a thread appeared in the Alternate Cryptocurrencies topic on BitcoinTalk announcing the launch of a new currency called Litecoin. Remember that the Bitcoin code is open-source, so there is nothing preventing someone copying it and creating their own identical currency. Trying to reproduce Bitcoin itself would be pointless, as Bitcoin has what is known as the network effect – brand recognition and an established history. But Charlie Lee, a young software engineer who had worked at Google, saw the opportunity to create 'silver to Bitcoin's gold', as Litecoin is often described.

In 2011, Lee forked the Bitcoin source code – but it was not a straightforward copy-paste. Lee had a vision for his coin, which was to focus on the idea of a network in which many people would participate, and in which payments would be cheap and fast. Unlike Bitcoin, which has been programmed to have just 21 million tokens by the time the last one is mined in 2140, Litecoin has 84 million. And unlike Bitcoin's 10-minute block time, Litecoin has a block time of 2.5 minutes. The puzzle that has to be solved for proof of work is still a necessary part of the process, but Litecoin uses a different algorithm (Scrypt, as compared with Bitcoin's SHA-256). One of the primary differences between the two algorithms is that solving Bitcoin's puzzle can be made easier and quicker by throwing more and more computing resources at it and running the computations in parallel. For the Scrypt algorithm, there is no advantage in this brute-force approach of simply increasing computing power, and all computations have to be run one after the other, so it does not penalize people who do not want to invest in expensive hardware and specialist premises where the huge racks of computing power have to be cooled. By allowing more people to participate in the mining process, so the argument went, it would encourage currencies to remain decentralized rather than allowing companies with large amounts of computing power to take over.

Litecoin had appeal for would-be crypto buyers who wanted the thrill of owning a 'whole coin', and also the lower mining difficulty meant it was easier for amateurs to get involved again. As time went on, more coins were launched based on the Scrypt algorithm, and hardware manufacturers did brisk business selling specialized mining equipment cheaply to hobbyist miners. Something else doing brisk business was the aforementioned Alternate Cryptocurrencies board, where threads prefaced with [ANN] (for 'announcement') proliferated like mushrooms in a damp forest, marking the launch of yet another Bitcoin imitator. While it was not compulsory for a new crypto to have what was colloquially known as an ANN thread, it was the first port of call for any new miners or traders who wanted to ask technical questions, cast aspersions or out-and-out troll the coin creators.

The principles that had inspired the creation of Bitcoin were less important to many of the new breed of coin creators than the chance to make a quick buck. Developers offered their services to entrepreneurs who wanted to copy the Bitcoin code, make a few quick tweaks and give their coin a memorable name and a marketing spin. There were even websites such as CoinGen where you could generate your own altcoin with nothing more than a snappy name and some arbitrarily chosen numbers for supply, issuance schedule, etc. New cryptocurrencies used clever marketing to attract attention from would-be traders, and memes and in-jokes became a huge part of crypto culture. Thus, it was no surprise that one of the best-known currencies started as nothing more than a meme.

The cult of Dogecoin

In 2012 and 2013, the internet was awash with a classic meme – a Shiba Inu dog giving great side-eye, captioned with thought bubbles in which he communicated his bafflement with the human world in Comic Sans. The misspelling of dog as 'd-o-g-e' was a pre-existing meme dating from some years before, but by 2013, generally the word 'doge' suggested a Shiba Inu with a Comic Sans interior monologue.

In December 2013, two individuals on different continents who met in a cryptocurrency IRC room (Jackson Palmer, a marketing professional at Adobe in Sydney and Billy Markus, a programmer from Oregon) decided to make their own fun cryptocurrency based on the Doge meme.

Dogecoin was to be an easy-to-mine, high-circulation, low-value altcoin designed for tipping and generally spreading joy. After launching on December 6, 2013, the coin's early days were marked by extreme volatility, rising 300 per cent in the first month, and subsequently crashing 80 per cent. By now, cryptocurrency exchanges were listing cryptocurrencies other than Bitcoin, and popular new entrants into the crypto ecosystem such as Dogecoin were very heavily traded.

As any would-be cryptocurrency developer would acknowledge, having a strong community to encourage the adoption of your coin is key to the success of any altcoin or token. Dogecoin had – and even now continues to have – one of the strongest and most colourful communities in crypto, one that presented (in public, at least) a kinder face than any other. Dogecoin enthusiasts were quick to rally around good causes such as raising sponsorship for the Jamaican bobsled team's Olympic bid in 2014 and collecting funds in Dogecoin for the World Water Day charity effort. Because of the native token's low value – a tiny fraction of a cent – it was extremely popular for developers who wanted to create tipping applications and extensions.

One can never underestimate the feelgood factor of receiving an unexpected goodwill payment via social media – even if the value is minuscule.

We cannot mention Dogecoin tipping applications without digressing into the subject of the much-loved DogeRain app, an integral part of the Berlin crypto scene, which went global. DogeRain was a simple but genius idea – you kept the app open on your phone and random strangers opening the app all over the world would automatically and randomly tip you. Then you could do the same in return. Topping it up only cost a couple of euros or pounds or dollars or whatever, and you had the instant gratification of seeing the names and locations of your fellow Dogecoiners, on whom your bounty was literally raining, to the sight and sound of falling doges and Comic Sans WOWs. You could even get together with friends and have an impromptu DogeRain session where you shook your phones in unison and made it rain DogeCoin. In the heady early days of the cryptocurrency revolution, it filled everyone with a warm feeling of optimism and possibility, uniting crypto enthusiasts across the world. It was community-building at its best.

However cute and heartwarming the Dogecoin story might be, it still presented an opportunity for making money. I've tried to keep my own personal journey out of these pages to make the book as objective as possible, but I will confess that I learnt my lesson about keeping cryptocurrency in web wallets and exchanges – anywhere you don't hold your own private key – the hard way. But I didn't lose Bitcoin in a hack. At the risk of compromising any credibility I may have left, my first experience of crypto-theft was with the Dogecoin web wallet DogeVault in spring 2014, when it was hacked and $56,000 of the currency was stolen. I think I lost $100 in total, but it was a lesson that paid for itself many times over. This was a reminder – as was the high trading volume of Dogecoin on the many crypto exchanges that were springing up – that it was not really possible to have a cute and fun altcoin that was not ultimately all about the business of making money.

Dogecoin co-founder Jackson Palmer has been a vocal and ethical voice in the crypto community calling out bad and risky behaviour where he sees it, which has not always made him popular. He disassociated himself from Dogecoin in 2015, openly stating that he had not made a cent from the launch of the altcoin. His reason? The toxic community. People are generally in cryptocurrency either because they want to make money or because they want to change the world. Sometimes the two intersect, but in the case of Dogecoin, the former faction won.

I remember speaking to people in 2014 who were utterly convinced that Dogecoin was the currency that would change people's minds about crypto, and would be the first cryptocurrency to cross over into the mainstream. Some coin-holders were evangelical about it, going around persuading retailers to accept Dogecoin in exchange for goods and services – no mean feat when only a tiny percentage of the population had even heard of Bitcoin.

Exchanges and trading tools in the early days of crypto

In 2013, many people who traded altcoins did so via strictly unofficial channels, such as dedicated forums on Reddit, or via IRC. But where Bitcoin went, other cryptocurrencies followed, and soon there were crypto exchanges springing up all over the place: Cryptsy, MintPal, Poloniex, C-CEX.

Along with exchanges came coin listing sites, altcoin block explorer sites and others, which promised technical analysis but were often just a front for people to shill their own copy-pasted cryptocurrencies. Along with the crypto news sites mentioned above, information aggregators such as CoinMarketCap and CryptoCompare displayed the latest prices for this strange new breed of digital money.

Some traders were experienced forex traders and old hands at charting and analysis. Others were chancers and even schoolchildren, all keen to make their mark – and make their fortune. Preposterous claims about profits were made on a daily basis. Traders garnered tens of thousands of followers on Twitter, posting live updates about their huge trading wins. Some of these claims were true, others doubtless exaggerated. But one thing all these people had in common was tenacity. In the early days, trading cryptocurrencies was not simply a matter of transferring dollars to an exchange via your bank account: most exchanges would only accept Bitcoin, so first you had to acquire Bitcoin and then familiarize yourself with how wallets worked so you could send it on to the exchange.

The early exchanges were all unregulated, often set up by enthusiasts who were as much chancers as many of the people who traded on them. They were often big characters – although this did not always presage honesty. Very much in the spirit of Bitcoin's creators, there was total freedom to trade, no matter who you were or where you lived. This was especially important for traders in the United States, where only 'accredited traders' are deemed knowledgeable enough to take these sorts of risks in the traditional markets. All you needed was Bitcoin to send to the exchange and a modicum of knowledge about the different cryptos.

Of course, it was not that simple. Some fortunes were made, but others were lost. In February 2014, there were just over 100 different altcoins available that were being actively traded on exchanges, but these were shortly to become thousands. Just like in the most barbaric of horse races, coins fell at every hurdle. Every week, new coins were launched and old ones disappeared from view, potentially to re-emerge months later with a new development team. Unbound by laws like insider trading regulation, and anti-boiler-room rules, a whole subculture of boom and bust lay largely hidden from the view of the general public.

The normal pattern went like this: developer decides to launch a new coin. Developer announces this in BitcoinTalk and other relevant channels. Traders, seeing a chance to make a buck, jump on this news and begin frantically shilling the coin anywhere they can – on Crypto Twitter, but also on Facebook and Instagram, in Telegram and WhatsApp channels, on Reddit and anywhere else they can think of. The coin is listed on several exchanges and hysteria drives the price sky-high. Everyone makes money and everyone is happy. Then the first movers dump their bags and the price crashes. The experienced traders are out and everyone else loses money. The amazing thing about pump and dump schemes, as these are known, is the human capacity for somehow assuming things will be different next time around.

Six years later, I still see people shilling totally worthless coins via all the usual media – including paid Telegram channels, where hapless newcomers pay so-called experts to be mis-sold useless tokens. To make cryptocurrency ticker symbols searchable on social media, traders began using cashtags in the same way that stock exchange ticker symbols are tagged: $ETH for Ethereum and $LTC for Litecoin, for example, just as people tweeting about Microsoft will use the cashtag $MSFT. Sometimes cashtags for altcoins and stocks would collide when the same tag was used for both a company and a cryptocurrency, with some confusion for both parties, one imagines.

Counterparty and Mastercoin

While the majority of the coins that were launched in this heady period have crashed and burned, there was genuine progress taking place on some fronts. Among these was a standalone project that was destined to become one of the most talked-about in the crypto space and beyond: Ethereum. But before we discuss Ethereum, let's have a look at a project that took a different approach: extending the functionality of the Bitcoin blockchain, rather than creating an entirely separate network.

The Counterparty team described their project as 'writing in the margins of Bitcoin transactions', which is a vivid way of describing how Counterparty leverages the security of Bitcoin to build a layer on top, allowing people to create their own tokens and assets and trade them securely. Counterparty also allows the automatic execution of digital agreements known as 'smart contracts'. We will hear a lot more about these later.

Counterparty is open-source, so anyone can download the software and create their own custom cryptocurrency or token. The Counterparty website describes a wide range of examples, but two that are worth highlighting are the use of custom Counterparty tokens for crowdfunding or voting; or to represent digitally unique assets, such as artworks or collectibles. In order to use the Counterparty functionality, you need to own Counterparty's own tokens, XCP. These are not magically created out of nothing: each XCP token is generated by 'burning' a small amount of Bitcoin. The Bitcoin 'burnt' is destroyed by sending it to a wallet address from where it can never be spent. This is what gives the XCP token its value and enables users to interact with its network.

The Counterparty team were not the only people to focus on using Bitcoin's protocol instead of starting afresh with their own block-chain. The Mastercoin project, for example, started with a white paper written by a cryptographer called J R Willett in 2012, and remains active to this day, although it has gone through several rebrands. Now known as Omni, the Mastercoin project is best known these days for being the first platform on which the stablecoin Tether was issued. More on this in the next chapter.

Let's return for the moment to this idea of smart contracts. Along with straightforward payments, the idea of agreements that are auto-matically executed on a decentralized network is one of the funda-mental concepts that has generated so much interest in blockchain technology. While Counterparty, Omni and various other protocols built on Bitcoin offer developers the ability to write smart contracts, some developers believed that it was necessary to develop an entirely separate platform with a completely different set of features for this purpose. Today, the best-known public blockchain for smart contracts is Ethereum.

Ethereum and the world computer

While Ethereum's token (Ether) can be used for payments just like Bitcoin can, its creator's ambitions were much more grandiose. Ethereum was conceived in late 2013 by the precocious Russian-Canadian developer Vitalik Buterin, who was just 19 years old.

Buterin learnt about Bitcoin from his computer scientist father Dmitry at the age of 17, and was soon writing articles for Bitcoin-related websites. In 2013, he co-founded the well-regarded *Bitcoin*

Magazine, but while he was primarily a Bitcoin enthusiast at this point, his mind was now preoccupied with a nascent idea about how one might use a blockchain not only to record transactions but to record the result of code execution. While this sounds like a terrible idea in principle – having thousands of computers of varying performance all over the world running the same code is an inherently wasteful process – there was logic behind it.

Buterin envisaged this new network as a fully decentralized world computer – the Ethereum Virtual Machine (EVM). Just as a transaction broadcast on the Bitcoin network can be viewed by anyone in the world, and must be validated by individuals who need no permission to join the network, so Ethereum's 'smart contracts', as they came to be known, would be executed by miners, who would be rewarded for their efforts by earning the native currency of the Ethereum network – Ether.

An undertaking on this scale was not to be taken lightly, and Ethereum's gestation period was lengthy. However, there was one great benefit to having a relatively long ramp-up period: the amount of interest that this new venture generated among other developers, who were able to download and experiment with the software and use a pre-release version of the Ethereum blockchain known as a testnet. All cryptocurrencies of any standing have a testnet. This is essentially a sandbox environment where code can be thoroughly tested before changes are approved to be released to the main network.

Anyone who works on an IT project will be familiar with the idea of these pre-release environments where bugs can be fixed and discrepancies smoothed out before any breaking changes happen. Of course, the practice does not always match the theory, and often unexpected bugs are not spotted while they are on the test environment. But this process is far better than the alternative – launching untested software changes into the live network. One of the prerequisites for a successful transition of a software release from a test environment to a real (or 'production') environment is that it behaves as much like the real one as possible. To give an example, it is hard to find a bug that only happens when thousands of people are using the system, when you are testing it on your own computer and only you are using it.

Hence, blockchain test environments – testnets – have tokens that can be mined, just like the real networks, and anyone can download and run the software and help maintain the testnet. Of course, because there is no real incentive (other than being a good citizen and particiating in the health of your chosen network), the numbers of people who choose to validate transactions on testnets is much smaller. But they still provide a useful tool for developers who are either making changes to the network or who want to make transactions or run code on top of it.

One of the quirks of the Bitcoin testnet is that it is reset every so often. Because it is possible to acquire small amounts of test Bitcoin for nothing via an online tool that is known as a faucet, and because test Bitcoin are also much easier to mine than the real thing, rumours intermittently go around among less experienced users that test Bitcoin have a monetary value, and this means that people hoard them instead of returning them to the faucets for other people to test with when they are finished. The solution to this is to start the network afresh every now and again so that the test bitcoin that people may be stockpiling do not exist on the blockchain any more.

I wanted to talk about testnets at this point, because the launch of the first Ethereum testnet was probably the most hyped launch of a test environment in the history of software. Because of Vitalik Buterin's existing profile and connections in the Bitcoin community, the release of his Ethereum White Paper in December 2013 generated a huge amount of interest. Unlike the Bitcoin network, development work on the Ethereum network was to be funded by a public crowdsale. It would be possible to mine Ether with a proof of work algorithm when, eventually, the main net would be launched, but 50,000,0000 Ether were pre-sold by the Ethereum Foundation for a value of just over $15.5 million. Selling them was not difficult: everyone wanted a slice of this much-hyped technology.

For Ethereum to be successful, people had to use it. But using it was a rather more complex experience than interacting with the

Bitcoin blockchain. Unless you were developing a Bitcoin wallet or a payment system that needed to interface with the blockchain, there was no great need for a huge community of developers building applications that run on top of the Bitcoin network. But, as Ethereum had been expressly designed as a platform on which applications could be built, it was imperative to attract as many developers as possible to build high-quality applications to which normal users would be drawn. This was the theory, anyway.

So, between the Ethereum presale in July 2014 and the main net launch a year later, there were various eagerly awaited milestones. The demand among blockchain-literate developers was high, it seemed, even if the general public as yet knew nothing of the benefits of decentralized applications. In May 2015, Ethereum's development team released their final proof-of-concept testnet, Olympia, and just three months later, in July of that year, Frontier was released. Evoking a pioneering spirit, Frontier, while public, was quite raw, and lacked most of the tooling and refinements that would later lower the barrier to entry and allow a wider audience of developers to participate.

However, the release of Frontier enabled people to see for the first time what the network they had crowdfunded actually looked like, and the more technically able could try writing their own smart contracts and deploying them on the live network. In the early days, it was comparatively difficult to interact with Ethereum because the client software through which people access the network was also in its infancy. Documentation existed – which was better than many other previously launched cryptocurrencies or public blockchains – but it was sketchy and presupposed a level of knowledge above that of most would-be Ethereum developers.

New programming languages were developed to enable developers to write applications for Ethereum: Solidity was slightly like JavaScript and Serpent was modelled on Python. Much of the logic went into working out how much it should cost to execute a smart contract on the network.

Why should it cost anything? Let's pause for a minute and imagine a blockchain where you could deploy anything because it was always absolutely free. The network would grind to a halt in no time. People would start spamming the network, placing free advertising such as sending microscopic tips, or else using the processing power of the network to run memory-heavy computations. Sometimes there might be absolutely no commercial purpose: the 'because it was there' clause is usually enough to tempt mischief-makers who have nothing to lose into the most pointless of ventures. Embed *War and Peace* with the first letter of every paragraph changed? Sure, no problem – that could be fun! Or else people who simply did not like the idea of Ethereum might attack the network by running computations that deliberately did not end, such as functions that ended in an infinitely recurring number.

The creators of Ethereum had already pondered this question, and the answer was to charge a small fee for each contract execution or piece of stored data. The significant difference between Bitcoin and Ethereum in terms of fees is that Ethereum fees are not paid directly in Ether, while Bitcoin fees need a certain amount of Bitcoin included as a transaction fee. Instead, Ether is powered by a parallel crypto-currency called Gas, which is tied to the price of Ether. (Effectively you are still paying for the transaction in Ether, as your Ether is directly convertible into Gas.)

The other similarity with Bitcoin is that as the demand and load on the network increases and decreases, so does the transaction fee you have to pay to get your transaction mined quickly. Paying a higher transaction fee is a way of influencing whether your transaction is processed before others are, so calculating the correct amount of Gas to add to a contract is a challenging task.

It is this unpredictability of working with a completely public network that puts a lot of people off using public blockchains such as Ethereum. This is a shame because if you think of Ethereum's current state of development as a tiny stepping-stone on the way to something amazing and revolutionary, you gain a completely differ-ent impression than you do if you regard its slow and impractical performance now as the finished product. Over the last four years, Ethereum has had its share of controversies, but despite the price fall-ing 93 per cent from its peak at over $1,000, there has also been much interesting development.

One of the main public relations problems that Ethereum suffers from is caused by the personality politics and the interwoven relationships between the maintainers of the network itself, the wider Ethereum community, and the developers of the clients, services and applications that are built on top of it. Because Ethereum's creator, Vitalik Buterin, is not anonymous like Satoshi Nakamoto, he is able to exert – even unwittingly – an undue amount of influence over what is supposed to be a decentralized network. As proof of this, we need to look only to the $4 billion instant loss in Ethereum market cap that happened in June 2017, after the infamous 4Chan messaging board posted a hoax story that Buterin had died in a car accident. The flash crash turned out to be short-lived once Buterin proved he was still alive, but it was a salutary warning (Roberts, 2017).

Ethereum and its growing ecosystem

The story of Ethereum's price rise is almost as legendary as that of Bitcoin, and for a while the mainstream media was full of reports of fortunes that had been made after the value of the native Ether token rose parabolically from $0.30 in the pre-sale to a high of more than $1,310 in January 2018. Much of the development activity that has helped make Ethereum such a success among developers creating applications on top of a blockchain has been the support network of enthusiasts, and also companies, creating tooling to make the process easier, and writing documentation and tutorials to help people get started more quickly.

Some of these companies are run by individuals who were at the heart of the original Ethereum development effort or who have always been members of the Swiss-based Ethereum Foundation. Two of these are ConsenSys, whose founder is Joe Lubin; and Parity, started by Dr Gavin Wood and Dr Jutta Steiner.

In some cases, developers who have worked tirelessly to develop great tools have later been hired by ConsenSys so they can support the Ethereum ecosystem in a more formal manner. An example of this is Tim Coulter, who developed the Truffle framework, which provides a brilliant one-stop shop for would-be Ethereum developers, wrapping deployment, testing and even a mock blockchain into one easy-to-use code repository.

ConsenSys is a sprawling octopus of an organization, providing capital for startups, managing training and publicity for Ethereum and also providing consultancy services for companies wanting to use Enterprise Ethereum, which allows clients to deploy private, consortium and hybrid implementations of the Ethereum codebase for business applications. Unlike ConsenSys, Parity are focused on one thing – software – and have been instrumental in creating some of the most widely used tools in the Ethereum space: a client for interacting with the blockchain, wallets and also networks such as Polkadot, which allow assets and data to be ported between individual blockchains.

Parity have created a succession of interesting products, but in 2017, some software created by the company twice became the target of hackers, causing its users to lose access to tens of millions of dollars. The Parity multi-signature wallet is a popular product that was used by many companies for their ICOs (initial coin offerings), which we will discuss later on. A multi-signature wallet – this is not an Ethereum-specific creation as the first multi-signature wallets were developed for Bitcoin – allows several users to have access to funds in the same wallet. Each has their own private key and there may be rules around which people are allowed to withdraw specific amounts without having the transaction signed by other participants. Just like a company bank account with several signatories, multi-signature wallets have an important role when cryptocurrencies are used in a business or community context.

This is not a book aimed at developers, so I will not go deeply into the technical reasons for the two hacks. The first hack, in July 2017, was a straightforward exploit, where an attacker managed to steal more than (at the time) $30 million worth of Ethereum. But it was the second hack, in November, which was to raise questions about the fundamental governance of Ethereum. In simple terms, every Parity multi-signature wallet was dependent on one code library, which contained an insecure smart contract. The part of the contract that was insecure allowed anyone in the world to update it in such a way that it became frozen. Thousands of users of the multi-signature wallet, which collectively contained millions of dollars of Ether, found that their funds could not be moved. They could see their balances but they could not withdraw them. In a double blow for Parity, the wallets affected included their own wallet, which they had created for their Polkadot crowdsale.

In Chapter 8, we will discuss the concept of DAOs (decentralized autonomous organizations) and explain how the first attempt to create a DAO resulted in a massive hack. The process by which investors' funds were returned to them was hugely controversial. Hence, when the idea was floated that in order to unfreeze and restore all the Ether that had been frozen in the second Parity hack, a similar operation could be attempted, it was quickly dismissed as unworkable. At the time of writing, the funds remain locked.

Monero and other privacy coins

Unlike Ethereum, another popular token, Monero, was used specifically for payments rather than complicated smart contracts. Monero was created to redress one of the problems that its creators saw with Bitcoin – its lack of privacy. We will return to this theme later, in Chapter 11. Monero has remained popular for five years, with a vibrant community to support it, but it is not the only privacy-focused cryptocurrency, and its key technology, the use of ring signatures, is not the only way to ensure untraceable transactions.

In 2016, a team led by cryptographer Zooko Wilcox-O'Hearn launched a new cryptocurrency called Zcash. Like Bitcoin, Zcash has a fixed ultimate supply of 21 million coins, but there are some important differences. Zcash relies on a type of zero-knowledge proof called zk-SNARKS (a zero-knowledge proof is something that allows you to prove you know something, or are allowed to access something without giving away details of facts you would like to remain confidential).

Zcash is a powerful idea that offers users the chance to send transparent transactions, which work in the same way as Bitcoin from one type of address, or shielded transactions from another type of address. Transactions work under a type of 'shielded disclosure', where users can choose to reveal a transaction to a particular third party – for example, an accountant or tax inspector.

If one accepts that freedom to keep payments private is an important facet of free speech, it is obvious that cryptocurrencies like Monero and Zcash are important. It is notable that the press coverage of Bitcoin and other cryptocurrencies focuses heavily on their use to purchase goods and services that may be illegal in various countries, rather than highlighting the many cases where privacy of payment is desirable for other reasons. If one needs an example of why this privacy is so important, spare a thought for the American teenager whose unplanned pregnancy was revealed to her family by junk mail she received from Target, after the store data-mined the purchases she had made (Hill, 2012). Or consider the case of political dissidents buying books or magazines that are frowned upon by a repressive government, whose purchase may put them at risk of surveillance or arrest.

Ripple

A chapter on altcoins and payments would not be complete without at least mentioning Ripple, or 'bank coin', as its detractors would have it. Ripple is the antithesis to the privacy coins I have just described, and has stirred antipathy in the cryptocurrency community because its advocates, the 'XRP Army' – named after the Ripple token, XRP – have actively engaged in trolling behaviour on social media, and are vociferous in promoting their financial interests in the coin.

Ripple is a network that operates in a rather different way from any of the cryptocurrencies we have described so far. To begin with, it does not work on a blockchain, and neither is it decentralized in the true sense of the word. Instead, it is a cross-border payments network that is designed for use by banks and other financial institutions. There is no concept of mining: all 100 billion XRP tokens were created at launch, and Ripple Labs, which is a private company, retain 60 per cent of the supply. The circulating supply is under the control of Ripple Labs, who distribute a certain amount of the tokens each month. While the list of companies reported to be interested in Ripple's technology is impressive, it is a matter of conjecture whether the token itself, unlike Bitcoin, is necessary for the network to run. Another key difference between Ripple and Bitcoin is that Ripple does not remove the need for trust: in fact, Ripple Labs recommend that their clients use a list of identified, trusted participants to validate their transactions. This trade-off between decentralization and efficiency means that Ripple is highly scalable, with potentially tens of thousands of transactions per second.

We have looked at a tiny subsection of the cryptocurrencies that came into existence in the first crypto bull market, their points of difference and the narrative of how these competing altcoins evolved. In Chapter 8, we will look at the bull market of 2016–2017 and focus on the tidal wave of near-useless tokens that were created in the ICO gold rush that took the crypto world by storm. We will talk about the concept of tokenizing activities and assets later on as it is a very important concept, but the coins we have discussed so far – with the exception of Ethereum – were designed primarily as peer-to-peer payment mechanisms. Speculation and hype have been a big part of the cryptocurrency phenomenon, and tales of stratospheric gains of several thousand per cent have made regular appearances in the mainstream media over the last few years. However, despite the 2016–2017 ICO-fuelled boom, the idea has now been well and truly put to bed that copy-pasted altcoins are the path to riches. While CoinMarketCap lists thousands of coins, many trade at near-zero volumes, and at least as many again died a death some years ago, with no developers working on their code, no miners validating their blockchains and no one trading them.

A handful of genuine projects continue to survive and thrive, and the cryptocurrency ecosystem has become a more productive and low-key place, with teams focused on building instead of speculation. We have so far looked at Bitcoin, Litecoin, Counterparty, Mastercoin, Ethereum, Dogecoin, Monero, Zcash and Ripple and talked a little about what makes these different from each other. In later chapters, we will examine the ICO craze and other cryptocurrencies created from forks of Bitcoin and Ethereum. But now we will jump forward in time and look at the game-changing developments that led to the 2019 announcement by Facebook of an entirely new kind of digital currency.

References

Hill, K (2012) How Target figured out a teenage girl was pregnant before her father did, *Forbes*, 16 February. Available from: https://www.forbes.com/sites/kashmirhill/2012/02/16/how-target-figured-out-a-teen-girl-was-pregnant-before-her-father-did/#6a1996668 (archived at https://perma.cc/KCP4-ZFJV)

Roberts, J J (2017) Hoax over 'dead' Ethereum founder spurs $4 billion wipe out, *Fortune*, 6 June. Available from: https://fortune.com/2017/06/26/vitalik-death/ (archived at https://perma.cc/CCK8-T2HV)

4

Libra: how Big Tech moved in on digital currencies

By mid-2018, a rumour began circulating about Facebook. The company had been recruiting blockchain engineers for some time, and while some people theorized that their blockchain initiative revolved around secure data storage or a blockchain-based identity system, word soon began to circulate that the new division, headed by Facebook VP David Marcus, was in fact a digital currency project.

No hard news emerged about the project throughout the rest of 2018, but by February 2019, it emerged that more than 50 engineers were working on the project, and enough information had leaked about it that the *New York Times* was able to run a speculative story about Facebook's plans (Popper and Isaac, 2019). If the *New York Times* story provoked a storm of speculation and commentary, this was nothing compared with reactions when the project was formally announced in June of the same year. This planned currency, Libra Reserve, was announced as a partnership between Facebook and a consortium of other household names, and has proved to be a game-changer in how journalists, governments and legislators talk about digital currencies. We will examine the project in more detail later in this chapter, but let us first think about the intersection of digital currencies and social networks, and how social media companies might leverage their huge captive audiences in order to get them using their own forms of private money.

Perhaps it was not that surprising that Facebook, with its 2.4 billion users worldwide, would choose to go down this route. Not only was David Marcus a former president at PayPal, which had itself been a major disruptor in the fintech industry, but Facebook was not the first social media company to take tentative footsteps into the digital currency arena. While Facebook's plans created huge waves in the mainstream media, there had in fact been two previous ICOs (initial coin offerings) which, while they had attracted the attention of the crypto press, had largely sailed under the radar of the wider business world. Both were launched by companies who also owned social networking platforms: Kik and Telegram, with their Kin and Gram tokens respectively.

The Telegram and Kik ICOs

Perhaps the failure of the mainstream media to pick up on these ICOs at the time can be attributed to demographics, as journalists working for traditional news outlets are not the same people who use messaging apps targeted at teens and Generation Z. One of these messaging apps was Kik, which at its peak had more than 300 million users worldwide. The Canadian-based Kik, founded in 2010, worked in a similar way to WhatsApp or Telegram, using internet connectivity to allow users to send text messages, photo messages or to chat over video, but its unique selling point was its anonymity – unlike other messaging apps, users did not need to provide a phone number to sign up. While this anonymity feature attracted controversy after stories circulated of bullying, harassment and sexual grooming of minors, it quickly became the type of app that teenagers loved but which most adults had never heard of.

With privacy also being a major drawcard for the sorts of people who invested in cryptocurrency, the Kik team assumed that there would be an appetite for a Kik-related token. In Chapter 8, we will discuss how the stringent rules around accredited investors in the United States had created a pent-up demand for investment among people who did not meet these criteria. Kik's announcement of their token, Kin, was the first time an existing, centralized and successful company had dipped their toes into the shark-infested waters of the ICO market. In 2017, carried along by a cresting wave of ICO hysteria, Kik raised more than $100 million in Ether in their crowdsale.

It is sufficient to say here that Kik's CEO Ted Livingston envisaged Kin as the native token for app usage, allowing users to reward each other for useful content, and developers to monetize their work. By some measures, Kin has been a success in terms of its usage: 300,000 transactions per month, making it the fifth most widely used cryptocurrency in the world by the end of 2019. However, two years after its crowdsale, events caught up with Kik. While the SEC (Securities and Exchange Commission) in the United States realized the difficulty of pursuing action against fully decentralized token ecosystems where there was no clear owner or responsibility, their response to centralized companies issuing blockchain-based tokens was to come down on them like a ton of bricks. In September 2019, Livingston announced the closure of the Kik app (which was later retracted), but vowed that the Kin token would live on. The token immediately dropped 36 per cent in value, taking it more or less to zero (it had fallen to $0.000008 from a high of $0.0012).

FIGURE 4.1   Value of Kin token 2017–2019

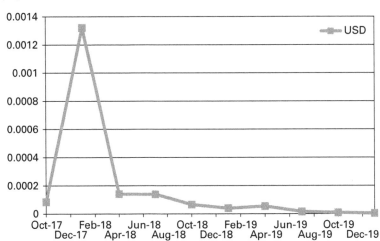

Kik was not the only social media company to announce a token offering in 2017. Telegram, another privacy-focused messaging app, drew up plans for a complicated, two-phase ICO for its Gram token, designed to be run on a public blockchain called TON (the Telegram Open Network). The first part of the token sale was aimed squarely at accredited investors, including capital funds, and was highly successful, raising more than $1.7 billion. By making the token available only to accredited investors, Telegram was able to avoid taking heat from the regulators, and plans for the proposed second part of the sale, which would have been a crowdsale to the general public, were quietly dropped.

In a precursor to Facebook's ambitions for Libra Reserve, the Gram token was presumed to have been designed to enable value transfer directly between Telegram users without leaving the app or involving banks. It was also designed to drive monetization of content by Telegram users so that developers building useful apps on, and integrations with, the Telegram network could be rewarded, as could those providing content, for example, in Telegram groups. The Telegram user base was a prime target for this kind of token: their messaging platform is the medium of choice for most cryptocurrency and ICO chat groups, attracted by Telegram's slick user interface on both phone and desktop, its privacy-focused qualities and the fact that, unlike WhatsApp, it is possible to create channels with no upper limit on the number of members.

There was thus huge interest in Gram's potential, and even before the token was released, its price was subject to large speculative price rises. The tokens were sold to investors using a special mechanism called SAFT – Simple Agreement for Future Tokens, which is effectively the right to buy the tokens before they come into existence. A Korean company known as Gram Asia, decided to sell their SAFT rights on Liquid, a Japanese crypto exchange, for three times the price they had paid in the crowdsale. Retail customers who bought the tokens (for a hefty $4 apiece) were not allowed to withdraw the tokens or sell them on and were forced to wait until the token launch before they could get their hands on their investment. This is a huge gamble, as it means that even if the future price of the token began falling before its release, they would be locked in and unable to sell.

Unfortunately for Telegram, in October 2019 the US Securities and Exchange Commission (SEC) secured an emergency action and restraining order, forbidding them from selling their tokens in the United States while they investigated whether Telegram had breached existing securities legislation. In January 2020, Telegram issued the following statement on their blog, clarifying that they had always intended their TON Blockchain to be a fully decentralized network and that there was no implication that Telegram itself would develop applications on top of it: 'Telegram and its affiliates have not made any promises or commitments to develop any applications or features for the TON Blockchain or otherwise contribute in any way to the TON Blockchain platform after it launches. In fact, it is possible that Telegram may never do so' (Telegram, 2020).

The ongoing delays prompted Liquid to cancel their token sale of Grams and return all funds. A January 2020 post on their blog stated: 'Under the Gram Token Sale Terms of Sale, Liquid is required to return all funds committed by Liquid users in the Gram Token Sale due to the fact that the TON mainnet was not launched by 30 November 2019.' (See Palmer and Baydakova, 2020.) Telegram announced in May 2020 that their active involvement with the TON network was over.

Stablecoins – Tether, MakerDAO and a host of other collateral-backed currencies

Both the Kin and Gram tokens were designed in a similar way to the cryptocurrencies we described in the last chapter, whose prices rise and fall according to supply and demand. However, there is one class of digital currencies which have been designed to eliminate this volatility: so-called stablecoins. A stablecoin is a type of digital currency whose value is always fixed in relation to (usually) a fiat currency, or a basket of several fiat currencies. While there is truth in the statement that 'one Bitcoin is always worth one Bitcoin', the volatility of Bitcoin and other tokens meant that it was often difficult for people to predict or manage their outgoings in a world in which most payments are made in pounds, dollars, euros, yen or yuan.

Living only on Bitcoin is not without challenges. Many cryptocurrency- and blockchain-focused businesses have offered their employees the chance to be paid in Bitcoin, and there are mechanisms and software to make this easy: for example, agreeing a dollar value for a salary and then paying the corresponding amount in cryptocurrency on payday. Naturally, this means that employees whose rent was due have an anxious time waiting to see what their Bitcoin would do in the intervening days. Of course, many people have profited from agreeing this kind of deal, but those who are paid on days when cryptocurrencies sink precipitously are not so happy.

There are many instances where, when goods and services are priced in dollars, pounds or euros, it can make sense to have a digital payment method that can represent a predictable value in terms of fiat currency. As the ConsenSys report The State of Stablecoins says: 'Stablecoins are designed for any (decentralized) application which requires a low threshold of volatility to be viable on a blockchain' (ConsenSys, 2019).

While there was an upsurge of interest in stablecoins during 2018–2019, the idea of a digital currency that is pegged to one or more fiat currencies is almost as old as Bitcoin itself. While there are subtle differences in stablecoins, we will look at one example from each of the two main categories: Tether, which is issued by one centralized company and which is, partially at least, backed by US dollar reserves, and Dai, which are managed by a foundation and issued on the Ethereum blockchain.

In order to maintain stability, the idea is that a stablecoin is backed by a reserve of some other type of currency or asset. If a corporation issues a token whose value is pegged to, for example, a fiat currency, then the user needs to be reassured that the corporation holds enough reserves for the token to be redeemed at face value.

As discussed in the previous chapter, networks such as Counterparty and Mastercoin were among the first to leverage and extend the features offered by the Bitcoin blockchain. Mastercoin was later rebranded as Omni, and this network was used to launch the precursor to Tether, known as Realcoin. The first Realcoin were issued in October 2014. There was a pressing use case for these tokens: the purchase of Tethers (exchange code USDT) would enable cryptocurrency traders to hold reserves, denominated in US dollar equivalents, on exchanges so that trades in and out of Bitcoin could be made easily, without actually using dollars. In January 2015, this facility was enabled on the Bitfinex exchange.

There have also been questions raised about how Tether is backed, and whether the company has sufficient dollar reserves to guarantee the entire issuance of the currency. As rumours flew around in 2018 that reserves were insufficient, this stablecoin proved itself anything but, briefly falling to a price of $0.88 as panicked traders moved their funds into Bitcoin, concerned that they would not be able to redeem their Tethers if anything went wrong. But in April 2019 lawyers for Tether confirmed that they had sufficient reserves in cash and short-term deposits to cover 74 per cent of the issuance (De, 2019 and Kharif, 2019) and the price stabilized back to parity with the dollar. In an environment where cryptocurrency enthusiasts have placed a high value on decentralization and transparency, perhaps it is inevitable that any kind of project where trust must be placed in audits offered by private companies should attract suspicion.

Like Tether, the stablecoin Dai is pegged to the US dollar at a 1:1 ratio, although they sometimes rise slightly above and fall slightly below. They maintain their peg and therefore their stability through automatic pricing mechanisms built into Ethereum smart contracts. Anyone could decide to lock up their Ether in a smart contract to generate Sai. (Confusingly, the coin that was generated from collateralizing Ethereum was originally called Dai. Now, users can deposit several different types of token as the collateral for Dai, while the stablecoin generated from Ethereum alone was known as Sai before it was discontinued in May 2020.). As we know from the previous chapter, Ethereum is a public network where anyone can view transactions and token movements, so unlike Tether, there is no need to trust a third party (Manrique, 2019).

The code, however, needs to be trustworthy. As we saw when describing the principles behind Bitcoin, when code can be viewed by anyone in the world, it also means that anyone in the world can contribute to its security. If a private company has a bug in its code, the consumers of its product have to hope that the software engineers working within the company are able to find it and fix it. A good example happened to MakerDAO in autumn 2019, after a software update. Many public blockchain companies use bug bounties to help catch defects in their software, paying benevolent hackers a bonus to uncover bugs in the code before they cause problems. Luckily, this bug never got near enough to the live network to cause any problems, but it could have been devastating, allowing a bad actor to create indefinite numbers of Dai for very little collateral. You can view this narrow miss in one of two ways: a flaw in the system, which shows a vulnerability, or a process of collaboration and transparency, which allows many eyes on a problem.

MakerDAO (sometimes shortened to simply 'Maker') is regarded as a successful and interesting project. The first Dai were issued in December 2017, and although its market capitalization is a fraction of Tether, it is closely watched by analysts as an interesting and evolving technology. To explain in detail the principles of Collateralized Debt Position smart contracts, and the technology behind the price adjustment mechanism would take at least a chapter in itself, so if you are curious to know more about the process, I would recommend reading the Dai white paper (https://makerdao.com/en/white-paper/ (archived at https://perma.cc/54Y8-3RPN)). In Chapter 10, we explain the role of Dai within the booming DeFi (Decentralized Finance) ecosystem, but it is sufficient for now to note that they have a use case that goes far beyond simple payments.

There are more than 60 stablecoins in existence, some used primarily as a fiat-to-crypto mechanism on exchanges, and others whose teams have grander ambitions. Additionally, there are more than 100 in development. Some are backed by fiat money reserves (Tether, TrueUSD, Gemini), others by cryptocurrencies (Dai, BitShares) and yet others by precious metals (for example, PAX Gold or Digix Gold). Stablecoins are clearly a technology with great potential – and this

FIGURE 4.2   Leading stablecoins and their capitalizations

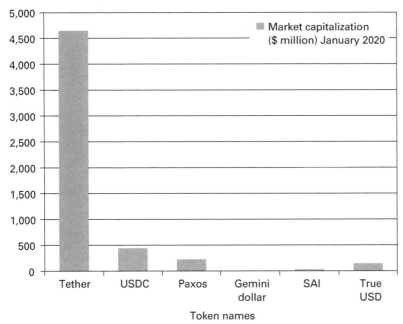

has not been missed by some of the largest of the world's corporations. Work is already taking place on a so-called JPM Coin, despite
the scathing words that the bank's Chair and CEO, Jamie Dimon,
has had to say about Bitcoin. Retail giant Walmart has also already
applied for a cryptocurrency patent for a stablecoin project. But the
headlines about developments such as these have been rendered
insignificant by Facebook's work on their new stablecoin, Libra
Reserve. We will devote the rest of the chapter to discussing this
because, whether or not the project is a success, it is a game changer
in many different ways.

Facebook and the Libra Reserve project

Normally, the launch of a new stablecoin is something that is not
announced with great fanfare. Traders, analysts and venture capital-
ists will sit up and notice if they think either that there is money to be

made or there is some technical innovation that can be put to use. However, in June 2019 Facebook made an announcement that made the headlines not only of the financial newspapers, but of the mainstream media worldwide: they were about to release their own white paper detailing the digital currency they had been working on with a consortium of partners, including Mastercard, PayPal, Stripe and others. The project was to be called Libra, and it would involve the creation of an entirely new cryptocurrency, which would be administered by a foundation.

One of the statements that took industry observers by surprise was the relatively advanced status of the project. Many cryptocurrency white papers contain vague promises about testnets that will be developed in the future, yet Libra's testnet, along with an entirely new programming language, were ready to be released, ready for developers to start building third-party apps. Another surprise was the extent to which Facebook were willing to relinquish overall control and embrace a degree of decentralization and create open-source software instead of locking their code away from prying eyes. A cynic might say that they had seen the long-term threat of truly decentralized currencies tempting a new generation away from the established banking system, and were acting now to mitigate this threat, rather than out of a sense of excitement and innovation.

Whatever the motivation, this bold and ambitious project set out to solve some of the problems that the global banking system does not solve: financial inclusion for some of the poorest people in the world, who are too poor for banks to want as customers; cheap, fast payments between individuals whose only other option would be to use a service such as Western Union, where fees might swallow nearly 20 per cent of the remittance; and a native token for Facebook's messaging service WhatsApp, allowing users to send units of value as quickly and privately as sending a photo or a text message.

The Libra project consists of many different moving parts, from the wallet developed by a team at Facebook, which will allow users to spend and receive tokens, to the Libra blockchain itself and, most importantly, the Libra Reserve, a custodian service for fiat-denominated assets, which is headquartered in Geneva, Switzerland.

While Facebook are driving the project and have carried out all the technical development to date, they state unequivocally in the white paper that once Libra Reserve is launched, they will be just one stakeholder among many companies who are underpinning the new global currency. The list of consortium members is impressive. The full list can be seen below, but the original 20 members spanned many different sectors as well as payments, including transport (Lyft and Uber) and entertainment and ecommerce (Spotify and eBay).

While many facets of the project remain under discussion, and the timescale of Libra's launch may be subject to change, most of the big issues confronting this ambitious global undertaking will remain the same, whenever or however it finally launches.

Challenges for Libra

Just like Dai and Tether, in order to issue new Libra, a commensurate value of assets need to be deposited into the reserve before new Libra coins can be created. Every Libra token that is issued will be backed by an agreed sum in collateral. Or, as the first white paper puts it: 'For new Libra coins to be created, there must be an equivalent purchase of Libra for fiat and transfer of that fiat to the reserve. Hence, the reserve will grow as users' demand for Libra increases.' However, there are important points of difference between Libra and other stablecoins. One of the most crucial of these is that unlike Dai or Tether, one Libra will not always equal more or less one dollar. While Tether or Dai will always have a value that is very close to $1, Libra may fluctuate. Yes, it is a stablecoin but it is stable against a basket of assets, rather than simply a single currency. Other important points of difference include the fact that Libra will run on computers administered by partner companies, rather than anyone who wants to join the network – in other words, it is permissioned.

Let's explore further this idea of Libra's peg against a basket of assets. Facebook's original vision of Libra as a truly global currency means that it should not simply become a way for people in different countries to hold US dollars. Instead, the Reserve is designed to hold:

'a collection of low-volatility assets, including bank deposits and government securities in currencies from stable and reputable central banks'. This means that a unit of Libra may not always have exactly the same exchange rate against any given national currency, but in the same way that the US Dollar Index is valued against a basket of currencies, it should maintain roughly the same purchasing power over time. Of course, we then need to consider the idea of 'purchasing power' and what that means when faced with an inflationary situation in one or more countries.

The following is a list of the 21 confirmed Libra Association members at its inaugural meeting:

- Anchorage
- Andreessen Horowitz
- Bison Trails Co
- Breakthrough Initiatives, L P
- Calibra, Inc
- Coinbase, Inc
- Creative Destruction Lab
- Farfetch UK Limited
- Iliad
- Kiva Microfunds
- Lyft, Inc
- Mercy Corps
- PayU
- Ribbit Capital
- Spotify AB
- Thrive Capital
- Uber Technologies, Inc
- Union Square Ventures
- Vodafone*
- Women's World Banking
- Xapo Holdings Limited

SOURCE Libra Association (2019)
*Vodafone announced their withdrawal from the project in January 2020

The white paper goes on to note: '... the [above] basket has been structured with capital preservation and liquidity in mind. On the capital preservation point, the association will only invest in debt from stable governments with low default probability that are unlikely to experience high inflation.'

While this commitment to stability means that people will not be tempted to use Libra as a vehicle for speculation, this depends to a certain extent on the stability of the national currency in countries where Libra will be used. We do not need to look back as far as the Weimar Republic to see the devastating effects of hyperinflation. Anyone who lived in Zimbabwe during 2007–2009, Argentina in the 1990s or present-day Venezuela would attest to the misery that is caused once this death spiral takes hold. But humans are inventive creatures, and we saw in Chapter 1 how more or less any item can be used for payment if both parties agree it.

People will always, based on the information they have available, want to put their money where it is in the best-case scenario, going to earn them interest or, in the worst-case scenario, at least not depreciate in value. In an economy where there are capital controls, which governments tend to impose in times of currency crisis, the ordinary person in the street has little access to the financial tools that large corporations and high net worth individuals can use to protect themselves. This gives governments an overwhelming and unreasonable stranglehold on their citizens, allowing them to penalize individuals as a consequence of their own economic mismanagement.

As mentioned above, Facebook has more than 2 billion users across the globe. Providing them with access to Libra as a payment method means that 2 billion people suddenly had the opportunity to circumvent their national currency. In Venezuela and Zimbabwe, there has already been an upsurge in Bitcoin use (Meredith, 2019), but this has been limited to those whose risk appetite is high and also whose knowledge of technology allows them to acquire and hold a decentralized cryptocurrency safely. In contrast, the tools that are being built to integrate Libra with Facebook's products, such as WhatsApp, will allow even the less technically adept to participate in this new economy. It is interesting that the second Libra white paper responded to these concerns by replacing the idea of a universal currency backed by a basket of assets with the idea of a stablecoin backed in each country by the national currency – a major retreat from its original principles. In Chapter 11, we will examine in detail the regulatory approach to digital currencies in general, but we cannot talk about Libra without discussing the initial reaction to it from global governments.

Government reactions to Libra

Analysts have been puzzling over Facebook's approach and the timing of their announcement. For an innovation that could threaten systemic risk to national currencies, it seems strange that they did not have initial talks with certain key regulatory authorities before sinking significant development resources into the project and announcing it. Yet the SEC seems to have been caught completely off-guard by the announcement, and governments in countries such as France and India were quick to denounce the project. It seems that people in many governmental positions were ignorant of the rapid development in cryptocurrencies and digital money, and being suddenly presented with a fully formed plan for a decentralized digital currency, backed by some of the largest companies in the world, was a huge shock.

The potential influence of Libra goes beyond systemic risk to individual currencies in countries where the government has exercised poor economic policy. If even a modest percentage of Facebook users begin to use Libra, the arbiters who decide the composition of the collateral assets against which it is pegged begin to have an undue influence on the markets. It is important to realize that the type and proportion of assets that make up the Libra basket are not set in stone and will change over time. If the economists who decide on the composition of the assets in the reserve decide, for example, to reduce the proportion of a particular national currency because they feel that the government's policies may lead to inflation in that currency, then this could become a self-fulfilling prophecy. It is entirely possible to envisage a situation where inclusion, or not, in the Libra basket becomes an important economic indicator. These risks have been mitigated by the later decision to make available to individuals stable-coins tied to national currencies, rather than one that is based on a basket of assets.

When Libra launches, it will truly be a first: a form of money that could ultimately be used by anyone, anywhere in the world. Facebook envisage it as a frictionless, virtually free method of sending value: a transformative payment facility that can help the unbanked take advantage of digital payments. However proud its creators may be of its inclusive and truly international potential, this feature is definitely a bug as far as many governments are concerned. Not only does Libra, in extreme scenarios, pose an existential threat to fragile national currencies and limit the ability of governments to impose capital controls, but even in countries with healthy economies, politicians are uneasy about a supra-national form of money being available to their citizens.

While Mark Carney, former governor of the Bank of England, who has been cautiously positive about the potential for blockchain-based currencies in the past, was the first to comment publicly on Libra, saying in the week of its launch that the currency would need 'direct regulatory oversight', his reaction was positive compared with many of the opinions voiced in the following months. Facebook's move appears to have taken governments and regulatory bodies entirely by surprise. Bitcoin and other cryptocurrencies had been such a niche concern, that perhaps complacency and a strongly held belief that the current system would never change had blinded them to the elephant in the room.

While many countries, although not expressing their reservations in such adversarial terms, were dismayed at the disproportionate power a US company would wield within their borders, few regulatory authorities expressed anywhere near the fury and panic of the United States' own regulators. US Federal Reserve Chair Jerome Powell declared on 10 July 2019 during his regular testimony to the US House of Representatives Financial Services Committee that there should be a moratorium on Libra until regulatory concerns had been addressed.

While he also touched on concerns around money laundering, privacy and financial stability, his comments were mild compared with that of Representative Brad Sherman, who not only described Libra as providing 'privacy to drug dealers, human traffickers, terrorists, tax evaders and sanctions evaders' but also compared Mark Zuckerberg's actions with those of Osama Bin Laden in an impassioned speech (The Week, 2019): 'We're told by some that innovation is always good,' Sherman said. 'The most innovative thing that happened this century is when Osama bin Laden came up with the innovative idea of flying two airplanes into towers. That's the most consequential innovation, although this may do more to endanger America than even that.'

Meanwhile, Representative Maxine Waters, a long-time Facebook critic, weighed in with a statement demanding not only a moratorium on Libra's development but also the institution of a new regulatory framework for cryptocurrencies (The Week, 2019). She stated:

> With the announcement that it plans to create a cryptocurrency, Facebook is continuing its unchecked expansion and extending its reach into the lives of its users. The cryptocurrency market currently lacks a clear regulatory framework to provide strong protections for investors, consumers, and the economy. Regulators should see this as a wake-up call to get serious about the privacy and national security concerns, cybersecurity risks, and trading risks that are posed by cryptocurrencies

while also demanding Facebook executives appear before Congress to testify on these issues.

To understand the visceral fury with which US policymakers greeted Facebook's proposal, it is important to be aware of two things: the fear that governments are ceding control to Big Tech, and also the very traditional view that many lawmakers have regarding the rule of government. Representative Carolyn Maloney spoke for many when she stated at the 17 July hearing: 'I don't think you should launch Libra at all because the creation of a new currency is a core government function.'

While even Representative Maloney, despite her reservations, was prepared to countenance the idea of a small pilot programme, with

Libra rolled out to a million or so customers with full regulatory oversight, some policymakers in other countries took an even more hard-line approach. There has been a history of various European Union nations going into battle against Silicon Valley's tech giants over matters such as privacy (with the recent GDPR legislation being a case in point), and while France has displayed a reasonably accommodating attitude to Bitcoin and other cryptocurrencies – more on this in Chapter 11 – French Finance Minister Bruno Le Maire announced on 12 September 2019 that he was minded to ban Libra from Europe entirely.

Quite how such a ban would be implemented he did not detail, but his words left no doubt that there were many challenges standing in the way before the EU would agree to Libra's launch in Europe: 'All these concerns about Libra are serious. I therefore want to say with plenty of clarity: in these conditions we cannot authorize the development of Libra on European soil,' he thundered (Jones, 2019). At the same time, the Swiss regulators, mindful of the Libra Association's base in Geneva, called for international cooperation in regulating the new currency. By late autumn 2019, France and Germany seemed more intent on blocking Libra altogether, rather than engaging with regulators, issuing a joint statement calling for an accelerated approach to issuing government-backed digital currencies.

France and Germany were not the only countries who wanted to ban Libra. Before Facebook even announced their plans, India had brought in some of the world's most draconian laws surrounding cryptocurrency, with a proposed law threatening 10-year jail sentences for digital money traders. Despite – or perhaps because of – Facebook's involvement, Libra appears no more welcome in India than the shadiest of altcoins, and so 260 million Indian Facebook users seem set to miss out on getting their hands on it.

Even countries where Facebook does not operate seemed unnerved by Facebook's bold move. At first sight, Libra would seem of little interest to China. The yuan is not expected to be one of the pegged currencies in the Libra Reserve basket; the Chinese are working on their own digital currency; and Facebook and WhatsApp are banned in China. Yet Chinese policymakers are carefully watching to see what the systemic impact will be in the global financial system, and are also mindful that whatever local regulations they put in place, Libra will eventually trickle into the country via various back-channels that are currently used for trading Bitcoin and other cryptocurrencies.

Whether or not their reaction was prompted by the regulatory response to the project, in autumn 2019 there was something of an exodus from the original list of partners in the Libra project, with Booking Holdings, eBay, Mastercard, Mercado Pago, PayPal and Stripe all pulling out and Visa clarifying that they were not in fact part of the project. The remaining 21 members officially signed a charter in October 2019 enshrining their support (although some would withdraw three months later), and in January 2020 a technical steering committee was formed.

Leaky national borders

This latter point is probably the most important. When travellers cross borders, we are used to seeing signs at the airport advising us of the limits for assets such as gold or cash that must be observed. Not only is there customs legislation around this, but different countries also have criminal laws against money laundering, and there may or may not be capital controls put in place to stop assets draining out of weaker economies. In the pre-cryptocurrency age, it was easy for the authorities to see exactly who was moving money where, because it would either have to be transferred via a bank account or physically carried.

Cryptocurrency changes this. While it would be highly inadvisable to carry several million pounds in a Bitcoin wallet on your mobile phone, or even – if you trust your memory – by carrying in your head the 12-word mnemonic that would restore your wallet, this is now possible. People can cross borders in the blink of an eye, and it would be impractical for border officials to stop every single person and search their phones. It is interesting that some countries, including New Zealand, have now brought in a law specifying that visitors to the country must be prepared to have their phone searched, but in reality, this is like looking for a needle in a haystack.

You do not in any case have to cross a border physically to transfer cryptocurrency between countries. As we saw in Chapter 2, while Bitcoin payments are not entirely anonymous – there is always some kind of trail unless you take special measures to hide your activity, meaning that payments are pseudonymous rather than totally private – it is very difficult to prevent Bitcoin from being transferred in and out of a geographic area, such as a nation state. Countries such as China and India are planning draconian measures to prevent cryptocurrency dealing within their borders, but people will often take a calculated risk. Technology such as VPNs (virtual private networks) mean that even when governments block particular websites or technologies at a national level, the truly determined can circumvent these.

One of the popular ways that governments or companies restrict access to particular websites is by detecting the IP address of the device that the person is using and blocking access to IP addresses within a certain range. As IP addresses are associated with particular locations and can be identified by their country, this should be easy to do. However, as most users of the internet are aware, using a VPN can route your activity via a server that is in another geographic location entirely, whether this is an IP address based at your company if you are working remotely, or in a different country. Use of VPNs to get around geographic restrictions is common, and so it is easy to see how there might be movement of cryptocurrencies from one region to another without explicit regulatory approval.

The KYC (Know Your Customer) process undertaken by exchanges is one way to ensure that local laws are followed, but the growth in the DeFi sector, which we will examine in a later chapter, goes some way towards mitigating the effect of government actions. Quite often, companies will themselves implement IP-blocking of addresses in certain countries to ensure they do not face sanctions, but this is often more for cosmetic purposes than because it serves a real purpose.

In conclusion, we have seen that Facebook has taken on an almighty challenge, not only in terms of investment in software development and coordinating with other large tech companies, but also in taking on the world's governments and facing down their fury. They would not be doing this if the incentives were not enough, so let's consider for a moment what is in it for them. It seems fair to assume that, along with many other influential people in the tech and finance sector, decision makers at Facebook have decided that digital currencies will be the payment rails of the future, and rather than sit back and wait until someone else develops a stablecoin that can be used for cheap, frictionless payments, they have decided to go for it and do it themselves. It is also significant that one of the stated aims of the Libra Foundation is to use some of the interest generated from collateralized assets to incentivize companies to start accepting Libra. This suggests that Facebook are prepared to promote their new currency aggressively and that, with a market of 2 billion users, usage of Libra will outstrip previous social media tokens and other stablecoins by a factor of many multiples.

So far, we have talked about digital currencies almost exclusively as simply another form of money, used to transfer units of value electronically. However, it is important to understand that along with being a cheap, quick and reliable payment system, cryptocurrency tokens have special properties that can make them even more useful than 'only' money. In the next two chapters, we will look at how tokens evolved for specific purposes, how smart contracts work, and examine how tokenomics plays a part in the design and implementation of these new currencies.

References

ConsenSys (2019) The state of Stablecoins, 2019, 16 August. Available from: https://media.consensys.net/the-state-of-stablecoins-2019-40c3eca990f4 (archived at https://perma.cc/77NY-L2RW)

De, N (2019) Tether lawyer admits stablecoin now 74% backed by cash and equivalents, *CoinDesk*, 1 May. Available from: https://www.coindesk.com/tether-lawyer-confirms-stablecoin-74-percent-backed-by-cash-and-equivalents (archived at https://perma.cc/695U-UQ2V)

Jones, C (2019) France says it won't allow Libra in Europe, *Financial Times Alphaville*, 12 September 2019. Available from: https://ftalphaville.ft.com/

2019/09/12/1568281687000/France-says-it-won-t-allow-Libra-in-Europe/ (archived at https://perma.cc/7YHQ-2LDM)

Kharif, O (2019) Tether says Stablecoin is only backed 74% by cash, securities, *Bloomberg*, 30 April. Available from: https://www.bloomberg.com/news/articles/2019-04-30/tether-says-stablecoin-is-only-backed-74-by-cash-securities (archived at https://perma.cc/HXN4-5Y66)

Libra Association (2019), Libra Association fact sheet, 14 October. Available from: https://libra.org/wp-content/uploads/2019/10/Fact-Sheet.pdf (archived at https://perma.cc/NF9C-FGM9)

Manrique, S (2019) What is DAI and how does it work? *Medium*, 7 February. Available from: https://medium.com/mycrypto/what-is-dai-and-how-does-it-work-742d09ba25d6 (archived at https://perma.cc/7BJ8-5GYQ)

Meredith, S (2019) Bitcoin trading in crisis-stricken Venezuela has just hit an all-time high, *CNBC*, 14 February. Available from: https://www.cnbc.com/2019/02/14/venezuela-crisis-bitcoin-trading-volumes-hit-an-all-time-high-.html (archived at https://perma.cc/7DHG-BZBV)

Palmer, D and Baydakova, A (2020) Liquid exchange cancels sale of Telegram's Gram Tokens, *CoinDesk*, 16 January. Available from: https://www.coindesk.com/liquid-exchange-cancels-sale-of-telegrams-gram-tokens (archived at https://perma.cc/AR7E-MHE8)

Popper, N and Isaac, M (2019) Facebook and Telegram are hoping to succeed where Bitcoin failed, *New York Times*, 28 February. Available from: https://www.nytimes.com/2019/02/28/technology/cryptocurrency-facebook-telegram.html (archived at https://perma.cc/FWZ3-CZFQ)

Telegram (2020) A public notice about the TON Blockchain and Grams, 6 January. Available from: https://telegram.org/blog/ton-gram-notice (archived at https://perma.cc/SR3L-J26C)

The Week (2019) Democratic congressman says Facebook's Libra 'may do more to endanger America' than 9/11, *The Week*, 17 July. Available from: https://theweek.com/speedreads/853333/democratic-congressman-says-facebooks-libra-may-more-endanger-america-than-911 (archived at https://perma.cc/L3FU-2JRK)

5

Tokenomics and governance

We are used to thinking of the word 'token' as meaning a unit of cryptocurrency – or, at least, this is the way it has been used in this book so far. Before we start talking about tokenomics, let's look at the meaning of the word, independent from any specific association with cryptocurrency.

The Oxford English Dictionary (OED, 2010) defines the noun 'token' as:

> - A thing serving as a visible or tangible representation of a fact, quality, feeling, etc; or
> - a voucher that can be exchanged for goods or services, typically one given as a gift or forming part of a promotional offer.

Additionally, as the US National Institute for Standards and Technology reminds us in their Computer Security Resource Center (NIST, nd), a cryptographic token is:

> - A token where the secret is a cryptographic key.

Perhaps, then, we can think of a token in the cryptocurrency sense as lying somewhere between all these three definitions. Rather like a physical token such as a parking meter token, a supermarket reward voucher or a subway ticket, a cryptocurrency token represents some representation of value, which may or may not be tradable between willing parties for other tokens or for fiat money, and which entitles the bearer to a specified unit of goods or services. It may seem that we are playing with semantics by conflating the meaning of a physical token with a digital one, but in fact the underlying philosophical idea of representing real-world assets and behaviour with digital tokens is key to understanding how token engineering and tokenomics work.

Tokenomics is a recently invented portmanteau word, which combines the words 'token' and 'economics' to describe the rules and frameworks that determine both the internal economy of a given blockchain, and how it interacts with the outside world. While traditional economics is divided into macroeconomics and microeconomics, this distinction is less clear within what we call the token economy. Some analysts have divided this new study into microtokenomics (mining incentives, inflation rate and other things related to the blockchain itself) and macrotokenomics (the externalities of how participants interact with the token, liquidity on exchanges, governance), including Sean Au and Thomas Power in their book *Tokenomics*, but I feel that this distinction could be somewhat arbitrary, depending on the structure of the token economy under discussion.

How accurately do tokenomic theories map to traditional economic models? Partially but not wholly, is the probable answer. While in traditional economics, microeconomics refers to the study of decision making by individuals, firms and other small associations, while macroeconomics studies the structure and performance of an entire economic system, one can see that examining the incentives and inflation rate within an intended overarching global system such as Facebook's Libra project could more fairly be designated as macroeconomics. Within such a new field, definitions are fluid and subject to change, and because such systems as Libra do not exist within traditional economics, it is fair to question how existing terms relate to new entities in this emerging new system.

While we are on the subject of definitions, is cryptoeconomics an interchangeable term for tokenomics? I think not. If we look at various definitions, including that of the MIT Cryptoeconomics Lab, we see that this term relates more to the use of cryptography to solve incentive problems, and focuses on the mathematical/game-theoretical approach to networks. It is thus a subset of tokenomics. Drill down deeper into cryptoeconomics and we see the sub-specialism of institutional cryptoeconomics, which looks at how blockchains (or distributed ledgers) can use rules to structure data in ways that can bring organization to human society: 'the institutional consequences of cryptographically secure and trustless ledgers' (Berg, Davidson and Potts, 2017).

Outlier Ventures have some of the leading thinkers in the emerging tokenomics discipline, and the paper by Outlier head of crypto-economics Eden Dhaliwal and Dr Zeynep Gurguc is recommended reading for anyone interested in token design (Dhaliwal and Gurguc, 2018). Within the paper, the authors emphasize the importance of assembling a team of people with the requisite skills to discover requirements, specify, design and implement one of these entirely new economic systems, recognizing that few people are likely to exist who possess the precise matrix of expertise required.

Smart contracts

Tokens issued on Ethereum or similar blockchains are defined in a smart contract. 'Smart contract' is rather a meaningless term, but it is widely used in blockchain circles. We have mentioned smart contracts many times in the book so far; maybe it is time to think about definitions. It is often said about smart contracts that they are not smart and they are not contracts: they are nothing more than chunks of computer code that are executed on distributed systems. They usually define some rules around an agreement and what actions should be taken in response to particular events: for example, when Alice pays Bob, Colin should receive a percentage of the payment. When smart contracts are executed on a platform that has its own token, such as Ethereum, transaction and payment are inextricably bound up with each other.

Before a token can be used in the smart contracts that make up the wider token economy, the token and its metrics need to be defined

FIGURE 5.1   Ethereum smart contract example

```
contract ERC20Interface {
    function totalSupply() public view returns (uint);
    function balanceOf(address tokenOwner) public view returns (uint balance);
    function allowance(address tokenOwner, address spender) public view returns (uint remaining);
    function transfer(address to, uint tokens) public returns (bool success);
    function approve(address spender, uint tokens) public returns (bool success);
    function transferFrom(address from, address to, uint tokens) public returns (bool success);

    event Transfer(address indexed from, address indexed to, uint tokens);
    event Approval(address indexed tokenOwner, address indexed spender, uint tokens);
}


// ----------------------------------------------------------------------
// Contract function to receive approval and execute function in one call
//
// Borrowed from MiniMeToken
// ----------------------------------------------------------------------
contract ApproveAndCallFallBack {
    function receiveApproval(address from, uint256 tokens, address token, bytes memory data) public;
}


// ----------------------------------------------------------------------
// Owned contract
// ----------------------------------------------------------------------
contract Owned {
    address public owner;
```

and the token needs to be issued. This is done with a smart contract, which has to conform to a particular standard. The contract needs to specify how many tokens are going to be issued, the token's symbol and its divisibility, as well as the ability to send and receive tokens and express their balance within a wallet.

In its simplest form, the code that makes up an ERC-20 token smart contract in Ethereum looks like the example in Figure 5.1.

You don't need to be able to read a computer program to understand the salient points of this template. Usually, tokens may contain much more detailed specifications than this. But the contract that is represented here contains the minimum instructions in order for it to be transported around the Ethereum network in a way that other smart contracts understand. Token smart contracts on other blockchains tend to follow this same pattern: for example, the NEP-5 template on the NEO blockchain, while it is written in a different programming language, also contains fields for token supply, decimal places and symbol (in this sense, its call code, such as ETH for Ether or ADA for Cardano).

Within the contract, it is possible to define some of the other rules that are specific to your particular blockchain network and its rules of engagement, such as how and when the tokens may be transferred, or the precise sequence of events that must happen in order for tokens to be created.

Now we have defined some of the themes we will be examining in this chapter, let's turn our attention to some specific metrics that determine the value and use of a token within a token economy.

Token taxonomy

It is no surprise that token templates for different platforms share many of the same characteristics. The Token Taxonomy project that is being coordinated by the Ethereum Enterprise Alliance is a technology-agnostic initiative in which many different companies are involved, including Accenture, Banco Santander, ConsenSys, Digital Asset, EY, IBM, ING, Intel and JP Morgan. The project, which is deliberately accessible for non-technologists, identifies certain characteristics of tokens (are they fungible? Divisible? Transferable?) and allows tokens to be categorized according to these properties, so that it is easy to map use cases to a matrix of these characteristics.

Eden Dhaliwal feels that while this taxonomy is useful, it is less important at the token design stage than the process of actually figuring out how your network will behave and grow. 'Growing your network, driving the adoption that will make your token necessary and getting the behavioural aspects right are all more important than getting tied down by taxonomy', he points out.

Market capitalization

In Chapter 1, we looked at the evolution of fiat currency, and compared the national currencies that we have today with the items and goods that were first used as units of exchange and value. We saw that while the first forms of money depended very much on their scarcity to maintain their value, since fiat currencies ceased to be backed by gold, this notion of scarcity no longer applies. We can no longer look with certainty at the circulating supply of a government-issued currency and draw a direct mathematical conclusion about its worth.

There is a general principle that the more money circulating within a country's economy, the lower its exchange rate will be. For countries that export a lot of goods, a weaker currency can sometimes be better – although it tends to make imported goods more expensive for the people who live there. Modern measures of money circulating within an economy are much more complex than they used to be when one simply had to add up the supply of notes and coins that had been minted by the government. Today, in our digital economies, the money supply in a country like the UK, France or the United States counts commercial bank deposits, central bank credit and even institutional money market funds. In 2010 in the UK, for example, notes and coins made up only 2.1 per cent of the total money supply (Lipsey and Chrystal, 2011).

When we attempt to value tokens on a blockchain, the process is simpler. It is easier to factor in the total supply of tokens as a criterion that influences price by looking at the laws of supply and demand. Of course, this is not the only measure of value. A token on a public blockchain that has 10,000 tokens, but which does something completely useless that means no one will ever buy the tokens, will still be worth less than a token belonging to a useful project where there are millions of tokens. But the idea of having a hard cap written into the computer code that runs the blockchain is often necessary to give potential users an idea of whether the token will retain its value or not. The law of supply and demand is usually one of the first things students learn in Economics 101: we are used to the price increasing if the item is rare. This is why a Stradivarius violin or a Van Gogh can command an eye-watering price at auction, while a grain of sand is almost without value. (I deliberately said 'almost' without value, as of course a tonne of sand has a price.)

Hence when potential buyers look at a token, one of the likely metrics they will consider is the number of tokens that can be generated by a particular blockchain. Projects have different approaches: some tokens are designed to be produced over time, according to a particular schedule, while others are created in a 'big bang' at the project's inception and gradually distributed. Whichever approach is taken, analysts will look at two specific figures: the circulating supply and the maximum supply.

The market capitalization (market cap) is the price multiplied by the number of circulating coins, not the maximum number of coins. If the number of circulating coins suddenly doubles, one would expect the price to fall (in the absence of any other changes, such as good news related to the project signifying future value increases). Bitcoin advocates point to the hard limit of 21 million Bitcoin that will only ever exist as proof that Bitcoin has a value as a 'hard money' such as gold. In comparison, Cardano has a maximum possible supply of just over 31 billion ADA tokens, which is one of the factors that means the price of ADA is a tiny fraction of that of Bitcoin. Stablecoins, where the value is pegged to a fiat currency, will always circulate at a number that is equivalent to the currency that backs the token, as we saw in Chapter 4.

The issuance schedule is also important. Where the number of tokens that will come into existence at any given time is determined by the underlying algorithm of the blockchain, it is easy for users to price in these expected supply changes. Again, to use the example of Bitcoin, the number of Bitcoins that are generated as a reward for miners validating blocks of transactions, is due to halve at predictable and regular intervals, which can be predicted months or years ahead with some certainty. Unless something dramatic happens in the short term to counter this, it means that the rate of increase in the supply will slow down, and the price should tend to go up. Generally, the issuance schedule will be defined in the smart contract, for tokens issued on blockchains such as Ethereum. However, where tokens have all been pre-mined (generated at the beginning of the project) and where issuance is determined by humans via some voting mechanism, users would have good cause to be wary. We will discuss governance issues further at the end of Chapter 11.

Incentives

One of the hardest conceptual leaps we need to make when thinking about cryptocurrencies – public ones, anyway – is to move away from the idea of centralized decision making – for example, by a government or a private company. In some instances, the organizations who build a blockchain network may be public limited companies, registered under the legal framework of the country where they are based, but they are just as likely to be structured as foundations – or, in the case of Bitcoin – to be completely decentralized and have no legal entity whatsoever.

Even where the software for a particular network has been built by a company, and the company's developers are responsible for making further updates to the network, once the software is released into the wild and anyone can run it, this means that the decision-making process has to be controlled in some other way than one person or one group of people issuing directives that other people have to follow. If you are an employee of a company, your contract will specify that you need to obey certain orders and carry out activities that are in the interests of the company. Occasionally, people will deviate from this if they find out that the company is acting in a way that contravenes their own morality, but this is rare. For most purposes, we can assume that the interests of the employee are aligned with the company.

If your company develops a distributed network (some kind of ledger that shares some attributes of a public blockchain) that is running entirely within the company, or perhaps is shared with a few other companies where there is a legal contract to specify who is responsible for what, incentives are not needed in order for the nodes (the computers that run the network) to exist. The employees of the company will simply set up servers (these days most likely to be cloud servers provided by the likes of Amazon, Google or Microsoft), install the software on them and allow them to connect to other machines on the network.

The running costs, whether these are the upfront costs of the hardware, the electricity consumed, the employee time or the payment to the cloud provider, will be paid by the company and accounted for as part of its business model. A cryptocurrency token will not be needed in these circumstances. We will delve deeper into the question of public versus private blockchains in Chapter 9. But for now, let's simply assume that we are talking about a public network where a cryptocurrency is needed.

The incentives that influence a public network such as Bitcoin are very different from the incentives offered to the employees of a firm. Above all, public cryptocurrency networks operate on the assumption that humans are rational creatures who seek to earn money in order to improve their quality of living.

There is no CEO of Bitcoin, so no one can simply direct people to purchase a server and start running the Bitcoin software. There is no contract between some mythical Bitcoin entity and a miner who decides to download the Bitcoin code. Instead, people and companies are incentivized to maintain and interact with the network based on the mathematics contained within the code itself. This is the hallmark of a truly decentralized network.

It would not be much of a network if only two or three people belonged to it: transactions would not be trustworthy (because they would be under the control of a tiny minority) and the token would be almost worthless. We can see this reflected in the value of Bitcoin over time, from the early months when hardly anyone knew about it. Hence people need to be incentivized to use the token and also to participate in the network and validate transactions. Ideally, these two activities should be intertwined, with anyone who uses the token for payment and investment also contributing to the health of the network by running what is known as a full node – a copy of the blockchain containing all transactions since the beginning of time. Since the size of the Bitcoin blockchain has grown, and the energy needed to mine new Bitcoins has increased, these two functions have become largely detached from each other, with Bitcoin holders not necessarily being miners, although initiatives such as the Casa Node (a copy of the Bitcoin blockchain running on a Raspberry Pi) aim to redress this balance.

There are three main incentives driving the adoption of Bitcoin, both for users and for miners: scarcity, mining rewards and transaction fees. Users need to believe when they buy a cryptocurrency (or choose to earn it through working or contributing value) that it will at least retain its value, if not increase. As we saw when we discussed stablecoins, this is not necessarily a given, if someone has acquired a token at an inflated price. In the case of Bitcoin, its scarcity is one major element driving its value. For other tokens that are not scarce such as Ethereum (with a potentially unlimited supply), users believe that it is demand generated by people using the underlying technologies that will maintain the price at its current level or drive it higher.

There are various mechanisms that are used to secure public networks, for example proof of work and proof of stake, but from a token-holder's perspective, the most important factors are that the mechanism is fair, reliable and unable to be gamed. The incentives for a miner (or a validator of another kind) are purely mathematical: are the tokens I gain in exchange for running the network worth more than I have to pay in electricity or other infrastructure costs? Given that Bitcoin was the first of its kind, and that Satoshi Nakamoto had to model the formula that defined the production schedule of new bitcoins and the rewards for producing them, without prior experimentation or running focus groups to assess people's motivations and feelings about the incentive structure, this makes Nakamoto's feat all the more remarkable.

Because block rewards shrink with each halving, with the very last bitcoin scheduled to be mined some time in 2140, what will incentivize miners to keep validating blocks? The truth is that Satoshi Nakamoto, of course, built this into the incentive structure, and it is presumed that the miners will make their money from transaction fees alone, with fees rising gradually as the block rewards fall away. This bootstrapping of the Bitcoin network with block rewards to generate enough interest and participants in order to keep the network running is a creative and elegant solution, which every public cryptocurrency that has followed has emulated in some way, either by copying wholesale or incorporating at least some elements.

Penalties

Behavioural economics dictates that where there are incentives, there are also usually disincentives. Transaction fees are a particularly hard part of the equation to get right. Too high and you run the risk of alienating users, whose business model may not be able to pay to use your network. Too low and you risk bad actors spamming the network, congesting it with useless transactions. A particularly vexed question is how transaction fees on a network relate to the price of the network's native token. During the 2016–2017 ICO bubble, token prices shot up on exchanges, but where the token's purpose was to purchase a certain unit of interaction with the network, this quickly made these interactions unpredictable and expensive to run.

Let's take Ethereum as an example. As we saw in Chapter 3, fees for executing a smart contract on the Ethereum blockchain or for sending a certain amount of Ether are not directly priced in Ether: instead, they consume units of Gas. While the Gas price is not fixed, when you deploy a smart contract, you can specify the Gas price (in Ether) that you are prepared to pay, and also set a Gas limit for your contract. So, while the price is not directly correlated, the Gas price tends to go up when Ethereum goes up, and vice versa, although network activity is probably a better indicator. To visualize how fees can rise and fall with network activity and with the dollar price of a cryptocurrency, Figure 5.2 shows an example of average Bitcoin fees over several years.

Reducing unnecessary traffic is an important element of developing public blockchain networks, and transaction fees are a big part of this. In Chapter 13, we will look at some of the scalability improvements that are being proposed and trialled, including so-called second-layer solutions such as Lightning, for Bitcoin, and Ethereum's move towards a proof of stake system, among other things. While everyone agrees that keeping unnecessary transactions to a minimum is important, not everyone agrees on what is 'unnecessary'.

A good example of this perception gap is the network congestion that overtook Ethereum in December 2017. While teams with serious prospectuses were trying to raise tens of millions of dollars for their

FIGURE 5.2   Bitcoin transaction fees over time

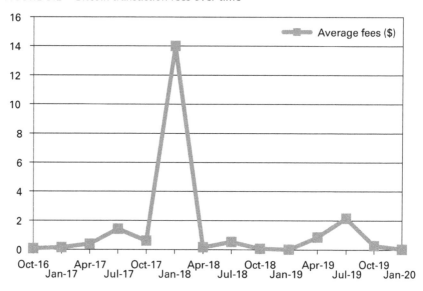

innovative decentralized project proposals, those users trying to crowdfund these exciting projects found that their contributions were getting stuck in the system, taking days to reach the smart contract for which they were intended. The cause? An engaging game called CryptoKitties in which players were invited to breed and sell cute cartoon cats, their transactions all being registered on the Ethereum blockchain. Coming, as this did, right at the tail end of the ICO boom, this was a stark reminder that perhaps Ethereum's technology was not quite ready for prime time, and that the incentive/penalty balance was perhaps not appropriate to all circumstances.

In October 2019, a game called FairWin was blamed for another round of Ethereum network congestion. However, it is not just avoiding spamming and inappropriate usage where a good tokenomic structure is crucial. Having an algorithm that correctly offsets the energy expended to acquire the token against its market price is essential to stop fraudsters from gaming the consensus system. This is not a technical book, so we will not discuss this in depth, but what this means in the real world is that a thief wishing to make a large purchase with Bitcoin and then rewrite the history of the blockchain so that they could spend the same amount twice, would have to waste more value in creating enough computing power on enough different computers than the profit from the theft. This perfect balance of rewards and penalties is what makes Bitcoin – and some of the other public networks that have followed it – such a resilient and elegant solution.

Distribution and burning mechanisms

Token distribution is probably one of the most controversial aspects of token engineering and design. In the early days, before Ethereum launched and before the consequent rush to crowdfund a new idea via the mechanism of an ICO (initial coin offering), coin founders would often conduct a pre-mine before making the software for the network publicly available. While there was some acceptance that for a cryptocurrency to be successful, the team who wrote the software and conducted other business activities should be remunerated properly to ensure their ongoing participation, pre-mining was generally frowned upon, especially if it did not observe reasonable limits.

Pre-mining is carried out so that the developer(s) get the first shot at generating tokens before anyone else has the chance. Either these tokens are kept as a way to remunerate the team, or as a personal reward in the case of the sketchier coins, or else they are pre-mined and held back to be sold in a crowdsale, as happened with Ethereum. While Satoshi Nakamoto was able to mine a large number of bitcoins, this was not a pre-mine, as the software had already been released to the public and other people were free to participate. It is worth noting that with the high initial block reward (50 bitcoins until the first halving, in November 2012), anyone who started mining Bitcoin early enough and managed to hold on to their coins would by now be a multi-millionaire.

Other cryptocurrencies that did not conduct pre-mines include Dogecoin, Litecoin and Monero, all of which remain in the top 20 cryptocurrencies to this day. Cryptocurrencies that were notably heavily pre-mined include Auroracoin, PayCoin and FuelCoin, all of which have either sunk without trace or, in the case of Paycoin, were revealed as an out-and-out scam. So, while a pre-mine is not always carried out for nefarious purposes, it can sometimes be a marker for when the founder of a coin simply wants to make a fast buck and exit as fast as they can.

After Ethereum was launched and startups began using smart contracts for managing their ICOs, there was even more scope to retain a generous share of the crowdsale for the development team. While this was ostensibly for paying office rents and expanding the team, many of the anecdotes of 2016–2017 – indeed, supported by the Instagram and Twitter accounts of some of the more shameless founders – revealed that individuals had made millions by allocating generous sums of tokens to support development and marketing efforts; it was, of course, pure coincidence that so many founders of the time were photographed driving around in Lamborghinis or other performance cars!

These coin allocations, accompanied by coordinated 'pump and dump' schemes are what earned ICOs such a shady reputation. Unlike a traditional cryptocurrency where the pre-mined blocks would be obvious as their timestamps would be dated before the official public release of the code, tracking down the movement of tokens in an ICO requires a little more detective work. The founders, and sometimes their advisors, receive value from two sources: the Ether that is sent to the smart contract in payment for the newly created tokens, and the proportion of tokens that is sent back to finance the project. As the earlier generation of ICOs were largely unregulated (more of this in Chapter 11), there was nothing to compel the founders to work on further development and build out the ecosystem once they had raised their ICO riches.

It is true that developer time is a reasonably expensive resource, and that projects need to make sure they are adequately funded to give themselves time to create a long enough runway to take off. But projects that were clearly designed more or less to line the pockets of their founders have attracted much bad press and given the whole cryptocurrency scene a bad name. There have also been cases where the initial development team have made so much money upfront that they do not remain committed to the project and instead are tempted to take their gains and move on elsewhere. Founder rewards and the proportion of fundraising that goes to this cause are therefore something to be taken into consideration when designing the economic model of your blockchain.

If your token is not a stablecoin, there is also a question around how its price might be set at a level by the market that optimizes engagement with the network. As we have seen above, while crypto traders love the volatility of altcoins, and millions of words and thousands of podcast hours have been devoted to the art and science of picking a coin that will increase in value 100 times or more, price instability is a bug rather than a feature when it comes to the smooth operation of a blockchain network.

Some organizations introduce conditions such as locking up the tokens for a certain length of time after the sale, and in this way deterring speculators who want to buy only in order to offload quickly, causing an initial stratospheric price rise and thereafter a crash. One of the mechanisms for doing this is by introducing the idea of a SAFT (simple agreement for future tokens). However, as token models have become more sophisticated, analysts and regulators have proposed the idea of RATE as a suitable model, which stands for Real Agreement for Tokens and Equity. This model is based on an initial token allocation that falls under security token regulation, after which, at some future point, the token that will be used on the network is distributed to security token-holders as a perk.

If a mandatory locking of tokens for a certain time is one way of preventing precipitous price rises and falls, there is another stability mechanism that can be brought into play. As we have seen, one of the main determinants of a token price is its supply and demand. Thus, by eliminating a certain number of tokens from circulation, the price should rise. The primary way of doing this is by destroying tokens, which is referred to as 'burning' them. Despite the dramatic name, all this means is that the tokens are sent to an address to which no one has the private key: in other words, they become unspendable. On a public blockchain, this action is of course able to be viewed by anyone, hence we talk about 'proof of burn'. It is important that the schedule and rules for token burning are laid out clearly and adhered to. If token destruction and consequent price rises are seen as being ad hoc actions that are left to the discretion of the people who run the project (and who presumably will benefit from the rising price), then the project should be viewed with suspicion. Such actions would signify that a project is not decentralized at all.

Eden Dhaliwal reminds us that if there are decisions to be made about token monetary policy once the network is live, decisions such as expanding or contracting the token supply should ideally be made programmatically and determined by algorithms, potentially using machine learning to enable automated processes to get the issuance right: 'Decentralization is a journey, rather than something that is achievable from day one, and of course things will change and evolve. But as long as these changes are automated as far as possible and can be understood by all the participants, then you are moving in the right direction.'

Governance

For a truly decentralized system, all incentives, parameters, numbers of tokens and issuance schedule should be predefined in code so that anyone investing in the system, either as a token buyer or as a validator, can know in advance what they are signing up to. The guiding principle of open-source software is that once it has been released into the world, the developer effectively loses control of it. As there is no governing body that represents Bitcoin (this has been a distinct advantage in scenarios where regulators have sought to clamp down and may well have prosecuted, had there been a single person to prosecute), if the software needs to be upgraded, the only way to do this, once it has been tested, is to push the fix out, communicate the reasons behind the upgrade and hope that enough miners in the network install the upgraded software and run it. If there is no clear consensus over which version of the software to run, then the network runs the risk of forking (splitting). We will talk in some more detail in Chapter 8 about the Bitcoin forks that happened in 2016 and

2017, some following bitter disputes about the entire direction of Bitcoin, and others that were purely money-making exercises. Although there have been concerted efforts at a corporate level to win over particular mining consortiums and to coalesce public relations around a certain point of view, the protocol itself has remained remarkably resilient to such politicking. The fact that Bitcoin has managed to survive and thrive for more than 10 years shows that human intervention can do more harm than good in some situations.

Let's revisit the scenario we briefly touched on in Chapter 3 and which we will revisit in more detail in Chapter 8, when Ethereum suffered a controversial hard fork as the remedy for returning DAO investors' funds. As illustrated by the wild 4Chan rumour of his death, which sent prices tumbling, Ethereum's creator Vitalik Buterin continues to exert a deep hold over Ethereum's future direction, although this is not necessarily his intention. While the Switzerland-based Ethereum Foundation holds some 0.6 per cent of Ether in circulation, following the 2014 crowdsale, the Foundation's activities tend to be focused on research and development, as well as disbursing grants to companies building applications within the ecosystem. Meanwhile, decisions about the direction of Ethereum's protocol layer tend to be taken by the network's core developers, many of whom work for Ethereum-affiliated companies. While the conference calls to discuss acceptance and implementation of EIPs (Ethereum Improvement Proposals) are live-streamed and are designed to be transparent, it is fair to say that the most senior and long-standing developers, as on any software team, wield a strong influence.

The DAO hack was an interesting case in point. The DAO smart contract had just become the biggest crowdsale in history and with more than $150,000 at stake, it was difficult for anyone with an influence to remain truly subjective. According to the original guiding principles of Ethereum, the 'code is law' argument should have prevailed and nothing should have been done that compromised the immutability of the data in the blockchain. If you are running a network whose primary strength is the fact that data can automatically be trusted, then the ability to rewrite parts of it in extreme circumstances is a weakness, not a strength.

Observers have claimed since the controversial decision was made to rewrite history and restore the stolen funds at the expense of Ethereum's integrity, that this path was chosen partly because the decision makers stood to lose money themselves; this is, I think, overly cynical. Others believe that it was instead a well-meaning attempt to redress damage done and make people feel more confident about investing in DAO-like contracts in the future.

We see in our daily lives that traditional corporations stand or fall on the strength or weakness of their human leadership. Even companies whose primary product is about to be made obsolete by technology can pivot to something new if their leadership team is sufficiently innovative and forward-thinking. Decentralized structures such as blockchains aim to eliminate this unpredictability by removing this dependency on human decision making, and ensuring that token incentives and penalties are sufficient to keep the network running without management decisions being taken.

The big question: why do you need a token?

While this is the last discussion point in this chapter, this question is probably the most important. Token incentives promote decentralization and – as we shall see in the next chapter – enable entirely new business models to exist. The idea of the cryptocurrency revolution as a whole is predicated on these models. However, the history of many so-called decentralized startups leads us to believe that there were unfortunately many ideas where a token was not really necessary, but was shoehorned into the business model anyway so that the founders could raise large amounts of money with an ICO.

In order to establish whether a token is really necessary for a particular business model, ask the question: could this be done using fiat payments, or even payments with Bitcoin or Ether. If the answer to this question is 'yes', then you don't need a token, and the whole question of tokenomics is moot. The next question is how likely users are to use your product if they need to buy a token, and how they will acquire that token. In the idealistic days of 2016–2017, many businesses made the assumption that somehow the general public would want to purchase their token in order to use the product, regardless of the extra time, cost and the fact that most people had barely even heard of Bitcoin.

Eden Dhaliwal feels that the question of providing users with an 'on ramp' where they can easily exchange fiat currency for tokens is critical: 'People need to be able to access tokens – they need to be able to do this easily and cheaply, and the whole user experience needs to be there so that the process is intuitive. We also need decentralized applications to be really compelling, so that users are motivated to acquire tokens so they can use them.'

In this chapter, we have looked closely at the factors that come into play when deciding how many tokens should be issued, how they should be distributed and what sorts of rights they should confer. We have also seen how many companies created businesses that did not genuinely need a token so that they could run an ICO and raise funds without having to go through the due diligence of offering securities. In the next chapter, we will look at the opposite case: some real-life examples of where tokenized systems using native cryptocurrencies could indeed be useful, and how tokenization could have revolutionary consequences for the way we do business and interact with each other.

References

Au, S and Power, T (2018) *Tokenomics: The crypto shift of blockchains, ICOs, and tokens*, Packt Publishing

Berg, C, Davidson, S and Potts, J (2017) The Blockchain Economy: A beginner's guide to institutional cryptoeconomics, 27 September. Available from: https://medium.com/cryptoeconomics-australia/the-blockchain-economy-a-beginners-guide-to-institutional-cryptoeconomics-64bf2f2beec4 (archived at https://perma.cc/WSY5-DLRU)

Dhaliwal, E and Gurguc, Z (2018) Token Ecosystem Creation: A strategic process to architect and engineer viable token economies, October. Available from: https://outlierventures.io/wp-content/uploads/2018/10/Token-Ecosystem-Creation-Outlier-Ventures-PDF.pdf (archived at https://perma.cc/VU5J-TUJS)

Lipsey, R G and Chrystal, K A (2011) *Economics*, 12th edn, Oxford University Press

NIST (nd) 'cryptographic token' Computer Security Resource Center, Glossary. Available from https://csrc.nist.gov/glossary/term/cryptographic-token (archived at https://perma.cc/MV44-TVWS)

OED (2010) 'token', *Oxford English Dictionary*, Oxford University Press

6

Driving change with token economies: case studies

Before we start considering some of the areas where using a specific token could provide incentives for people to interact with a network, automate payments or create a monetized market where there was not one previously, let's define the scope of this chapter. This book is not about how companies are using blockchain technology to manage their existing data or to work with partners in a consortium. There are many existing books covering the implementation of blockchain frameworks within enterprises. See the Further Reading section at the end of this chapter for some recommendations.

Instead, the purpose of these case studies is to look at public networks where the incorporation of a token is critical to their operation and show how blockchain technology can work with a convergence of other 21st-century innovations such as the Internet of Things (IoT) in order to improve people's lives. The part about improving people's lives is particularly important: however innovative and interesting your idea is, if it is too complicated and expensive for people to obtain some very real benefits from adopting it, then there is very little point in trying to turn it into a business. This idea of the Convergence Stack has been developed by Outlier Ventures, and their paper 'Blockchain-enabled convergence' (Outlier Ventures Research, 2018) makes for interesting reading.

The other thing to remember is that these scenarios, while they may not sound plausible now, are quite probably business models that will become familiar over the coming years. If we cast our minds back a decade or so, it is easy to forget that 'sharing economy' businesses such as Airbnb and Uber would have engendered the same degree of scepticism. After all, who would get in a stranger's car or go and stay in a stranger's apartment in a different city in another country? People would have come up with all kinds of reasons why this business model was doomed to fail if they were asked to analyse the prospects of companies like this in 2000. So, it is useful to remember these examples as you read on, and bear in mind that expectations and social norms change along with technology.

Automotive

The automotive sector is a great place to start as an example of how token economies could work because it is already a market that is undergoing fundamental change, with autonomous driving, electric vehicles, vehicle connectivity and shared-ownership/rental schemes all disrupting the traditional business model of selling vehicles via local dealerships. If we look at a city like Berlin, where car-sharing schemes are popular, as early as 2016 it was estimated that ownership of private cars was 15 per cent lower than it would have been without the presence of schemes such as DriveNow and Car2Go (Giesel and Nobis, 2016). Analysis by McKinsey (Gao *et al*, 2016) sees this type of innovation as a positive change rather than an existential threat to the automotive industry, with the potential to add $1.5 trillion in economic growth via these new opportunities.

Moving away from the traditional 'one household, one or more cars' model has to be something that is convenient, desirable and financially sensible for the consumer, or else in a free society, such innovation simply will not happen. Modern car-sharing schemes such as DriveNow and Zipcar have customers because they have been able to use new technologies to smooth the rental process to the point where it is seamless and is able to compete with car ownership not simply in terms of price, but in terms of convenience. Compare the DriveNow experience to a legacy vehicle-rental service. If renting a vehicle from the latter, you have to show up at a specified location, which may or may not be near where you are; you need to take along paperwork to prove your identity and your address; you have to leave a deposit to guard against the possibility of damaging the vehicle; you are often upsold expensive insurance; you must return the vehicle within particular working hours so it can be checked; and so on.

Customers of modern car-sharing services, on the other hand, can sign up as a member and can then use a mobile app to locate any car within their vicinity, access it via Bluetooth using the same app, drive it to wherever they want to go and then leave it by the kerbside, while their journey is automatically charged to the nearest minute. It sometimes happens that people's lives change as technology and society change around us, and the old ways of doing things often do not mesh well with modern living. DriveNow and Car2Go are among many companies who stepped into this vacuum to provide a service that fits perfectly with the way we live now, and they are doing well as a result. The use of these new technologies is beneficial not only for customers but also for the company itself, as the connectivity built into modern cars gives the company a source of rich data to mine and analyse to help it with its business development.

So, how would a cryptocurrency token fit into the mobility – and specifically the automotive – sector? In order to understand some of these examples, it is necessary to make a mental leap where one regards transactions, whether on a blockchain or on some other kind of network, as something that can be made by and from machines and devices, rather than by and from one human to another. There are already more connected devices on the planet than humans, and most of these interactions are device-to-device rather than initiated by humans. Many of these will be on the same network, such as sensors within a factory or a warehouse, but where there is a need for payments to pass between these devices, which may be owned by different people, then there is an issue of trust. How does one device prove it is really what it says it is? How can a payment be authorized without human intervention – and what if the payment is so small that it would be inefficient for the banking system to process it?

If all of this sounds rather abstract, let's consider a concrete example. In 2017, a hackathon was held at an event in Dubai whose purpose was to promote technology ideas for smart cities. A team called Project Oaken was one of the three finalists, presenting their idea for allowing cars to pay for their own tolls automatically. As they explain: 'The Tesla tells the toll gate that it wants to pay the toll, causing the toll booth to trigger a smart contract transaction. The toll booth takes the raw Tesla data and communicates it to the blockchain in the form of an IPFS hash' (Higgins, 2017).

You may wonder what the problem is with the current situation where car drivers simply pay tolls by using cash or card, or in the case of special areas such as London's Congestion or Ultra Low Emission Zone, where the user sets up an account and is automatically billed. To begin with, fixed-rate toll stations where the driver pays manually are very inefficient. Not only do they cause queues when drivers have to stop and pay, they tend to be a blunt instrument as a flat fee is easier to charge and understand. To optimize traffic flow in smart cities, the ideal scenario is to be able to charge a variable fee, depending on traffic congestion at the time of day. If the vehicle could itself make a machine-to-machine transfer, while informing the driver what the fee was likely to be, then this would reduce the need for human interaction, smoothing the traffic flow and avoiding the need for the driver to provide their bank details and sign up for schemes that may vary from city to city.

The idea of making payments in some kind of global, cross-border currency is also appealing, while an automated process fixes the problem of drivers in new cities not being aware of what tolls they should pay, or how to sign up. A recent case made the news where an unwitting Spanish motorist ran up a fine of £20,000 for driving in and out of London 12 times while on holiday, without realizing his 4x4 violated the Low Emission Zone rule (Collinson and Brignall, 2019).

London's car-sharing schemes currently incorporate the Congestion Charge into their rental fee, and this could also be done on a pro-rata basis in a peer-to-peer network. Research done on the Ethereum blockchain by startups such as Slock.it predicts a future where one's possessions can use their spare capacity to earn their owners money in an entirely automated, decentralized way. If you park your car on the side of the street and inform it that you will not need it for a certain amount of time, the car can be made available for other people to rent. The hirer could identify themselves using a self-sovereign identity system, which would enable them to reveal as much or as little about themselves as they wished. It could, for example, identify them as a reliable renter of cars without revealing their name and address to the car owner. The car itself would then charge the renter for the time and mileage consumed, including any tolls or taxes, according to a pre-agreed formula. A geographical limit on where the car could be used would be written into the smart contract, and the car would be programmed to respond to the smart contract and not be driven outside the exclusion zone. Yes, much of this would be possible without a blockchain, but using a decentralized network means a lot of the hard work surrounding identity, payments and privacy is made easy and quick.

The data generated by our cars is not only useful for car-sharing and other new business models. Modern cars generate vast amounts of data – about weather conditions, other vehicles on the road and their geographic location, as well as information about engine performance and so on. This information is currently available only to the manufacturer or the dealership, but imagine the following scenarios:

- Owners of vehicles can allow their car to report road conditions to allow other cars' navigation systems to make better decisions about routes.

- Vehicle owners can be seamlessly paid to leave their car at home on certain days of the week, using location data.

- Insurers are empowered to make better decisions and drive down the cost of travelling for responsible individuals.

- Town planners can use geolocation data from vehicles, cyclists, pedestrians and public transport vehicles to make better infrastructure decisions.

The ability to receive micropayments in exchange for small pieces of data that can be aggregated and then consumed and analysed in order to make cities run more smoothly is just one part of the puzzle.

So, where do blockchains and integrated token payments come into this equation? Is all of this not possible without using a blockchain? The answer is that yes, of course it is possible, but a blockchain allows us to provide validated data that cannot be rewritten, thus allowing companies to make sensitive commercial decisions based on this source of truth, while cryptocurrencies allow frequent, ambient payments to be made to unknown individuals. For example, imagine you are driving somewhere on a busy road and you are not particularly in a hurry. The driver behind you, in contrast, is late for work and would like to overtake. A seamless microtransaction could be made between vehicles, allowing their car to overtake yours. You do not have to consciously make a decision or provide the other driver with your bank details – it happens automatically.

It might sound like science fiction now, but along with autonomous cars, drone-enabled takeaway deliveries and fridges that restock themselves automatically, it will become part of our daily lives at some point.

Energy

One of the reasons for using a blockchain for device-to-device transactions is that if the blockchain has a native token, data and payment is able to form part of the same transaction. Another interesting example is the idea of peer-to-peer electricity trading between neighbours – of particular interest for those who own renewable generation sources such as solar panels or windmills and want to be able to sell their excess power. How would this work in real life? Let's take the example of neighbours in a street of townhouses. Each house on one side of the street has a roof that faces south and is fitted with solar panels, while the other row of houses is north-facing. The houses on the south side of the road produce enough power to fuel their homes, particularly in the daytime when the residents are out at work and their batteries are filled to capacity.

In normal circumstances, this power would go to waste, as there is nowhere to store it, and the solar panel installation is not one of the expensive and complicated ones that is linked to the national electricity grid. However, in our example, the houses in the street are networked together, so that excess energy produced by one home can be consumed by another home, where the residents may not be at work, or which does not have a solar panel. This is a really neat solution, you think, but it must be tedious for the over-producers to monitor their electricity production and transfers, and to invoice their neighbours periodically for the power they have used, as well as checking their bank accounts to ensure that payments have been made on time.

Fortunately for the solar panel owners, this street has been chosen for an experiment in peer-to-peer energy trading, and all transactions are recorded on the Ethereum blockchain. A smart contract specifies the payment in Ether, which is transferred in exchange for the electricity sold, and the transactions are made between the solar panels, rather than between the residents. There is no need to know your neighbours' bank account details, or even their names, and no need to chase them for payment. Everything happens seamlessly and all you have to do is have an Ethereum wallet address in order to receive the payments.

OK, so some of the automotive use cases I have described above sound quite futuristic, but in this case, a practical proof of concept has already taken place: the Microgrid project in Brooklyn. The company behind it, LoEnergy, has since moved away from the idea of using Ethereum in favour of its own platform, Exergy, but the concept is the same. Just as devices that are connected to the internet now outnumber humans connected to the internet, so device-to-device cryptocurrency transactions will at some point outnumber those originated by humans.

Media

Since the earliest days of the internet, traditional media companies have been wrestling with the question of how to make their business model continue to work in an entirely new and unfamiliar world. While there are still many people who prefer to buy a newspaper in its print version, most prefer to consume their news online from the same organizations, or from sources online that have sprung up after being enabled by internet technology: social media, blogs or digital-only publications. The Covid-19 pandemic has hastened this trend. When newspapers, television and radio were the only available options, anyone who wanted to read an authoritative written piece that was more up to date than a book would turn to a newspaper because there were no other choices. The cover price of the paper, plus revenue earned from print advertising supported a business model that was centuries old and that has not changed much during those centuries.

The advent of the world wide web broke this business model. Readers became accustomed to content that was supplied online being given away for free. It is also true to say that, apart from a few visionaries, most journalists and executives working in newspapers saw the new technology as a threat, rather than an opportunity. Most editors fought against what they saw as the enemy within their news-rooms, subjecting their content to a digital embargo until after the print edition had gone on sale, and in some cases vetoing reproduction on the website altogether. Many editors thought that the online edition of their paper should be a faithful reproduction of the printed version, and this failure to grasp the different opportunities that presented themselves made them feel even more beleaguered. They were fighting resistance on two fronts: not only were their younger readers unused to paying for digital content, but their older and more established readership was, at least in the early days of the late 1990s and very early 2000s, suspicious of giving their bank details or credit card number to any website. Eventually, most legacy publications opted to install some kind of paywall.

The problem with paywalls is that they require some kind of minimum outlay, whether monetary or in terms of effort. Even if you admire the quality of the writing in *The New York Times*, for example, how can you guarantee that in your time-poor life you will eventually get around to reading the number of articles that will make your subscription worthwhile? And if you have clicked idly on a Twitter link to a newspaper story to find it paywalled, it is most likely that you will not even go through the boring process of activating a free trial sign-up. Some news aggregators attempted to negotiate with newspapers to set up a general news passporting service, where revenues would be shared, but this was rejected out of hand. In an archaic industry where even stablemates and sister titles such as the *Guardian* and *Observer*, and *The Times* and *Sunday Times* were bitter rivals, this collectivist approach made no sense.

On the other hand, while the old media was quietly dying, a new breed of content producers was rising. Fashion bloggers soon became more influential than fashion magazines, in recent years usurping the star writers of glossy magazines in the coveted front row at fashion shows. Other content producers created video: everything from political opinion to technical tutorials to DIY guides. Mobile phones meant everyone now had a video camera, and platforms such as YouTube, Vimeo and TikTok meant that previous unknowns now had followings of millions.

I have spent some time filling in the background to show that while media has been one of the sectors most disrupted by the arrival of the internet, it has also been one of the slowest to find a solution. How would tokens help? The answer is that, while many people are not prepared to pay for content, some are: and we can see this willingness in the writers and vloggers who are supported on a voluntary basis by programmes such as Patreon, which allow consumers to contribute to their chosen creators. However, even Patreon is a paywall of a kind, and unless you are particularly dedicated to the work of a particular person, it remains a barrier.

In the early days of crypto social media, an interesting phenomenon sprang up. Because money could be sent directly to a Bitcoin address, whether it was $10, a few cents or even a fraction of a cent, some content creators began to provide their public Bitcoin address, either as a string or as a QR code on their websites, their YouTube page or their Twitter profile. People were happy to send tips (which, of course, appreciated dramatically in value over the years between 2012 and 2017) and tipbot browser extensions were created, allowing users to send Bitcoin, Dogecoin or various other currencies to social media addresses of their choice to reward useful content.

Perhaps it was this that sowed the seed of several startups, and gradually the idea of micropayments for tiny quantities of content began to catch on. Building some software into a browser so that you could keep some cryptocurrency in a general-purpose wallet and allow it to release a fraction of a cent's worth of cryptocurrency in a steady stream while you read an interesting article or watched an entertaining video seemed to be an idea with genuine usability. As a content creator, all you had to do was sign up, place some code on your page and if a consumer stumbled across your article or video, they could read it and pay paragraph by paragraph. It was the perfect frictionless way to enjoy good quality media, while knowing that in the background the creator was being rewarded for your attention. Bitcoin was the original network chosen for this, but as transaction fees rose and micropayments became too expensive, startups such as SatoshiPay and Smoogs pivoted to other blockchains.

Since then, another solution has come along: the Brave browser, with its Basic Attention Token (BAT). Co-created by Brendan Eich, who not only invented the JavaScript programming language but also co-founded the Mozilla Foundation, home of the Firefox browser, Brave hosts its own advertisements, which readers can receive a small payment for watching. Brave also incorporates a reward system for content creators, where you can register to receive payments denominated in BAT if readers consume your content using Brave. At the moment, no one is making a living from Brave, but it is early days and the fact that many people are receiving at least some small payments from this so-called 'attention token' suggests that the idea of attention tokens is possibly an innovation worth watching. Reddit have since announced a Community Points system, built on Ethereum, which allows users to tip each other.

Gaming and art

As we discussed in Chapter 1, one of the precursors to cryptocurrencies were the forms of digital money that were used in games such as Second Life. While these were centralized and were issued and circulated very much at the discretion of the game manufacturers – if you were banned from Second Life, you lost your Linden Dollars – it showed there was an appetite for a form of money to use in games that had at least some kind of nominal exchange rate with dollars, pounds, euros or yen. The growth of whole parallel economies in cyberspace even before Bitcoin was invented, was a sign that to blend the economy of a virtual world with that of the real world was to solve a problem that really existed.

Not only did game players purchase land, avatars and superpowers, but there was also a market for collectibles and craft items. To browse the Second Life Marketplace is to gain an insight into a world of rich imagination and possibilities. However, where there is genuine creativity, there are always people looking to capitalize on that creativity with cheap imitations, especially when a game's economy is opened up to third-party traders.

How do we ensure that a digital item such as an artwork or a custom avatar cannot be copied and sold a thousand times over? The answer is to issue the item as a non-fungible token, or NFT. This is a special type of cryptocurrency token, which exists as a one-off on a particular blockchain and maps a digital asset (such as an in-game accessory or an artwork) to an entry on the blockchain. This has been carried out on various blockchains, such as the Counterparty network, but Ethereum lends itself well to this particular use case, and there are even special types of standard smart contract for this purpose, namely ERC-721 contracts.

Probably the most famous ERC-721 contract, at least at the time of writing, is the one that is used to create CryptoKitties, the game that took the crypto world by storm in 2017–2018 and attracted many users outside the hardcore crypto trading community. Just as real-world collectibles such as football cards or Pez are traded, so were these cute cartoon cats. To make the game even more appealing, once you had some specific kitties, you could breed them to create more, and even give them cool, marketable names. For a brief period, serious crypto traders poured into the game, as prices of these quirky collectors' items soared. The most expensive CryptoKitty sold for an astonishing $170,000 worth of Ether as the hype cycle kicked in. The game continues, although the prices are more sensible now: you can check the most recent Kitties sold on the Kitty Explorer website, which has all the historic prices and records a fascinating episode in cryptocurrency history. Despite the sudden craze bringing the whole Ethereum blockchain to a virtual standstill, CryptoKitties was a useful illustration of the type of thing one can do with NFTs. It is also worth mentioning here that for all its use of the Ethereum blockchain, CryptoKitties is not a decentralized project at all. While the buyer (or breeder) owns the token and can trade it, Dapper Labs, the company behind CryptoKitties, retains the intellectual property of the artwork.

Where CryptoKitties trailblazed, other similar projects followed, and there were soon CryptoPunks, CryptoPuppies and many others, including CryptoCountries. For some reason, the UK in CryptoCountries was bid up to $69,000 while the United States could only muster $10,000. Many of these collector games were cut-and-paste copies of the wildly successful CryptoKitties, but occasionally something came along that was of particular interest. For example, Decentraland is an interesting virtual reality project powered by the Ethereum blockchain. Players can use Decentraland's MANA token to buy plots of land within the game and build their own applications and experiences, which they are free to monetize. Creators retain all the rights to their creations, and the project is decentralized. The plots of land are represented by NFTs in the form of an ERC-721 token called simply LAND, and when the MANA token is exchanged for LAND, the MANA is burned. The focus of the game is on creativity as well as collecting: tutorials on the Decentraland website include instructions on how to place the NFT artwork you have bought or collected into a scene in the game. Blockade Games and The Sandbox are other well known names in this space.

While these companies are probably the most forward-looking blockchain projects in their treatment of, and vision for, in-game NFTs (which are, after all, a specialized type of cryptocurrency), it seems that they have to wait for the rest of the gaming world to catch up with them. While Decentraland can get developers building applications on its platform to obey particular coding standards that mean that Decentraland NFTs can move smoothly between applications, the same does not apply – yet – to other games. As Decentraland explain on their blog, and as other cryptocurrency and blockchain writers have pointed out, the end game for NFTs is for them to have a life of their own, independent of the game in which they were originally acquired. If your avatar has the perfect custom skin in one game, then why should your avatar in another game not be able to use it? If you buy a famous sword that was used to win a legendary battle that was streamed live on Twitch TV to tens of thousands of viewers, then provided that sword has an NFT representation, you should be able to sell that sword on an open crypto marketplace, not simply the marketplace aligned with the game in which you bought it. Similarly, if games makers were ultimately to agree some development standard for the representation of NFTs, there is nothing to stop the sword turning up in another game entirely. Obviously, there are all kinds of commercial and technical reasons why this is not yet a reality, but it is useful to bear in mind the ultimate vision that NFT enthusiasts are working towards.

Gaming is not the only arena where the idea of NFTs is making inroads – the idea of registering a digital artwork as a smart contract so that it can be marked as unique and traded as such has been a recurring theme in crypto circles for some years. If you own a painting or other physical artwork, someone has to go to great lengths in order to forge a copy of it and demonstrate its provenance. Previously, digital artists faced the problem that their art could be easily reproduced: how do you prove if you send someone a high-resolution JPEG that you have not just sold 100 more of these to other art collectors? The Forever Rose is probably the most prominent crypto-artwork that has been sold, although Parisian street artist Pascal Boyart has been conducting some interesting experiments in tokenizing his street art – the first part of his 'Daddy, What is Money?' mural sold on the OpenSea marketplace for 25 ETH ($5000 at the time) (Delafont, 2019).

In this chapter, we have covered several different examples of how data and payments can be combined in some programmable way to perform certain tasks. In this book so far, we have examined primarily public, permissionless networks, which anyone can join. In the next chapter, we will turn our attention to the main differences between true, decentralized public blockchains and their near neighbours, private distributed ledgers, and we will see how examples of each of these categories are being used in real-life scenarios.

References

Collinson, P and Brignall, M (2019) I was charged £20,000 for driving my car into the London emissions zone, *Guardian*, 31 August. Available from: https://www.theguardian.com/money/2019/aug/31/i-was-charged-20000-for-driving-my-car-into-the-london-emissions-zone (archived at https://perma.cc/9EPX-T7CU)

Delafont, R (2019) Crypto artist continues to innovate with tokenised street art sale, *News BTC*, September. Available from: https://www.newsbtc.com/2019/08/27/crypto-artist-continues-to-innovate-with-tokenised-street-art-sale/ (archived at https://perma.cc/6SQG-47JQ)

Gao, P, Kaas, H-W, Mohr, D and Wee, D (2016) Disruptive trends that will transform the auto industry, *McKinsey & Company*, January. Available from: https://www.mckinsey.com/industries/automotive-and-assembly/our-insights/disruptive-trends-that-will-transform-the-auto-industry (archived at https://perma.cc/7MCE-H6PF)

Giesel, F and Nobis, C (2016) The impact of carsharing on car ownership in German cities, *Transportation Research Procedia*, **19**, 215–224. Available from: https://www.sciencedirect.com/science/article/pii/S2352146516308687 (archived at https://perma.cc/8PS2-QPZT)

Higgins, S (2017) Ethereum IOT project wins $100k Dubai blockchain hackathon, *CoinDesk*, 14 February. Available from: https://www.coindesk.com/ethereum-iot-project-wins-100k-dubai-blockchain-hackathon (archived at https://perma.cc/5A5A-S5U6)

Outlier Ventures Research (2018) Blockchain-enabled convergence: understanding the Web 3.0 economy, November. Available from: https://outlierventures.io/wp-content/uploads/2018/11/Blockchain-Enabled-Convergence-Whitepaper.pdf (archived at https://perma.cc/E8TU-2F8V)

Further reading

Casey, M J and Vigna, P (2018) *The Truth Machine: The blockchain and the future of everything*, HarperCollins

Pejic, I (2019) *Blockchain Babel: The crypto craze and the challenge to business*, Kogan Page

Tapscott, D and Tapscott, A (2016) *Blockchain Revolution: How the technology behind Bitcoin and other cryptocurrencies is changing the world*, Penguin

7

Public blockchains versus permissioned blockchains

If public blockchain networks derive their security from running on many different computers to provide a single source of truth, one might reasonably ask the question: why on earth would someone want to use a private blockchain? The idea of a wholly private blockchain implies that a company replaces a normal database with one that is distributed across several different computers – or, more likely, several different virtual servers in a cloud provider's data centre – in which the data is cryptographically timestamped so it can't be rewritten. The only people who can access this data are those who have usernames and passwords that are issued by the company who has set up the network. This network's data cannot be read or written to by anyone outside a carefully selected group, just as a company does not let anyone write to their normal databases. This type of privacy is obviously a highly desirable feature where information needs to be kept confidential: commercially sensitive transactions, medical records, criminal records and so on. We are used to the idea that some data needs to be entirely private and should not be released to the outside world, even if encrypted. There are arguments for and against this approach, which we will consider later in the chapter, but let's assume for now that we want the data in our network to remain private.

Given that writing data in several different places and waiting for the network to reach consensus is time- and energy-consuming, and given that technology for limiting access permissions is so good, why would someone want to go to all the trouble of replacing a private database with a private blockchain to which the same people have access? This is a good question, and it is comparatively rare for companies to want to use a distributed ledger in this entirely private way, although naturally there may be cases when they want to present evidence to an auditor that information has not been rewritten or tampered with, and the cryptographic security of the data is provable. Instead, when people talk about 'private' blockchains, they are more likely to be talking about distributed ledgers to which more than one organization has access, but which are restricted to certain authorized individuals: in other words, a consortium. For this purpose, it is probably more useful to think in terms of 'permissioned' or 'permissionless' rather than 'private' or 'public'. You will often hear the acronym 'DLT' for distributed ledger technology, and this is often a more accurate term for these consortium networks than 'blockchain'.

Once we start thinking about these shared networks that allow access to timestamped, trustworthy data by multiple organizations, the idea begins to make more sense. A distributed ledger shared between several organizations allows these companies to share a common record of transactions while making the details of these transactions private unless a participant is directly involved. What this means in practice is that while Bank A, Bank B and Bank C can belong to the same network, Bank C cannot see the details of a transaction that had been made between Bank A and Bank B. Just as a fully public blockchain network means that members of the network do not have to trust each other because the record of all transactions is out there for everyone to see, so a permissioned distributed ledger can help solve the trust problem between organizations who may not necessarily trust each other but who need to share data while keeping some pieces of commercial information private.

Table 7.1 shows some examples of industry sectors where companies have grouped together to explore cooperation using blockchain technology.

TABLE 7.1   Table of DLT consortiums in various sectors

Sector	Consortium
Banking	R3
Insurance	B3i
Shipping	Tradelens
Internet of Things	Trusted IoT Alliance
Oil and Gas	Oil & Gas Blockchain Consortium
Automotive/Mobility	MOBI
Trade Finance	Marco Polo Network

Unsurprisingly, banks and other financial institutions are among some of the pioneers initiating proofs of concept and pilot projects in this area, not only for settlement of institutional transactions, which is currently a time-consuming process that makes use of decades-old technology in some cases, but also for retail customers. Accenture calculated that the use of distributed ledger technology could reduce central reporting costs by up to 70 per cent for some financial services companies (Accenture, 2017). Having said this, the subject of how blockchain technology or DLT can smooth existing processes and even create new business models in financial services is enough to fill a book in itself, so we will not be examining every single use case in this chapter. We will divide these examples into those which use a native token and those which do not.

Platforms without cryptocurrencies

There are now many companies working on launching their own proprietary blockchain platforms, and given that most do not use tokens, we will not be examining them in detail. However, the three best-known frameworks in the corporate space are Hyperledger,

Corda and Quorum. None of these has a public network, so unlike Bitcoin, Ethereum or any of the cryptocurrencies we have described so far, the company that wants to use the software needs to download the software, set up their own nodes and write integration code that will enable the distributed ledger to work with their existing systems. Hyperledger, Corda and Quorum are products that can be used and configured by anyone, which means businesses can configure their own networks to be private (limited to participants within their own company) or shared between other collaboration partners.

The Hyperledger project was born in 2015, as an umbrella project for the purpose of developing open-source blockchains and toolkits. It was initiated by the Linux Foundation, and participants over the intervening years have included IBM, Digital Asset, ConsenSys, Blockstream, Wells Fargo and Deutsche Bank. Its frameworks include Hyperledger Fabric, Hyperledger Sawtooth, Hyperledger Iroha and, most recently, Hyperledger Besu, which is an enterprise-grade Ethereum codebase. Companies using Hyperledger include Allianz, SAP, Santander, Nasdaq and many others.

While Hyperledger lends itself to many different sectors, Corda was developed very much with banking and financial services in mind. Developed by a software company called R3 in collaboration with some of the world's biggest banks, its free, open-source software allows developers to build interoperable ledgers with smart contract functionality, while keeping all or some of these transactions private. Just like Hyperledger and like Quorum, which we will discuss next, there is no public, overarching Corda network. Any company wishing to deploy smart contracts or build applications on Corda needs to set up its own network or join an existing consortium that another company has established.

In Chapter 9, we'll look more closely at how banks are streamlining their processes using blockchain technology, but to give a brief example of the sorts of applications Corda is being used for, an open platform called Voltron was built using Corda to facilitate settlement of letters of credit (documentary trade) which are used in 10–15 per cent of export transactions. It is also possible to use Corda – as with other blockchain technologies – to issue different types of assets and financial instruments. Remember that, although the software is free and open-source, in order to gain access to a particular network, an individual or company must be approved by whoever is administering the network and receive access credentials from them before they can read or write information to the ledger. It is the complete opposite of how a blockchain such as Bitcoin works, although some of the technical aspects are similar. Remember also that there is no mining process: computers join the network only with the permission of the administrator, and there is no currency or token.

While Hyperledger and Corda are both independently developed software whose code was not derived directly from any existing blockchain, Quorum was developed by JP Morgan as a variant of Ethereum. This illustrates that even blockchains that exist as public, permissionless networks with their own tokens can be run in a private context. What do we mean by this? Remember that Ethereum, Bitcoin and any other public cryptocurrency are open-source software. When you download and run the software on your own computer, you input certain configurable values to instruct your node to join a particular network. If you don't join any network at all, the software will still run. Or you could join two or three other computers in your house or your office, which have been configured to network to each other. This means that you will be mining your own tokens – but because you are not joined to a public network and validating other people's transactions, you will not be able to sell your tokens to anyone else and they will be worthless. Think of it as being like an economy where the circulating currency is a particular type of red bead, and you want to trade but you only have blue beads, or like going into a shop and trying to buy something with Monopoly money. It looks roughly the same, but everyone knows it has no value. You cannot, for example, use your Starbucks loyalty points in a Costa or in your local cafe, as the Costa loyalty points are recorded on their own system, and they don't have access to your Starbucks records.

It is with this in mind that we will take a look at Quorum's most prominent usage so far: a platform for issuing JP Morgan's own coin.

Permissioned ledgers with tokens

As any casual observer of the cryptocurrency scene will know, JP Morgan and Bitcoin have a chequered history. Chair and CEO Jamie Dimon is well known for his loathing of decentralized and unregulated currencies, describing Bitcoin in 2018 as 'a terrible store of value' (Marinova, 2017), and doubling down a year later, predicting that governments would find a way to stop Bitcoin if it ever became a threat to the dollar.

He may have hated the idea of Bitcoin, but it did not stop JP Morgan from taking the significant step of developing the Quorum distributed ledger software, whose launch took place in late 2017. Quorum is a private implementation of Ethereum, which adds extra functionality to make it suitable for enterprise applications, bringing speed and high performance as well as privacy. It is not exclusively designed for banking and financial applications: US insurance giants State Farm and USAA, for example, share a Quorum ledger that enables them to reclaim automobile insurance settlements from each other. While Quorum is a fork of Ethereum, there are some significant differences. You will remember that to deploy a smart contract on Ethereum, one must pay a transaction fee. Because Quorum's code is an enhanced version of Ethereum, the concept of Gas still exists, but in this case it is set to zero for every transaction, as there is no need to incentivize miners to run a public network. And, of course, specific data can be kept private if required. Increased privacy levels tend to reduce the speed of transaction throughput beyond a certain level, but at maximum performance, Quorum is capable of clocking more than 2,000 TPS (transactions per second).

Not only did JP Morgan develop Quorum, but they also created JPM Coin, a stablecoin that is pegged to the US dollar and which runs on Quorum. JPM Coin has various uses, but the bank envisages that one of the most important will be in the wholesale payments business. Currently, JP Morgan's huge corporate clients, like those of any other bank, have to depend on decades-old technology such as wire transfers, to move payments around the world. Using networks such as SWIFT means that delays can occur, not least if a payment misses the cut-off time in a particular country, and there are also inefficiencies and losses when converting from one currency to another.

JP Morgan's clients would not be able to use the stablecoin for money laundering, as such institutional clients have already undergone all the necessary checks, and it is not envisaged at the moment that the new currency would be rolled out to retail customers. The way it works is that the customer deposits US dollars at the bank, and the commensurate quantity of JPM Coin is generated. The transfer is carried out in real time, at any time of the day, and is almost instantaneous. When it arrives, the JPM Coin is destroyed and the equivalent amount reinstated into dollars. Such institutional coins have the ability to save financial institutions and large corporations billions in wasted time and money, and it is interesting to note that because of JPM Coin's limited circulation within banks, whose customers have already presumably been through all the appropriate identification processes, there has not been the same regulatory push-back from the authorities as in the case of Libra.

Given the advantages such 'bridge currencies' offer (JP Morgan prefers this terminology to 'stablecoin'), it is not surprising that other banks are following suit. Quorum is not the only game in town as far as bank digital currencies are concerned: early in 2019, IBM Blockchain announced that at least six banks had signed up to issue tokens backed by fiat currency on IBM's World Wire platform. Interestingly, World Wire uses Stellar as its protocol layer, although it does not incorporate the use of Lumens, Stellar's native cryptocurrency. Stellar is an open-source payment network that shares some characteristics with Ripple. Indeed, it was founded by Jed McCaleb, a co-founder of Ripple. It is interesting to see both JP Morgan and IBM, both household-name legacy corporations, opting to use innovative open-source technologies such as Ethereum and Stellar as the basis of their money transmission networks rather than starting from scratch with software developed in-house.

Unlike JPM Coin, World Wire has been designed to be crypto-currency-agnostic. As IBM explain on their website: 'Two financial institutions transacting together agree to use a stablecoin, central bank digital currency or other digital asset as the bridge asset between any two fiat currencies. The digital asset facilitates the trade and supplies important settlement instructions' (IBM, 2019).

It is rare for one bank to embark on a cutting-edge project like JPM Coin without others also following suit, and it is therefore not surprising that where JP Morgan leads, others have followed. At first glance, US rival Wells Fargo might seem to be imitating JPM Coin, with plans for its own digital token also announced in 2019. However, there are sufficient differences between the projects to keep them distinct from each other. To begin with, Wells Fargo uses R3's Corda software rather than Quorum, and its system targets payments exclusively within Wells Fargo's own banking network. The Wells Fargo stablecoin is designed to move money smoothly across borders when both payer and payee have accounts with Wells Fargo. We will discuss the SWIFT messaging network in more detail in Chapter 9, but it is sufficient for this chapter to understand the limitations and costs inherent in transferring value across national boundaries. While internal transfers between Wells Fargo branches within one country can be done easily, international transfers cannot be done via an internal network but must be transmitted via SWIFT. The new stablecoin will eliminate these external costs and allow Wells Fargo's branches to make cross-border payments without involving SWIFT. Following a successful proof of concept, Wells Fargo coin is expected to move to a pilot stage, allowing its international branches to move digital cash around effortlessly between themselves.

So far in this chapter we have talked about tokens expressly designed to facilitate the movement of money around the world without going through the notoriously slow bottlenecks of SWIFT and the other components of the existing banking system. But what about bank cryptocurrencies that might be used to represent other assets? We will talk in Chapter 10 about the issuance of new asset classes made possible by the use of cryptocurrencies and blockchain technology. But for now, let us focus on one specific token, which has been patented by Goldman Sachs. On 11 July 2017, Goldman Sachs was granted US Patent No 9,704,143, titled 'Cryptographic currency for securities settlement'. This token, which is to be called SETLCoin (note that is not related to the London-based blockchain settlements startup SETL), is designed to create an entirely new system for settlements of digitized securities between banks and institutions. The current system for clearing securities such as stocks or ETFs (exchange-traded funds) can take one to two business days and involves the clearing house matching the trading instructions from buyer and seller, taking on counterparty risk and executing the trade. Goldman Sachs' proposed new system would remove this delay and inefficiency from the process, offering instant settlement self-regulated by a blockchain, with the SETLCoin payments ensuring that no external services such as SWIFT had to be used.

It is worth reiterating that none of these proposed bank crypto-currencies are available to the general population or tradable on exchanges. They are all designed for intra-bank or inter-bank use, circulating solely on permissioned blockchains. In these instances, the token is being used as a unit of transfer rather than an incentive for validating transactions, so it is helpful to think of these 'bank coins' as representing a type of cryptoasset rather than a token that is used to incentivize participants in a self-sustaining network.

Private versus public

As we see above, permissioned distributed ledgers that aim to use 'bank coins' have been designed to speed up existing processes, rather than to rethink entirely the way such processes work. In technology terms, we talk a lot about 'disruption' and 'disruptive technologies'. But how disruptive, really, are the innovations we have described? I would argue that, while some entities and older ways of doing things might be bypassed – such as the need for clearing houses, or the dependency on networks such as SWIFT for cross-border payments – we are talking about enhancing existing structures and removing friction, rather than completely rethinking entire processes.

This cautious approach is understandable. When we encounter a new technology, the first thing we do is try to apply it to the things that we understand, and the shift towards a more decentralized model

TABLE 7.2   Private and public networks, with and without tokens

Network	Token?
Bitcoin	Yes
Ethereum	Yes
Tezos	Yes
Hyperledger	No
EOS	Yes
IIN	No
Marco Polo	No
Ripple	Yes

is simply too much of a leap for most legacy organizations to understand. As per the famous Henry Ford quote – 'If I had asked people what they wanted, they would have said faster horses' – it is often difficult to see beyond the status quo. It is therefore entirely predictable that the 'walled garden' approach, where a blockchain simply becomes another kind of centralized, permissioned database, has prevailed in many cases.

It is understandable that banking institutions need to keep their commercial transactions private, not least because regulatory authorities in different countries mandate that this is the case. And even where data is encrypted, an entirely public blockchain can reveal a surprising amount of detail when forensic analysis is applied (companies such as Elliptic, TokenAnalyst and Chainalysis specialize in this). Movements of value around the Bitcoin blockchain have caught out many a criminal who has supposed their actions to be private, and even if client details are obscured, a bank may not be ready to share such details as transaction volumes with the outside world... yet.

We may not be able to predict a future in which openness and transparency, even between companies, becomes the norm, but then previous generations would not have been able to comprehend the way in which individuals share intimate details of their lives on

Facebook or Instagram. Attitudes towards the way we share our information evolve over time, and even now – leaving blockchain technology and cryptocurrencies out of the equation – we are beginning to see the destruction of these silos. A good example of this is the OpenAPI movement, and the global trend towards Open Banking.

The OpenAPI movement and Open Banking

If you are not working in software or technology, the OpenAPI movement may not be something you have ever thought about. But it has led to a significant change in the way companies think about their businesses and their data. In simple terms, an API (application programming interface) allows developers to access data in a structured way so that they can interact with it and make use of it, whether this is to present the data to an end user in a website or mobile application, or incorporate it into some other process or application. The OpenAPI Initiative, which is a Linux Foundation project, provides specifications for how data should be presented to make it universally usable, interoperable and understandable.

So far, this might sound like a reasonably dull technical initiative, but it has far-reaching implications. The norm for all businesses in the past was to hoard all their data, hiding it away behind firewalls. Why would they want to share their data? It was a precious resource that they had spent money and effort aggregating. Perhaps in some cases they would consider selling to other companies if the payment was sufficient. In these cases, there would often be a disagreement about the way the data was presented: often it ended up being transported in Excel spreadsheets that would then have to be imported into databases by the company who had purchased it.

Over some years, the peer-to-peer, free-for-all approach of the world wide web began to rub off on other business practices. It is a cliché that data is the new oil, but perhaps it is true if we think of it as the type of oil that lubricates modern commerce and enables new opportunities in the same way that oil lubricates an engine, rather than the type of oil that is jealously guarded and sold as a commodity. Businesses came to realize that the process of having ideas and turning them into technological reality was an expensive one, and that perhaps allowing a wider group of people to come up with ideas and use your data to build their own applications was an idea that would have mutual benefit. Obviously there is some data that is more like solid gold than oil (such as real-time share market data) and that continued to be consumed solely by the company who had funded the infrastructure to acquire it, but gradually more and more companies decided to make various parts of their data available for public use, and also to structure it in a specified way to make it more accessible.

Thus bus and rail companies offered up their real-time travel data so that builders of travel information applications (from individual developers sitting in their bedrooms to billion-dollar corporates) could aggregate this information and use it. Government departments opened up certain data streams so that anyone could build a useful portal to filter the information in some way. Twitter and YouTube offered information to public feeds so that developers could build apps that presented information in a different way, or made some interaction processes easier. Of course, this approach was not without its risks. As a company, you could not control the quality of the applications beyond asking developers to sign up to some basic guidelines around the context of how the data would be used and therefore control how your data was presented.

However, overall, OpenAPIs have been key in fostering an upsurge in creativity and developer activity that would not otherwise have happened, and organizations who have embraced this shift have found that rather than hoarding data that they would not have had the resources to organize into usable apps or present to the public in a meaningful way, this collaborative approach has been generally beneficial, especially for consumers.

The retail banking sector has been slow to embrace these changes, at least in part because of regulations around data privacy. However, given that Europe has significantly lagged behind Asia in embracing financial technology innovation, governments have taken action to ensure that fintech companies are able to compete with established banks, and to level the playing field. As mentioned previously, WeChat Pay was ubiquitous in China before mobile payments became widespread in Europe, and adoption rates in both the UK and continental Europe have shown there was a pent-up demand to embrace new payment technologies, regardless of the glacial progress within the large legacy banks. Mobile apps that aggregate your bank accounts and allow you to pay with a single virtual card have recently been launched, and others that allow you to budget and invest from a one-stop shop. Sometimes these applications are launched by banks, but more often they are challenger fintech startups, taking advantage of the Open Banking legislation to enable them to gain access – under strict conditions, of course, and with customers' permission – to data from larger companies.

Set against this backdrop, then, we can see that while securing financial data is paramount, locking it up in a secure vault behind high walls is not necessarily the most beneficial approach. Collaboration and innovation can be beneficial for companies and individuals, and so, when designing security practices and architectures for these new ways of transacting, it behoves developers and executives to think carefully about the type of world they want to live in. A panellist at a conference I attended some time ago said something that gave me food for thought. He was a senior technical manager working for a large company that was actively putting together a consortium of companies in the same sector to develop a shared blockchain solution. While the technical challenges were significant, he said, the far harder part was the human element: getting people from companies who were traditionally competitors and thus very secretive about their development practices and business ambitions to open up to co-develop something with the opposition. He made the point, which others have done so many times before, that blockchain technology is a team sport, and that building human relationships is as important as building the technical solution.

If we are to see this kind of future, where companies do not rely on hoarded data, there needs to be a sea change in the way we think about online identity. While this is not cryptocurrency specific, there are so many conversations floating around about possible strategies for identifying ourselves in a decentralized future that it would be valuable to introduce the idea of self-sovereign identity.

Self-sovereign identity

In the distant past, identity was easy. When humans all lived in villages and most people did not travel very far, we rarely had to prove who we were. Everybody else knew who we were, and on the rare occasions when we met someone new, other people of our acquaintance would vouch for us. Sometimes there would be cases of mistaken identity – either accidental or deliberate and/or fraudulent – but these were infrequent enough to form the plotlines of books or plays, because it was presumably quite difficult to present yourself as someone else.

As the world opened up, every now and again it became important to prove who you were: when you got married, registered the birth of a child, bought a house or opened a bank account. In the pre-digital age, unless you were in an unusual situation, such as living in Spain and working in Gibraltar, where you literally had to cross a national border twice a day, you would not have to identify yourself very often. Some countries make it mandatory to carry a national ID card, but most do not, and many people went for years without having to prove their identity in the physical world.

Then, when the internet came along, everything changed. Businesses began to store information about people: if you ordered products online, the supplier kept your order history for you, so you could log in and reorder. Governments kept information about you online, which you could view and sometimes update through their portals. Other companies kept your email address and a password you had chosen together with a list of your interests so you could choose to receive newsletters from them. And also, companies with whom you had never dealt, such as credit-checking agencies, compiled information about you that you had never given them permission to hold. Banks kept information about your transaction history and your investments, along with security information.

Most people didn't think too hard about this – until it went wrong. It seems that the last 10 years have been a sequence of one personal information hack followed by another: millions of records containing confidential information that have been stolen by hackers whose intent was to either use them for financial gain or sell them on. The number of wasted hours, days and years people have spent remedying these leaks cannot be counted – and there has been human misery and even death as a result of some of the hacks (after some users of the Ashley Madison marital affairs website were threatened with exposure unless they paid a ransom, at least two people killed themselves (Thomson, 2015)).

So, why do we trust these faceless entities to store data for us: the same overlapping dataset in hundreds and hundreds of different companies? Every time we sign up with a new service, we present the same information, generally secured only by a password. And what if these companies decide to stop dealing with us, or go out of business? Social media profiles, while they did not exist 20 years ago, have become a virtual expression of ourselves and are, in many cases, the way we choose to identify ourselves to other third-party services. What if your profile is in the hands of a social media company and it gets stolen or deleted? There is usually no recourse in these situations, but the effect is just the same as if someone has impersonated you or stolen your identity in the physical world.

There is also the question of how much information we need to supply about ourselves in order to access certain services. Of course, companies love to acquire our data, the more of it the better, because as we have seen above, it is a valuable resource, which they can sell on, or from which they can extract vast amounts of information about us – information which sometimes we barely know ourselves, in terms of predicting what we will do or buy next. But, if you think about what companies are asking us to prove, we are often very generously giving them far more information than they need. Frequently, a company will ask us to identify ourselves simply because they supply services to people over 18 and need to know that we have reached the appropriate age. Or they need to know that we live in a certain area, or that we are using the right credit card and so on.

Now imagine that your digital identity was totally under your control, not something that depended on data other companies held about you. Ideally, this data would be presented in such a way that you would provide only the minimum amount of information that you needed to access a service – no more handing over your name, physical address, phone number, birthdate and political opinions in order to sign up for a newsletter. No more linking your Facebook account, with every single bit of your life exposed within it, to some random third-party service you have just signed up for, or to accept an RSVP to a networking event.

This also has massive implications for the way we hold and send cryptocurrencies, which is why it is included in this book. So, how might such a system work? Phillip J Windley, Chair of the Sovrin Foundation, explains in the Sovrin Protocol and Token White Paper (Sovrin, 2018):

> We're still a long way from an identity system for the internet that works the same way the internet does. The internet was designed to allow any machine to send messages to any other machine without any administrative authority's permission. In fact, it was designed to route around any attempts to keep those messages from getting through.
>
> An internet-like identity system would allow any person, organization, or thing to have an identity relationship (something we call a 'claim' in the world of identity) with any other. And to do this without the need for authorization from someone else. Because anyone can use these identities and the resulting relationships without an intervening authority, they're called 'self-sovereign.'

What does this mean for the dichotomy between public and private networks systems and cryptocurrencies, as we have been discussing in this chapter? It seems that advances in the way we think about privacy, identity and authentication could well change in the coming years or decades, and this would mean that straightforward decisions about what should be private and what should be public will become more blurred. However, as we have seen, for the moment there remain commercial reasons for institutions working in the existing banking ecosystem to want to keep some networks – and also some cryptocurrencies – private and limited to only permissioned participants.

In the next chapter, we will talk about the polar opposite: a type of investment that was available to literally anyone in the world, and how it turned the rules of startup fundraising upside down.

References

Accenture (2017) Banking on Blockchain, Accenture Consulting. Available from: https://www.accenture.com/_acnmedia/Accenture/Conversion-Assets/DotCom/Documents/Global/PDF/Consulting/Accenture-Banking-on-Blockchain.pdf#zoom=50 (archived at https://perma.cc/CJC8-3UMG)

IBM (2019) Transform cross-border payments with IBM Blockchain World Wire. Available from: https://www.ibm.com/blockchain/solutions/world-wire (archived at https://perma.cc/QT7J-NCTB)

Marinova, P (2017) Jamie Dimon: Bitcoin bad, blockchain good, *Fortune*, 13 September. Available from: https://fortune.com/2017/09/13/jamie-dimon-bitcoin-blockchain/ (archived at https://perma.cc/3PDW-SD6M)

Sovrin Foundation (2018) Sovrin™: A Protocol and Token for Self-Sovereign Identity and Decentralized Trust, January. Available from: https://sovrin.org/wp-content/uploads/Sovrin-Protocol-and-Token-White-Paper.pdf (archived at https://perma.cc/85C3-47TT)

Thomson, I (2015) More deaths linked to Ashley Madison hack as scammers move in, *The Register*, 24 August. Available from https://www.theregister.co.uk/2015/08/24/death_toll_ashley_madison/ (archived at https://perma.cc/F89Y-CP3N)

8

ICO mania

If you talk to anyone who bought cryptocurrencies between 2016 and 2018, the chances were that they would have participated in an ICO (initial coin offering). Now we've learnt about token economies, let's have a look at one of the biggest bubbles in recent history. Historically, a sudden rise in the price of a particular asset class, which is not matched with a corresponding increase in its underlying worth, has tended to be limited in geographic area. Think about bubbles in house prices, for example. But between 2016 and 2017, investors all over the world spent billions of dollars buying cryptographic tokens for blockchain networks that would mostly never do what their creators claimed, and in many cases, would never launch at all. These tokens are in some cases now selling for less than 1 per cent of their sale price. So, how did this all happen – and what are the positives that came out of this extraordinary piece of investment history?

In 2015, Ethereum had recently launched, and Bitcoin was ticking along. The latter was well down on its then-record price of around $1100 but more and more people were getting drawn into the cryptocurrency sphere. The big wave of cut-and-paste altcoins and out-and-out scams originating on sites such as CoinGen (all of which were described in Chapter 3) had slowed, and with the Bitcoin price sitting at $250 or so – it would briefly double at the end of the year to just over $500, causing a flicker of excitement – there was probably more focus at that time on growing the developer community than on easy money. Also, in November 2015, Ethereum developer

Fabian Vogelsteller proposed a set of rules for issuing tokens on top of the Ethereum blockchain. Under the protocol for suggesting such rules, this suggestion became known as ERC-20, with the ERC standing for Ethereum Request for Comment, and the 20 indicating that it was the 20th such recommendation.

Until this point, any developer was able to create a cryptoasset on Ethereum simply by executing a smart contract, but the crucial thing about ERC-20 was that for the first time, there was a consistent set of rules that governed how data was represented and how value was transported from one user to another. As an interesting footnote, it was nearly two years before the Ethereum GitHub page was updated to indicate that the standard was now formally adopted – September 2017. But well before this time, ERC-20 had become the most important three letters and two numbers in the history of startup crowdfunding, and by the end of 2018, more than 99 per cent of all token crowdsales were carried out on Ethereum, representing more than $4 billion.

The DAO

We touched on the infamous DAO hack in Chapter 5, but we are now going to revisit it in more detail. 'DAO' can be a generic term, but most people think of the original 2016 DAO when the term is used. While the DAO was certainly not the first example of ERC-20 tokens being issued for public sale, its scale overshadowed everything that had come before it. It is also a useful illustration of how and why tokens were used as a vehicle for crowdfunding. Interestingly, while a slew of negative publicity followed the hack, it did not put crypto investors off the idea of buying tokens, and indeed, could even have had some kind of Streisand effect in publicizing this type of investment, regardless of the suboptimal outcome. Observers of the crypto ecosystem are divided between seeing the event as a bold philosophical experiment that went wrong but which helped advance the decentralization debate, or a ham-fisted fundraising attempt that was poorly executed and in the long term damaged Ethereum's reputation.

So, let's analyse in detail exactly what happened. DAO stands for 'decentralized autonomous organization' and this novel structure was envisaged by its inventors as a substitute for a company or a foundation, which is represented by a smart contract on a public blockchain, whose governance is entirely carried out by economic incentives rather than by human decision making. This particular entity was created as an entirely automated venture capital fund where projects could apply for funding and could be voted on and awarded funds without a centralized decision-making body. Traditional venture capital funds depend on individuals, often with many years of experience, to allocate funds to projects and early-stage startups, but within a DAO structure, this is entirely replaced by a 'wisdom of crowds' approach where tokens confer voting rights, and participants can fund the project(s) of their choice by 'putting their money where their mouth is' and using their tokens to specify which projects should get funded. DAOs could be set up, in theory, for administering almost every field of human endeavour, substituting human hierarchies with a clearly defined set of programmatic rules for every eventuality. While many in the cryptocurrency and blockchain space had – and still have – an abiding fascination for this kind of automated governance structure, and it is true that game theory and careful structuring of incentives should make it possible and also eliminate some of the bias often associated with human governance, DAOs bring with them an entirely new set of challenges and are not (yet) capable of many of the things that their more breath-less advocates suggest.

One challenge is regulatory: if a governing board of humans is not present, and if the code is being run by thousands of computers all over the world, then who can be targeted by governments and regulatory authorities in the case of any perceived breach of financial rules in a particular country? Recently we have seen a worrying trend towards governments targeting developers of open-source code simply for writing code, even if they do not do so with any expectation of financial gain. However, any government that enacts laws such as this should think carefully, as it is a sure way to stifle innovation, and developers working on cutting-edge technologies would simply move to countries with less onerous laws if they felt that they were personally threatened by this.

Another challenge, of course, is that while it is entirely possible to automate governance, the rules that are applied will be dictated by the mindset, goals and ethical approach of the person(s) who programmed these rules, whether this is conscious or subconscious. In his excellent book *The AI Does Not Hate You* (Chivers, 2019), author Tom Chivers looks at the unforeseen consequences that may arise if one gives an omnipotent AI an instruction to maximize paperclip production. Such an AI might theoretically decide to kill all the humans in the world because the resources humans consume are diverting energy away from the task of paperclip production. The AI does not have the capability to rationalize that murdering all the world's humans would remove the end consumer of the paperclips, because all it has been instructed to do is maximize production. Hence anyone creating a DAO and writing code that assumes that a simple computer program will apply logic in the same way that a human would in a given set of circumstances should be wary.

It is also worth noting that while the source code for this particular DAO was transparent and decentralized, some provisions were put in place to allow the organization to interface with the real world, including the legal aspects of contracting individuals or companies to carry out funded work on its behalf. These participants were known as Contractors. In order to make these contracts legally enforceable, a limited company (DAO.link) was set up in Switzerland. Along with Contractors, there was a class of nominated individuals and companies called Curators, whose task it was to ensure the independence and decentralization of the network and prevent the DAO from falling victim to a 51 per cent attack. One of the major Contractors pitching for funding from the DAO was Ethereum startup Slock.it.

However, the reason this particular DAO foundered was nothing to do with regulators. It was something much more prosaic: a programming error – not that anyone knew this, of course, on 30 April when the DAO was deployed on the Ethereum blockchain to much fanfare. Investors were quick to want a piece of the action, and

FIGURE 8.1   Timeline of the DAO hack

Smart contract deployed	30 April 2016
$100m deposited	15 May 2016
Vulnerability discovered	5 June 2016
Hacker begins to syphon funds	17 June 2016
Ethereum is hard forked	20 July 2016
SEC determines DAO tokens were securities	25 July 2017

word spread like wildfire. For every 1 Ether that investors gave to the fund, they received 100 DAO tokens in exchange. Within six weeks, 14 per cent of the entire Ether supply, worth $150 million at the time, was wrapped up in this fund, but there were already rumours circulating that showed the smart contracts that ran the DAO were not as watertight as they seemed. On 17 June 2016, disaster struck. An unknown attacker managed to exploit a coding error and withdrew $70 million worth of Ether. For many observers, the surprise was that this mistake was not spotted earlier, although as anyone working on software projects knows, it is easy to be wise in hindsight. Without going too far into technical details, the contract allowed users to withdraw funds over and over again without checking their balance – as though you could withdraw the same $100 from your bank balance over and over without your bank account ever being debited.

Fortunately, the DAO rules specified that any withdrawn funds were frozen for 28 days, and this gave some breathing space while furious debate raged in developer forums and on Reddit about how to recover the stolen tokens. Some people think that even after the 28-day freeze, the thief would have struggled to offload the tokens.

'It's like stealing the Mona Lisa', said Stephan Tual, chief operating officer of Slock.it, at the time. 'Great, congratulations, but what do you do with it? You can't sell it, it's too big to be sold' (Finley, 2016).

When it became clear, after a less invasive suggestion proved impossible, that recovering the funds came down to a straightforward choice between doing nothing or implementing a hard fork where the offending transactions would be rewritten to divert the stolen Ether to a refund wallet, the issue was delegated to the Ether-holding community to vote on, and both sides made their arguments.

To summarize, the group that wanted to keep the status quo felt that as Ethereum's whole purpose was to provide an immutable, trusted record and that the quote 'Code is law' had been frequently employed as a shorthand for the reliability of smart contracts, then the sanctity of the blockchain should be respected and events should be allowed to take their natural course. However, the group who wanted to restore investors' funds argued that the ecosystem was evolving, that code was not yet law, however much it remained an aspiration, and that more reputational damage would be done to Ethereum if attempts were not made to remedy the situation. The fork went ahead and the appropriated funds were returned to those who had contributed them, but when the new version of Ethereum's software was released, a proportion of individuals who remained ethically opposed to the fork continued mining and transacting on the older version of the software. In practical terms, this meant that there were now two Ethereum currencies, sharing a common history up until the moment they diverged. 'New' Ethereum continued to use the currency code ETH, while Ethereum Classic, as the original version of the code was quickly dubbed, gained the code ETC.

While the fork caused much argument and bad feeling at the time, Ethereum Classic has continued as a separate network, albeit on a smaller scale, and more than two years on, the focus is on being prag-matic and releasing software updates that keep Ethereum Classic interoperable with Ethereum. For users who held Ethereum, the prac-tical effect was that they now had the same amount of ETH and ETC. This sounds like it was a great way of making money out of thin air, but in fact the whole DAO hard fork debacle had hit the Ethereum price so badly that even with the bonus of now owning two currencies, Ethereum holders were out of pocket. We will return to the concept of forks later in the chapter, in the context of Bitcoin. As for Ethereum, it would be some time before anyone would attempt another DAO, but the idea had now solidified that Ethereum was the perfect platform for crowdfunding in the form of token issuance.

A tidal wave of ICOs

While the DAO was not the first token sale on Ethereum – Augur, who operate a prediction market on the Ethereum platform, were one of the first, if not the very first, issuing their tokens in August 2015 – it was by now the most notorious. The DAO debacle had not dissuaded startups from the idea of crowdfunding via a smart contract. So, what is the mechanism via which this is done – and what does the acronym ICO mean, anyway?

Put simply, ICOs matched a huge pent-up demand for startup investment with a huge pent-up demand for assets. ICO simply stands for initial coin offering (or, as some analysts would have it, initial cryptocurrency offering). The term is derived from initial public offering, which is the point at which a company releases its stock on a public stock exchange for sale for the first time. In most countries – but particularly in the United States – one must meet qualification criteria in order to be eligible to invest in these often highly profitable offerings. To gain accredited investor status in the United States, sophisticated or experienced investor status in the UK, or the equivalent elsewhere, usually requires the prospective investor to show they have an existing portfolio minimum (in the US it is $1 million) and also meet other criteria, such as knowledge of financial markets. While these laws were presumably enacted to protect naive investors from falling prey to scams, many people who did not meet the criteria but who judged themselves perfectly able to make their own decisions, even bad ones, felt aggrieved that they had been unfairly excluded from the opportunity to make money this way, and saw it as yet another example of the wealthy hoarding the best buying opportunities for themselves.

Just as the first wave of cryptocurrency trading had drawn in a new wave of Millennials and Generation Z-ers, who had not necessarily participated in other types of trading before, so the ICO boom gave free rein to those excluded from IPOs to buy a stake in what they felt would be the tokenized economy of the future. Because an ICO was executed by a smart contract running on all the computers all over the world that made up the Ethereum blockchain, and because the tokens being sold did not come with any kind of promise that they conferred any ownership rights over the organization who issued them, it was a common assumption on the part of both buyers and sellers that there was no pressing need to comply with any regulation, particularly in the beginning.

So, if someone bought a token, what exactly were they buying? Apart from the cynical explanation that many people probably did not think about this very hard – tokens normally went up in price once they were released on to exchanges, so many people bought them purely for their speculative value – the general idea is that the token represented some kind of stake in a future system that would allow you to participate in the network and make use of it. For example, if you bought REP tokens in the Augur sale, your tokens would allow you to create a bet on the platform or to bet on someone else's proposition. Similarly, the Golem network, whose ICO took place in 2016, issued GNT tokens, which would allow users to purchase the unused processing power of other computers participating in the network. In the case of the DAO, owning tokens allowed users to vote for their preferred projects; STORJ tokens allow users to purchase distributed storage; STEEM rewards social media engagement on a dedicated platform, and so on.

One of the most significant things about ICOs that were carried out using Ethereum's ERC-20 tokens is that they enabled startups to issue tokens with little more than an idea. Previously, if you were going to launch a blockchain crowdsale, you had to first develop all the underlying technology: a blockchain network with the appropriate consensus mechanism, wallets and software clients, and you also had to hope that miners would participate in validating your transactions and persuade cryptocurrency exchanges to incorporate your bespoke wallet software. Now, you could issue your token as an ERC-20 token with the promise that one day you would build your own blockchain and develop your own network with all the technical challenges that this implied, and at this point, you would swap ERC-20 tokens held by investors for the actual tokens that would be needed to participate in your network.

This was a seismic change, which opened the door for marketing companies who did not even have their own development teams and even for out-and-out scammers to carry out token sales in this unregulated space. The period from 2016 to the beginning of 2018 was like the Wild West during the gold rush. *Forbes* calculated in late 2018 that more than $20 billion had been raised by ICOs so far (Kauflin, 2018). Tutorials proliferated online showing even the least technical of people how to create and deploy an ERC-20 token. Whole industries sprang up around supporting ICO launches, some of which were sustained only by a website and a shoddily written white paper, offering nothing in the way of new technology. The worst of these used white papers plagiarized from other projects and websites that featured photographs of advisors who did not exist, and whose photographs had been taken from the social media profiles of models or actors, with fake names attached. Or sometimes projects would claim that a prominent cryptocurrency expert was advising them, display the expert's photograph and credentials on their site and hope that no one noticed.

YouTube investor channels and paid newsletters and paid Telegram groups sprang up, creating jobs for moderators who would create content, dispense bounties in exchange for engagement and answer questions from investors keen to know when the token they had bought would 'go 100x'. Stories emerged of founders driving around in Teslas while lines of code remained unwritten and marketing teams went unhired. By 2019, there were more than 200,000 different ERC-20 tokens deployed on Ethereum, although many of these are likely to have been trainee Ethereum developers or the simply curious trying out the technology, courtesy of the many online tutorials that sprang up. Remember that the barrier to entry is low in terms of expenditure: deploying a simple smart contract can cost as little as a few cents. While it's true that people were using Ethereum for a variety of interesting purposes, much of the network's capacity during this time was taken up with token sales. It seemed that providing a distributed platform for this type of fundraising was to be Ethereum's primary use case.

The proliferation of outright scams clouded the fact that many projects were, in fact, genuine. Some were teams who had been working on bona fide decentralized projects and saw tokenization as a valid way to generate a network effect and engage people in their community, as well as raising money. While most of the projects that launched in the heady days of 2016 and 2017 have sunk without trace, some are still pursuing their goals and are making steady inroads, having met their software release milestones and swapped the ERC-20 tokens for tokens running on their own network.

Some projects started out small in scale, with teams of three or four people, while others were massive in their scope and ambition. Two of the highest-profile were Tezos and EOS. Tezos was to become a cautionary tale for token sales, going from raising a record $232 million to becoming mired in legal issues and acrimony (Lewis-Kraus, 2018). EOS, launched by the blockchain company block.one, ran a hugely ambitious uncapped crowdsale, which ran for a whole year and raised $4 billion. The huge sum raised enabled them to hire a large team and also to fund multiple events in some of the tech hub cities around the world aimed at encouraging developers to build on their blockchain. Both have subsequently launched their networks – and both have become the target of retrospective scrutiny by regulatory authorities, though EOS's fine of $24 million imposed by the SEC in the United States in 2019 was such a small proportion of the $4 billion they raised that a cynic might look at this ratio and think it was well worth the risk.

Cryptocurrency exchanges flourished with this huge influx of new tokens and once again, like the boom days of 2014, exchanges found it hard to keep up with the demand from new traders. The first wave of crypto exchanges had been taken over by a new breed, and the slickest of all of these was Binance, founded by the charismatic Chinese-Canadian Changpeng Zhao ('CZ'), who was a veteran of Blockchain.info and OKCoin. Compared with most other crypto exchanges, the Binance interface was easy to use and its customer support was excellent, and it quickly became the exchange on which everyone wanted to list their tokens. However, getting your token listed, even on one of the smaller and more sketchy exchanges, was not a given. Many exchanges charged listing fees. Some exchanges were upfront about these charges, while others preferred to negotiate deals with startups based on what they thought the token sale might raise. Listing fees for some tokens were rumoured to be in the millions (although the average was only $50,000, according to the August 2018 Blockchain Transparency Institute Market Surveillance Report (Blockchain Transparency Institute, 2018)). In 2018, Binance took the step of not only making their listing fees transparent, but also stating that they would be donated to charity – a smart PR move over a topic that was becoming more controversial.

It was not just EOS and Tezos making headlines – every entrepreneur with a good idea jumped on the bandwagon. There were tokens for payment systems, distributed computing, peer-to-peer energy sales, gaming, peer-to-peer medical records: anything you can think of was getting tokenized. Except in many cases, it wasn't – marketing teams would frequently pay a developer to deploy a standard ERC-20 token, write a white paper that was hugely optimistic about the technological possibilities of their proposition, do the rounds of blockchain conferences and only then start thinking about hiring an outsourced team to complete the most important part of the equation – the technology. Meanwhile, the scammers had a field day. Many people who had been involved in the crypto ecosystem for some time could spot a scam a mile away, and were quick to call out the culprits, making fun of them with memes and generally not taking them seriously at all. But unfortunately, many startups were able to appeal to the newbie investors who were now flooding into the space, drawn in by friends' tales of spectacular gains. The founders of OneCoin managed to raise $4 billion with their so-called private blockchain before a warrant was issued for their arrest. BitConnect was a lending platform with a token that rose to $500 apiece before sinking back to $1 when it was revealed as a Ponzi scheme. It was best known in crypto circles for its gathering in Thailand in late 2017, at which New York investor Carlos Matos whipped up an evangelical frenzy and became a meme for his enthusiastic cry of 'BitConeeeeeeect!', which was immortalized on YouTube.

FIGURE 8.2   Highest-funded ICOs of all time

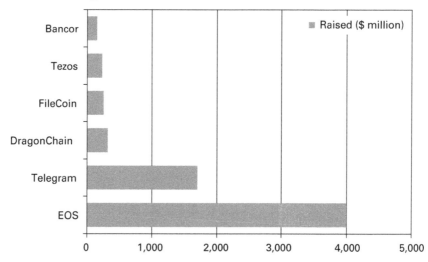

While many people have lost considerable sums of money buying tokens at inflated prices, the ICO boom was positive in many respects, stimulating debate about how small investors might be allowed to spend their own money. It is not just ICOs that have shown there is a huge pent-up demand for this, but the popularity of platforms such as Kickstarter, Indiegogo, Seedrs and Crowdcube has also shown that ordinary people would very much like the opportunity to get in on the ground floor and participate in funding good business ideas.

Regulators step in

By the end of 2017, even the keenest promoters of ICOs admitted that the market was beginning to become saturated. Social media groups that had begun for the sole purpose of promising exclusive access to oversubscribed token offerings lost their appeal. Tokens launched and then dropped in value instead of rising vertiginously. Some token sales failed to make their targets and rumours circulated over which would be the next venture to feel the weighty hand of the regulator on the back of their neck.

The problem was that although ICOs were a great way to crowd-fund your company while fitting the decentralization ethos perfectly, and while there were no specific laws against running a token sale because ICOs were such a new development, the SEC in the United States, the FCA in the UK and their equivalents around the world knew that they did not need to introduce specific legislation because there was already a ruling that applied. In the United States, this was known as the Howey Act. While most ventures were careful to present their tokens as having a specific purpose without which their proposed blockchains would not function, somewhat akin to owning a voucher for a service or a pre-paid API key for application data, the distinction between 'utility tokens' and what were now starting to be called 'security tokens' was blurred, to say the least.

On 25 July 2017, the SEC issued a press release, which can be viewed in its archive, referencing its report (https://www.sec.gov/litigation/investreport/34-81207.pdf (archived at https://perma.cc/V8PU-K4YD)), which detailed its investigation into the DAO sale and cautioned that 'tokens offered and sold by a "virtual" organization known as "The DAO" [were] securities and therefore subject to the federal securities laws'. While the literature accompanying various ongoing token offerings suddenly became more scrupulous about implying that the tokens would become tradable assets or making promises about on which exchanges they would be sold, a shot had been fired across the bows of all these projects. If even a supposedly decentralized entity such as the DAO could be described in such terms, it meant that many of these projects, with bricks-and-mortar addresses and real people beaming from the photos on the Team pages of their websites were effectively issuing unregistered securities. The irony was not lost on Bitcoin enthusiasts, who lost no time in pointing out the advantages of true decentralization.

The decider on which these warnings – and the Howey Act itself – hinged was the so-called Howey Test, arising from a 1946 case in which the judge ruled that something was a security if: 'a person invests his money in a common enterprise and is led to expect profits solely from the efforts of the promoter or a third party'. While it is obviously a US ruling, the arm of the SEC is long, and securities laws apply to the location of both the investor and the entity offering the investment. Hence, even if the token issuer was not based in the United States, if investors from the United States were permitted to buy tokens, then the issuer could in theory be extradited to face charges in the United States.

The impact of the SEC ruling had an immediate effect, with fund-raisers initially restricting purchases from the United States based on their geographic IP address (some founders were prepared to over-look the existence of VPNs, feeling that they would be judged on a 'best efforts' approach) and being more cautious about the way they described the sale process on their social media but otherwise carry-ing on as normal. The larger projects, often with executives on board who were experienced in financial compliance, began to take a differ-ent approach and went down the route of registering their tokens as securities, packaging them up and offering them to accredited investors as a stake in the company. This was a costly process, requir-ing the services of lawyers experienced in compliance, and many startups could not afford the upfront cost. People talked a lot about the difference between security tokens and utility tokens, but in real-ity, only a very small number of tokens issued between 2015 and 2018 were genuine utility tokens.

Security tokens of the nature described above (often abbreviated to STO) therefore differ from utility tokens in that they represent a formal investment contract with legal ownership of a physical or digital asset. If you participate in an STO, you are purchasing some-thing like a fraction of a company, or a bond, or even an asset such as a precious metal, fractional ownership of a bricks-and-mortar property or something else that could reasonably be expected to give you a return. Most usually, they were issued for equity in a new venture, and thus found themselves sitting somewhere between an ICO and a traditional IPO.

Amid this confusing proliferation of acronyms and abbreviations, another one soon popped up: IEO – initial exchange offering. Whereas ICOs had been carried out entirely by the ventures who issued the tokens, once people became mindful of the need to at least verify the identity of their investors, it became obvious that there was a gap in the market to be filled. If you were running a token sale and you had to negotiate with exchanges and pay them a listing fee, why not simply involve them at an earlier stage and piggy-back on their KYC systems, as well as capitalizing on all the publicity and exposure of a popular exchange. The exchanges were keen to do this as they already had all the infrastructure to hand, and they also received a proportion of the tokens in addition to the listing fee.

Binance were one of the first to offer IEOs, through their LaunchPad platform. BitTorrent elected to use LaunchPad for their token sale in January 2019 and raised $7.2 million in less than 15 minutes. This was Binance's first IEO: the second, for Fetch.ai, reached its hard cap in just 22 seconds, attracting $6 million in investment. While this process is the antithesis of a decentralized process – instead of sending funds to a smart contract, everything goes through the exchange's own accounts – this centralization appeared to offer reassurance to more traditional investors who were scared off by the idea of decentralized sales. Where Binance led, other exchanges followed, and soon Bittrex, Huobi and Kucoin had their own IEO platforms. With the exchanges staking their reputation on such offerings, putative investors had some reassurance that the exchanges themselves had done due diligence on the tokens being offered. It was the polar opposite of the DYOR ('do your own research') mantra of resilience and self-reliance which had been such a big part of the crypto scene until now. This stamp of approval did not, however, mean that the tokens raised in IEOs retained their value, though: most have lost a considerable proportion of their value.

My personal feeling is that the 2017 Cambrian explosion of ICOs revealed a demand for an entirely new way of fundraising, which benefited both company and investor when handled correctly. Demand for accounts on exchanges where tokens could be traded or for apps on which you could buy Bitcoin or Ether reached such a fever pitch that the exchanges could not keep up with the KYC process for new customers. Coinbase alone had acquired 30 million account holders by mid-2019. One of the attractions of holding your Bitcoin on an exchange, if you were prepared to overlook the security risks, was that for inexperienced users, airdropped tokens (sending free tokens directly to wallets) resulting from blockchain forks were handled in the background, without any need for technical knowledge. So, what exactly were these tokens, and why were they created?

Bitcoin Cash and other cryptocurrencies with 'Bitcoin' in their name

The process of agreeing upgrades to the Bitcoin network is a complex one. While anyone can contribute code to the repository, the process of deciding whose code is incorporated into the live version of the code is long and complicated, and involves discussions among the development team, which are made public. A dramatic change that would cause a hard fork, such as the one that happened on Ethereum following the DAO hack, is absolutely the path of last resort as it means that any nodes running the old software would produce blocks that would be judged invalid on the new chain, so just like a road that forks, you would end up with two parallel chains, each with their own transactions and there would no longer be a single source of truth once the fork had happened.

In 2014, an ongoing debate about how Bitcoin was going to scale up to accommodate more transactions came to a head. While many people now see that the future possibilities of scaling Bitcoin can be achieved in other ways, the focus then was on solutions such as simply making the block size bigger. Damien Ducourty, founder of B9lab, who are specialists in blockchain education and adoption, summarizes the debate thus: 'The conversation around scalability is now being entirely reshaped. Previously, we were talking about the scalability of the baseline protocol, but now we are talking about the scalability of the entire architecture.'

This was certainly not the prevailing view in 2014, and after many public debates, a group of developers went ahead and released new software that increased the size of each block, and thus the number of transactions that could be fitted inside it. The new block size was 8 megabytes, compared with 1 megabyte, so the difference was substantial. Many in the Bitcoin community feared that the idea would be popular among miners, and that Bitcoin XT, as it was called, would become the predominant flavour of Bitcoin. They had little to fear. While the fork was initially successful and had around 1,000 nodes mining it, it did not turn out to be an existential threat to Bitcoin, and although it still technically exists, interest in Bitcoin XT is minimal. When a blockchain undergoes a fork, this means that the transaction history up to the point of the fork is shared, so that if you have a certain amount of unspent coins at the time of the fork, you continue to hold the same number on both of the new chains.

Further debates continued about the best way to increase Bitcoin's throughput, and an improvement called Segregated Witness was introduced in 2017 after first being presented at the end of 2015. SegWit, as it was abbreviated, is a protocol upgrade that reduces transaction size rather than increasing block size. While most Bitcoin developers, miners and holders welcomed the change, which was implemented on Litecoin a few months earlier, some in the community still felt strongly that increasing the block size was the only way to proceed. In August 2017, a hard fork was implemented, which became known as Bitcoin Cash. It had the backing of some prominent Bitcoiners, including Roger Ver, and the move prompted bitter disagreements on social media, with both sides claiming the right to the Bitcoin name.

While Bitcoin Cash has been the most consistently successful of Bitcoin's forks, and has remained in the top four or five cryptocurrencies by market capitalization, many Bitcoiners regard it as an altcoin. Some time after its launch, it turned out that there was still considerable disagreement between camps within the Bitcoin Cash community, and the code was forked again in November 2018 to create a fork with even bigger blocks (128 megabytes). The new currency was named Bitcoin SV (standing for Satoshi's Vision). Bitcoin SV became associated with the controversial Dr Craig Wright, who had long claimed that he was Satoshi Nakamoto, and personality politics continue to loom large in the Bitcoin Cash and Bitcoin SV worlds. One of the claims made by both Bitcoin Cash and Bitcoin SV proponents is that the larger blocks make for greater throughput and thus make the network more suitable for everyday, smaller transactions. Bitcoin's supporters counter this by pointing out that new developments make it possible to do this in other ways. Both Bitcoin Cash and Bitcoin SV continue to be mined, although the former has less than a quarter of Bitcoin's miners and the latter has about five per cent. Some Bitcoin forks have also been criticized for allowing much of their mining to take place in cloud services provided by Chinese giant Alibaba, resulting in much greater centralization than the original Bitcoin network.

These disagreements preoccupied many participants and observers in the Bitcoin community, but went largely unnoticed by many casual Bitcoin holders, who simply registered with happiness the fact that their funds kept increasing every time a new fork was added. The new coins were never worth as much as Bitcoin itself – usually substantially less, but it seemed that the major beneficiaries of these wars over the future of Bitcoin were holders themselves, who were effectively airdropped money for nothing. Even if the coins you had been gifted from the latest fork were worth $100 or less, it was still a pleasant surprise. Meanwhile the developers and marketing teams behind the forks were left with the uphill battle of trying to drive adoption and interest. It was not a given that a newly launched Bitcoin fork would ever be listed on exchanges, and one of the toughest challenges was persuading miners that your insignificant new coin was worth diverting mining power towards, when mining, with all its hardware and electrical expenses, was an activity targeted at purely the most profitable networks.

Bitcoin forks continued to proliferate through 2017, with Bitcoin Gold launched in October, to be followed by Bitcoin Diamond, Bitcoin Private and various others. None of these altcoins, however, impeded the progress of Bitcoin which, despite a fall from its record highs at the end of 2017, continued to prove itself impervious to all the drama.

While unregulated ICOs flourished and Bitcoin forks abounded, there was another revolution taking place, far away from the headlines. The world's major banks and financial services companies had been eyeing Bitcoin and the technologies behind it for some time, and it was not long before innovation teams and startups began to imagine how traditional processes could be made more efficient with the use of blockchain technology. In the next chapter, we will look at some examples of where this is already being done.

References

Blockchain Transparency Institute (2018) Market surveillance report, December. Available from: https://www.bti.live/reports-december2018/ (archived at https://perma.cc/TVU4-C2N8)

Chivers, T (2019) *The AI Does Not Hate You*, Weidenfeld & Nicolson

Finley, K (2016) A $50 million hack just showed that the DAO was all too human, *Wired*, 18 June. Available from: https://www.wired.com/2016/06/50-million-hack-just-showed-dao-human/ (archived at https://perma.cc/PP5G-KX55)

Kauflin, J (2018) Where did the money go? *Forbes*, 29 October. Available from: https://www.forbes.com/sites/jeffkauflin/2018/10/29/where-did-the-money-go-inside-the-big-crypto-icos-of-2017/#3d4ac9b7261b (archived at https://perma.cc/EQ7E-UETJ)

Lewis-Kraus, G (2018) Inside the crypto world's biggest scandal, *Wired*, 19 June. Available from: https://www.wired.com/story/tezos-blockchain-love-story-horror-story/ (archived at https://perma.cc/XM3S-4GRF)

9

Banking and financial services

To understand the current status of blockchain technology implementation within the banking sector, we need to rewind to 2012. Bitcoin had been around for three years, and news of this strange new currency had started to spread beyond cypherpunk circles. Most financiers, if they thought about Bitcoin at all, saw it as an outlier used by anarchists and idealists who were convinced they could overthrow the world's banking system with their magic internet money. Many banking professionals, who had not themselves studied the technical mechanisms that underpin Bitcoin, assumed that it would simply be hacked or would be banned by governments. We have seen from earlier chapters that neither of these scenarios is likely, but it was a frequent refrain from many within the industry.

There were a few exceptions. Some banks had innovation teams or sometimes just one person who saw through the hype and understood what the technology could offer. The response to this potential took two different forms: banks wanting to invest in startups that directly leveraged the potential of Bitcoin and other technologies, and other banks where the technology teams could see that there was some advantage to be gained from using a system that shared certain attributes of Bitcoin's blockchain but were not directly associated with Bitcoin itself.

By 2015, there was a flurry of activity as banks tried to get a piece of the action. Their strategies varied from those who were interested in Bitcoin and were prepared to partner with, or invest in, cryptocurrency startups, to others who were more interested in having their innovation teams look into how efficiencies might be produced by using distributed ledgers internally and sharing them with key partners such as other banks. As we will see later in this chapter, the potential for working in new ways at an inter-bank or inter-company level was something that was sufficiently exciting to enough influential people that it enabled cooperation between competing parties at a level that had not been seen since the introduction of the internet.

In July 2015, history was made when Société Générale posted their first advertisement for a Bitcoin- and cryptocurrency-focused developer, to be based in Paris (Higgins, 2015). In the same year in London, Barclays worked on an initial proof of concept with remittances company Safello, and also accepted three blockchain-focused startups into its accelerator: Safello, Atlas Card and Blocktrace (Spaven, 2015).

However, it soon became clear that most banks were not yet ready to take advantage of the true potential of these new open networks. In many cases, their suspicion of Bitcoin meant that they were not prepared to understand the purpose of the token, or the incentive structure that keeps the network running. By 2016, 'blockchain, not Bitcoin' was the mantra, as executives tried to figure out how they could keep the useful technical parts that would bring efficiency to their business, while ignoring Bitcoin itself. In the eyes of many in the higher echelons of management, Bitcoin was a word that had been tainted by its association with idealists, free thinkers and revolutionaries, but 'blockchain' was an exciting buzzword that could be dropped into sentences containing other buzzwords such as 'big data' or 'AI' and packaged up into strategy documents that promised a great deal but delivered little.

Richard Crook, Director of financial services technology startup LAB577 and former Head of Emerging Technologies at NatWest/ Royal Bank of Scotland, believes that things have changed since then:

> We worked hard in 2015 to separate Bitcoin from blockchain so we could have a conversation about blockchain. That is now working very successfully in areas such as post-trade settlement, trade finance, netting, clearing and settlement. Those areas have tremendous touchpoints, both interbank and intercompany and those are using blockchain or DLT

technology very successfully. We've had many false starts with proof of concepts where people have mixed up digitization with decentralization.

What is really exciting is that the artificial split between Bitcoin and blockchain is now coming back together, and the crypto world is converging with the use of blockchain technology that I've just described.

To understand why these 'blockchain without Bitcoin' technology projects were so appealing to banks, it is important to first understand the processes they aimed to transform. The administrative systems that form the backbone of the world's financial infrastructure is creaking under decades of technical debt because so many of the critical services depend on other services and coordinating change on this great scale is both costly and risky.

In the United States, around 80 per cent of retail banking transactions are made on platforms that are written in the COBOL programming language. COBOL (Common Business Oriented Language) was invented in 1959 and is largely the preserve of a much older generation of programmers. Stories abound of retirees being paid small fortunes to keep creaking systems running, and there is even an apocryphal story of one bank putting in frantic calls to a resident of a nursing home who was the only person with the specialist knowledge to fix a bug in their system. Banking technology is slowly being migrated to new platforms that use modern programming languages. But it is expensive, as underlined by the 20 billion euros Spanish bank Santander have set aside for their ambitious digital transformation programme (Kahn and Devereux, 2019).

This may sound like an astronomical amount, but many within the legacy banking industry see such ambitious programmes as their only chance to compete with challenger banks such as Revolut, Monzo and Starling, or with the new breed of fintechs. Banks are not the only organizations in the FIRE (Finance, Insurance, Real Estate) sector who are struggling with the burdens of their antiquated systems, not only in terms of the technologies they use, but also in terms of the culture and tradition within their sector.

In the closely related and equally old-fashioned insurance industry, another apocryphal story tells the tale of how business used to be carried out with handwritten notes, which were taken from representative to representative and signed before being actioned. When the system went digital, the original note was scanned and emailed to the next person, who printed it out and signed it... and then scanned and emailed it to the next person, and so on. When systems have existed for hundreds of years, humans become prisoners of convention and it is difficult to imagine acting any differently.

As with much else in life, these generalizations are not true of many institutions. Following the liberalization of trading laws in the City of London's 'Big Bang' in the 1980s, some companies seized the opportunity to reinvent themselves and invest in new ways of working. Goldman Sachs stands out as a company that is now almost as much of a technology company as it is a bank, with software engineers now comprising almost a third of its workforce. No longer do the technology team lurk in back rooms, unnoticed except for when something goes wrong: they work in small, high-performance teams, integrated with traders.

Retail banking settlement

However, the Goldman Sachs model is far from universal, and some banking functions are still carried out in a primarily manual fashion in many organizations. The process of settlement (of securities, futures and options, as well as retail payments) is even now sometimes carried out using Excel spreadsheets, and reconciliation can take literally days. It is this one area that is a prime target for business transformation using DLT (distributed ledger technology).

Leaving aside the fact that many banks today also rely on Excel to conduct important parts of their settlement systems, let us think for a moment about the way settlements work between banks. As we discussed in Chapter 1, when an individual or a company has an account with a bank, the bank does not hold their money on their behalf.

If Company A has an account with Bank Y and their current account shows a balance of £100, this is a liability for the bank. It means that the bank owes Company A £100. Imagine Company A wants to send £50 of this amount to Company B, which has an account with Bank Z. Most people would imagine that the money is actually transferred between Bank Y and Bank Z and the records adjusted to reflect this new reality. But it is not what actually happens. Say Company B's account with Bank Z shows a balance of £25. After receiving the payment from Company A, Company B's account should be in credit by £75. What this really means is that Bank Z now owes Company B £75 instead of £25. Why would they want to do this? And how can they prevent their assets and liabilities from becoming completely unbalanced, depending on the daily whims and needs of their customers?

The answer is that Bank Y and Bank Z in this straightforward example also have reciprocal accounts with each other. So, Bank Y holds an account at Bank Z and vice versa. When Company A makes a payment of £50, which is transferred from Bank Y to Bank Z, what happens behind the scenes is that Bank Y sends a message to Bank Z to let them know that there is £50 more in the Bank Z account at Bank Y. So, the balance of assets and liabilities is now the same at both banks as it was before the transaction. In practice, it would be expensive to do this for each and every transaction made between Bank Y and Bank Z. So, transactions between particular banks are added up and settled in batches (a process known as 'netting').

This sounds relatively straightforward, but extra complexity arises when customers want to make payments between banks that do not have reciprocal accounts with each other. In this case, settlement has to be made via various intermediary banks that happen to have accounts with each other, forming a chain of liabilities. There is an added complication in that where substantial sums are involved and where one bank is much larger than another, it may not wish to have exposure to the smaller bank. If this sounds clumsy and as if there should be a better solution – well, there is. In countries such as the UK, banks all hold accounts with the Bank of England, and liabilities that are transferred between the banks are done via the accounts held at the central bank. So, in our case study, the transfer of £50 from Company A to Company B would be achieved by moving £50 from Bank Y's account at the Bank of England to Bank Z's account. This is known as real-time gross settlement and speeds up transaction times greatly. Despite the name, transactions are still not made in real time, although they are relatively fast. Would distributed ledger technology help here? The results from recent trials have been positive, as we see from the example below.

One of the most extensive blockchain trials was carried out in 2019 and involved 17 leading Italian retail banks. Reconciliation processes in Italy can be particularly complex, as there is a lack of standardization and if there is a mismatch of information about a final settlement, it can be a laborious manual process to resolve. This particular type of settlement is called 'spunta' in Italian, and the purpose of this particular pilot programme, carried out in partnership with the R3 enterprise software company in association with other collaborating organizations, was to use R3's Corda distributed ledger framework to bring transparency and consensus to settling retail banking transactions.

The initiative was led by ABI Lab, the innovation centre promoted by the Italian Banking Association. ABI's Research Manager, Silvia Attanasio, says interbank reconciliation was ideal because of the challenges with the current process. 'From the very beginning, it was very important to have a real business need that we could address with distributed ledger technology (DLT),' she says. 'The spunta process in Italy is reliant on a special kind of correspondence account – and so long as the ownership of the accounts rests with one bank, the other party can't see anything. So, the first need was for more transparency. The second was better efficiency in the matching rules and matching activities. And the third was better handling of the movements that needed further investigation.' (See https://www. r3.com/wp-content/uploads/2019/04/Spunt_CS_R32018.pdf (archived at https://perma.cc/M8F9-H3E9).)

While it is possible to gain an idea of how complex the existing settlement mechanisms are for payments between banks within one country – remember that these are competing private businesses, with absolutely no motivation or justification for trusting one another – the problems are greatly multiplied when dealing with payments between institutions in different countries. Payments between banks in different countries in the eurozone (the collection of states within the European Union that share the euro as their unit of payment) are complicated enough, but when it comes to sending payments between banks on different continents, the unit of payment, the time zone, the technologies used, the regulations that are enforced and the local settlement methods may all be different. It is essentially a miracle that anyone ever manages to send a cross-border payment, and in the end we pay a lot for a very slow process... optimization is calling.

Cross-border payments

Let's look at how international payments are currently administered. Imagine you are in London and you want to send a payment to your friend in Manila – and you have decided not to use Bitcoin for this purpose. Anyone who has ever sent a payment to a recipient in another country is familiar with the idea of an IBAN code: a reference code with up to 34 characters that is universally understood. However, when a retail customer makes a transaction to a bank account using an IBAN, frequently other information needs to be provided, which can vary from bank to bank, so that the sender is obliged to chase up the recipient to provide details such as the bricks-and-mortar address of the bank, or their own physical location.

In their report 'Blockchain and retail banking: making the connection' (Higginson, Hilal and Yugac, 2019), McKinsey estimated that applying blockchain technology to cross-border payments could save about $4 billion per year. However, it is also important to remember that the issue of slow and inefficient international payments could be solved in a multiplicity of ways, only one of which involves blockchains. Within days of Facebook's Libra announcement, payment processor SWIFT announced its own plans for transforming payments infrastructure – and there was not a blockchain or cryptocurrency in sight. In her article 'SWIFT's battle for international payments', Frances Coppola notes that: 'in fact, payments "plumbing" is undergoing perhaps the most radical change since the 1980s. Domestic payment systems are going real-time... As SWIFT says, banks must respond to these far-reaching changes if they are to survive – though of course, left unspoken is the fact that SWIFT and its member banks must also respond to the threat posed by cryptocurrencies if they are to survive' (Coppola, 2019).

As Coppola notes, lack of common standards is the biggest barrier to seamless international payments. SWIFT are unconvinced that blockchain technology will solve this problem, so their efforts towards instantaneous real-time payments, 24/7, are focused on more mundane initiatives such as adopting the open ISO 20022 standard, using OpenAPIs and standardizing technical architecture across borders and institutions. However, as she also points out, this pre-supposes a degree of cooperation and willingness to invest in new technologies that most banks have not shown until now. It is highly likely that the rapidly evolving payments landscape will expand to include both components of an improved legacy system and a block-chain/cryptocurrency/DLT approach rather than falling on one side of an either/or choice.

Unlike SWIFT, which is an entirely separate enterprise not owned by a particular bank, the main blockchain-based international payments network is the brainchild of a single organization: JP Morgan. Their Interbank Information Network (IIN) launched as a pilot involving just 27 banks in 2017 but has now grown to well over 350 global banks, around 40 per cent of them in Asia. IIN is the largest live banking blockchain project by any measure, and its purpose is to speed up cross-border payments, reducing friction and allowing them to reach beneficiaries faster. It is a peer-to-peer network based on Quorum, which you will remember is derived from Ethereum. The list of signatories to IIN reads like a *Who's Who* of global banking, including scores in Asia, Africa and the Far East, and JP Morgan has ambitions to spread the IIN net even further.

IIN's achievement is to allow banks on every continent in the world, however large or small, to exchange secure, validated settle-ment messages more or less instantly, without having to go via a central bank or other trusted authority. While JP Morgan's stable of blockchain projects contains both IIN and JPMorganCoin, it is important to make the distinction that the token is not required to make transactions via IIN. And, as you will have gathered from Chapter 7, the Quorum blockchain on which IIN is run is not open to the general public. So, someone who lives in Malaysia and wishes to send a payment to their relative in Ecuador would not be able to access the IIN ledger directly: they would have to go through their bank in the normal way. The difference is in the way the banks communicate with each other.

Collaborations

The world's global banks are traditionally competitors, rather than collaborators. Hence it is no surprise to see organizations such as JP Morgan and Goldman Sachs forging ahead with their own projects and reaping the later profits. In this sense, a project like IIN sees JP Morgan operating in the same kind of competitive sphere as SWIFT. However, even deadly rivals can work together if there is enough of a reward at stake, and there are win–win situations for both in some instances when the quantity of banking business grows overall due to their collaborative effort.

The R3 consortium is an example of such a joint effort. The collaboration we discussed earlier in the chapter, during which the Italian Banking Association joined forces with R3 and various Italian banks to trial digital ledger technology-based settlements for retail payments was not the first time R3 had worked with banks at scale. Founded in 2014 and headquartered in New York, R3 set themselves the task of developing DLT solutions for financial services, insurance, trade finance and many other usages. In 2015, the company formed a consortium to work with a small number of leading banks (original consortium members included Barclays, BBVA, Commonwealth Bank of Australia, Credit Suisse, Goldman Sachs, JP Morgan, Royal Bank of Scotland and UBS) on mutually beneficial software solutions. The platform developed by R3 is called Corda and is designed as a permissioned distributed system to allow peer-to-peer information exchange and transactions between cooperating members. Corda offers firm control of who is allowed to see what information, so that if Bank A transacts with Bank B on a particular Corda platform,

Bank C will not be able to view those transactions, while retaining full visibility of transactions between itself and either Bank A or Bank B.

Applications built on Corda are known as CorDapps, and in the years since 2015, both the range of potential Corda use cases and the number of banks in the R3 consortium have expanded rapidly. While JP Morgan, Goldman Sachs and a handful of other high-profile names have withdrawn to focus on their own DLT solutions, there are now more than 100 participating banks in the consortium, and in 2017 R3 raised $107 million in Series A funding (the first round of venture capital funding for a startup), showing the appetite for innovation in this area.

Not only do banks and financial corporates collaborate with each other: sometimes it suits blockchain software companies to join forces, too. Two of the other major players in distributed ledger research and development are Axoni and Clearmatics. Not only have Axoni previously collaborated with R3 and IBM to develop a framework for smoothing processes in derivatives post-trade events, but in 2018 Axoni also teamed up with London-based Clearmatics for a proof of concept in which a derivatives smart contract was executed on one blockchain and settled on another one. With Axoni having done much work in the area of derivatives, while Clearmatics have developed their own open-source interoperability protocol, this willingness to share knowledge in order to push research and development forward is a key attribute of many of the new breed of blockchain-focused software companies.

Richard Crook points out that collaboration is key in this new world of decentralized opportunities:

> There's only so much fun you can have on your own with a blockchain. Collaboration is difficult in an anti-trust environment, and therefore we watch the financial institutions coming together as they did around the internet. It doesn't matter whether you are a retail, corporate or financial institution: your banking is delivered over the internet now, which required collaboration across the industry on a very large scale. And that's what we see going on again now.

Of course, blockchain or distributed ledger solutions are not just for transferring value, executing smart contracts or settling trades: they can also be a resilient and trustworthy way to share information between parties, which is the next use case we will consider.

Know Your Customer rules, credit checks and data aggregation

One of the primary purposes of sharing information between institutions is to ensure that banks comply with money-laundering regulations both in their own country, and elsewhere. Blockchains offer instant information-sharing between peers, while minimizing the opportunity for information to be tampered with, making it a powerful tool for auditors and those tasked with ensuring compliance is adhered to.

The decentralized structure of blockchains eliminates overlapping KYC and AML compliance checks (banks share authenticating information), lightens the information burden and allows banks to disseminate data as it is updated. To give an example, Bluzelle, a blockchain-based data-storage startup, in 2017 worked with a consortium of three banks in Singapore – HSBC, Mitsubishi UFJ Financial Group, and OCBC Bank – to test a platform for KYC. The project showed that a blockchain platform would improve efficiency, cut the risk of financial crime, and heighten responsiveness to performance and scheduling needs. It was predicted to reduce costs by 25 to 50 per cent. (It is important to note here that Bluzelle is an independent organization offering a third-party product, rather than a proprietary software product created by a bank.)

This type of information is also used for credit checks on individuals and companies, allowing financial institutions to make decisions about how much money to lend out, or what types of financial products to offer, based on the credit history of the prospective customer. Companies such as Experian and Equifax hold substantial data on millions of people, often without their explicit knowledge. When the Equifax hack happened, exposing the private financial details of

143 million people, many of those individuals whose data was stolen were unaware that such detailed information was being held by an organization of which they had little or no knowledge.

Of course, it is not only for KYC and credit-checking purposes that companies require certain personal and financial data about us. We spoke briefly in the last chapter about the rise of fintech, aided by the Open Banking regulations in the UK, which is levelling the playing field not only for challenger banks but for apps offering all kinds of services, from mobile investment apps to card aggregation apps, such as Curve. Aggregation services that collect vast amounts of data about our spending and saving habits make a fortune from sitting on and charging for this data, but every once in a while an innovation comes along that threatens to upend their dominance in this sector.

In 2019, Visa announced the results of their pilot LucidiTEE project, which allows financial institutions to share and process data without using intermediaries. Visa's own research paper describes LucidiTEE as: 'the first system to enable multiple parties to jointly compute on large-scale private data, while guaranteeing policy-compliance even when the input providers are offline, and fairness to all output recipients' (Sinha, Gaddam and Kumaresan, 2019). How does it do this? In simple terms, the shared history of all the data that has been computed is available on a permissioned distributed ledger such as Hyperledger, while sensitive computations of the data itself are carried out in a TEE (trusted execution environment).

The TEE has to obey certain rules and policies, which are agreed on by all participants in the network, and anyone can check the history of the computations at any time by verifying the history of the ledger. This allows banks and other institutions to share their data directly with others, for example, to validate a customer's borrowing history or to aggregate consumer data, safe in the knowledge that this data will not be abused and will be used in a way that is compliant with regulations such as GDPR. Because the other institutions' ability to interact with the data is circumscribed by the computational rules that are embedded in the network, there is no need for the participants to trust each other, and no need for a third party such as an aggregator to supply and validate the data.

Audit trails and blockchains

As we saw above, one of the notable features of the way distributed ledger technology is advancing in the financial sector is a willingness of banks and institutions to collaborate with each other, and also of software companies to join forces for research and development in some cases. As the cliché goes, blockchain is a team sport, and there is little point in maintaining a distributed trustless network if you only allow people who are trusted to participate in it. Another significant feature has been a movement towards open-source software instead of institutions keeping a jealous hold of the code and architecture that their engineering teams have produced. One only has to look at Corda (open-source, developed by R3) and Quorum (developed by JP Morgan) to see the rapid change that is taking place in the sector.

Even so, if there was one piece of news in 2019 that encapsulated this new approach, it was the announcement by EY (the Big Five auditor previously known as Ernst & Young) that not only had they developed their own set of protocols for allowing entirely private transactions on the Ethereum blockchain, but that they were open-sourcing the results of their labour. This means that they are freely sharing the code they developed by publishing it in a public repository on GitHub. This library of smart contracts and microservices, which they called Nightfall and uses zero-knowledge proofs, was originally designed to help EY's corporate clients in areas such as supply-chain management and food traceability.

Explaining the decision to make the code freely available, Paul Brody, EY Global Innovation Leader for Blockchain, said: 'Making public blockchains secure and scalable is a priority for EY. The fastest way to spread this privacy-enhancing technology was to make it public. The gold standard in security is only achieved with the kind of intense review and testing that comes with public domain releases' (EY, 2019).

It is natural that auditing firms should have a strong interest in developing distributed ledger solutions: an immutable chain of transactions that is very difficult to tamper with makes the job of verifying accounts and processes much smoother and less time-consuming.

Trade finance – letters of credit

Of all the functions and services in which banks are involved, one of the areas that is widely considered ripe for disruption by blockchain-based technologies is that of letters of credit, a cumbersome system of documentation and guarantees that provides sellers of goods with an assurance that they will receive payment, or buyers the assurance that they will receive the goods they have ordered.

Damien Ducourty of B9lab agrees that letters of credit are the first area to see real inroads made by DLT: 'Usage of the blockchain technology from financial institutions we've seen mostly on the issuance of letters of credit... because it's a relatively simple application. Very useful, immediately applicable and it touches on a lot of economic activity that has been siloed for many years and to get those instruments more liquid.'

Letters of credit are profitable for banks and expensive for those who need to use them. The British government's own website warns against using them unless strictly necessary on the basis that not only are they expensive but can also cause delays and extra paperwork as they need to be processed.

However, many exporters have little choice but to engage a bank to provide these services, sometimes because the government in the importer's home country stipulates it as a legal requirement. It is a huge business: 1.2 million letters of credit worth $750 billion were issued into China alone in 2018 (John, 2019), and with five main types of letters of credit, standards that need to be adhered to and a great deal of inflexibility about the participants' need to stick exactly to the conditions laid down in the letter, it is unsurprising that there is now an impetus to reform the system with decentralized technologies.

One of the major movers in this direction is the Voltron consortium, which also uses R3's Corda software. Voltron's founding members included BNP Paribas, HSBC, ING, NatWest and Standard Chartered, and the consortium now has more than 50 banks and corporates as members, working in coordination with R3 and CryptoBLK. Live trials between participating members in 2018 and

2019, which involved generating letters of credit across 27 countries on six continents, proved that the time taken for this process can be reduced from 5 to 10 days down to less than 24 hours – a huge success by anyone's standards. Considering the initiative was announced only in October 2018, this reinforces Damien Ducourty's opinion that letters of credit are indeed a prime target for transformation by distributed ledger technology.

Trade finance – open accounts

Not all trading arrangements require letters of credit. We have seen from some of the examples above how cumbersome this process can be, so it is unsurprising that alternative solutions were found, long before blockchain technology became an option. Much of the world's trade payments are settled by open accounts, an arrangement by which goods are shipped by the exporter and received by the importer before payment for the goods is made. In a pre-blockchain environment, this required a higher level of trust than letters of credit, as payments might be made as much as 90 days after delivery, and companies in different countries do not necessarily have the same knowledge about each other as companies who routinely deal with each other. The Marco Polo trade finance platform, a joint venture between R3 and TradeIX, offers a solution to this, facilitating trade flows and removing barriers to international trade. Companies using its network include BNP Paribas, Commerzbank, ING Bank, Standard Chartered Bank, Sumitomo Mitsui Banking Corporation, Natwest, Natixis, DNB, Bangkok Bank, OP Financial Group, Danske Bank, Anglo-Gulf Trade Bank and many others.

Richard Crook compares the current wave of technological innovation in the financial sector to the birth of the internet: 'We have just watched for the last 25 years the rollout of an internet of information. And we are now watching over the next 25 years the rollout of the internet of value,' he says.

He sees tokens as an integral part of this internet of value. When asked about the role that tokens might play, for example, as part of the transaction process on platforms such as Marco Polo, he says:

The other part of that is those blockchain projects that are doing trade finance or reconciliation in the real economy are now recognizing that they need stores of value and transfers of value, in other words, tokens inside them. So, they've only got so far by shuffling invoices back and forward before they realize that what they really want is the payment inside the ledger itself… what Marco Polo and others are doing is exchanging the representations of the trade with the invoice, the letter of credit, the purchase order.

And then having to leave the new network to make the payments in an old-school system like SWIFT. This means you lose the transparency, you lose the customer experience and you gain fees and latency. And we've always made this point which is people don't send the payments for no reason – they send payments in receipt of goods and services. So if you've got an invoice going one way, then you want a payment going the other, and you want to do it on the same fabric on the same network.

The future for DLT in banking

Damien Ducourty feels that while progress continues behind the scenes in exploring the potential of blockchains in making efficiencies in many areas of financial services, this has stabilized and even cooled (with a few notable exceptions, such as trade finance), and for the first time there is more of a focus on the potential of crypto tokens themselves:

We've seen a willingness not to explore a number of potential applications for the time being because people are aware of the risks that are involved when existing processes are affected.

However, on the crypto side we have seen much more activity. Why is this? Because the potential is so much more exciting in this sphere: new products, new token issuances, new financial instruments that can be derived from crypto tokens. We have seen much more acceleration, especially around the emergence of STOs [security token offerings], which I believe will excite some people and scare others.

The next decade will be one of profound challenges and changes for legacy banks and financial institutions, many of whom have been around for literally centuries. Like giant oil tankers that cannot easily change direction, the huge sunk costs of technical infrastructure, existing agreements, cultural factors and working arrangements mean that such organizations can find it difficult to adapt to changing technology and market conditions. The more established the company, the more resistant shareholders tend to be to rapid transformation programmes, and companies that hold customers' money tend to be tightly regulated in all jurisdictions. Add to this the fact that rules on monopolies or cartels can also restrict vertical or horizontal expansion, partnerships and acquisitions and it is starting to look like something of a miracle that they have managed anywhere near the truly impressive innovations that some of them have achieved.

Of course, much of this innovation is patchy, even within companies. In 2015, while Barclays was supporting Bitcoin-based startups through its accelerator programme in London, the retail arms of high-street banks were busily closing down the accounts of individuals and companies because they were suspected of being involved in cryptocurrency. The availability of business bank accounts for cryptocurrency exchanges and other decentralization-focused businesses continues to be an issue in the UK, Europe, the United States and most of the rest of the world. Perhaps unsurprisingly, Switzerland leads the way in crypto-friendly banks. In summer 2018, Hypothekarbank Lenzburg became the first Swiss bank to provide enterprise accounts for blockchain and crypto-related fintech companies.

However, as the Bitcoin faithful are quick to point out, decentralized currencies were invented for a reason, and that reason was not to provide a source of efficiency savings for the world's financial incumbents. If one truly believes that Bitcoin exists because it is a way of disrupting rent-seekers and offering individuals the chance to exercise their right to cheap, quick and uncensored payments, then perhaps decentralized platforms can offer their own versions of other products and services offered by banks and the financial behemoths that dominate our world. Just as the internet is so much more than 'the real world, but online', blockchains offer a fundamental shift in the way we perceive money, value and financial instruments.

In the next chapter, we focus on some of these new ideas, starting with different ways in which Bitcoin can be traded without taking custody of Bitcoin itself, looking at ways in which tokens allow investors to invest in existing products, and finally presenting the concept of DeFi – Decentralized Finance, whose proponents believe has truly transformative power to open up a whole new world of products and possibilities to a new wave of traders.

References

Coppola, F (2019) SWIFT's battle for international payments, *Forbes*, 16 July. Available from: https://www.forbes.com/sites/francescoppola/2019/07/16/swifts-battle-for-international-payments/#10b432ca758e (archived at https://perma.cc/C9WP-9X6Z)

EY (2019) EY releases zero-knowledge proof blockchain transaction technology to the public domain to advance blockchain privacy standards, 16 April. Available from: https://www.ey.com/en_gl/news/2019/04/ey-releases-zero-knowledge-proof-blockchain-transaction-technology-to-the-public-domain-to-advance-blockchain-privacy-standards (archived at https://perma.cc/3AXT-BK5C)

Higgins, S (2015) French megabank Société Générale seeks Bitcoin expert, *CoinDesk*, 22 July. Available from: https://www.coindesk.com/french-megabank-societe-generale-seeks-cryptocurrency-expert (archived at https://perma.cc/Q4EB-7HMZ)

Higginson, M, Hilal, A and Yugac, E (2019), Blockchain and retail banking: making the connection, *McKinsey & Company*, June. Available from: https://www.mckinsey.com/industries/financial-services/our-insights/blockchain-and-retail-banking-making-the-connection (archived at https://perma.cc/FX45-AVUL)

John, A (2019) HSBC processes first blockchain letter of credit using Chinese yuan, *Reuters*, 2 September. Available from: https://uk.reuters.com/article/us-hsbc-hldg-blockchain/hsbc-processes-first-blockchain-letter-of-credit-using-chinese-yuan-idUKKCN1VN1QL (archived at https://perma.cc/4RGG-9GWJ)

Kahn, J and Devereux, C (2019) Banks waking up to fintech threat throw billions into digital, *Bloomberg*, 10 May. Available from: https://www.bloomberg.com/news/articles/2019-05-10/banks-waking-up-to-fintech-threat-throw-billions-into-digital (archived at https://perma.cc/9TNB-QZZR)

Sinha, R, Gaddam, S and Kumaresan, R (2019) LucidiTEE: A TEE-blockchain system for policy-compliant multiparty computation with fairness, *Visa*. Available from: https://eprint.iacr.org/2019/178.pdf (archived at https://perma.cc/U6RL-FEE9)

Spaven, E (2015) Three blockchain startups selected for Barclays Accelerator, *CoinDesk*, 23 March. Available from: https://www.coindesk.com/three-blockchain-startups-selected-for-barclays-accelerator (archived at https://perma.cc/32LB-A4KM)

10

A revolution in financial products

The previous chapter dealt with how the banking system is leveraging blockchain technology and similar systems to bring efficiencies and improved processes to traditional assets and value flows. From the end user's point of view, a letter of credit or a cross-border payment appear to be pretty much the same product, whatever happens behind the scenes. Customers will undoubtedly reap the benefits of faster transaction times, although it remains to be seen whether cost savings will be passed on to end users or retained by institutions as a cost saving.

In contrast, this chapter examines the disruptive potential of cryptoassets in their many different forms, from new products offered by established players to innovations whose potential has scarcely been tapped yet, and which are only made possible by decentralized technology.

Of course, cryptocurrencies such as Bitcoin are assets in themselves, particularly since Bitcoin began to be viewed as a store of value as much as a means of exchange. Tokens such as Bitcoin and Litecoin are traditional bearer assets, meaning that the owner of the private key is the owner of the asset. Many Bitcoin holders prefer to simply hold their assets themselves, rather than rely on trust-based fiat currencies, but others are keen to combine the ideas and structures of the legacy financial system with cryptographic assets in order to leverage their worth in new and exciting ways.

Some ideas can be expressed as simply doing something familiar with a new product, such as Bitcoin futures or ETFs, while others, such as the new concepts made possible by DeFi platforms (DeFi stands for Decentralized Finance and is a concept we will return to later in the chapter) represent a massive shift in the way people think about value and how it is stored and used to generate wealth.

Bitcoin futures

For some years, Bitcoin was simply Bitcoin. Early adopters were keen to use it, and while some were keen to trade, many of those original holders (or 'hodlers', as the meme would have it), eschewed the traditional financial markets, with their products built around leverage and centralization. However, as the years went on and traditional investors finally began to see in Bitcoin the qualities of censorship resistance and independence from central banks that the cypherpunks and cryptoanarchists had seen from the outset, it became obvious that this new money was stoking a demand for the kinds of products that already existed in the commodities and securities markets.

Futures are nothing more complicated than a bet on the price of something at a predetermined time in the future. If the Bitcoin price is $8,000 and Alice decides that one Bitcoin will be worth $10,000 by the end of the month, she can enter a futures contract that allows her to take a long position on the Bitcoin price. Futures contracts usually also allow leverage, meaning that Alice can stake a bet of $20,000 for example, if she only has $10,000. If in our example the Bitcoin price falls to $7,000, Alice loses her bet and has to pay $2,000 – the difference between the price times the multiplier she is leveraged. The leverage is one of the risk factors that makes financial products such as futures so dangerous. Of course, it is attractive to be able to put down 10 per cent of the stake you are betting, and to gain the ability to win 10 times the reward. But the potential to lose money is also great, especially in a volatile market such as Bitcoin where liquidity can be low, and where the influence of large stakeholders ('whales') can cause disproportionate swings.

After months of rumours, the first regulated Bitcoin futures were launched in December 2017, by the CME Group, launching a

FIGURE 10.1   Volume of CME futures in the first year

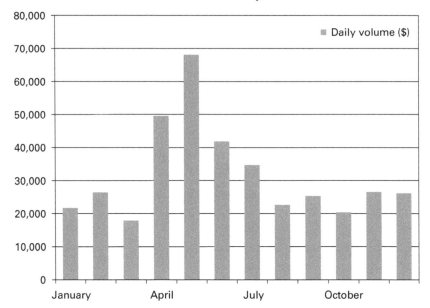

Bitcoin-based trading product into the mainstream for the first time. However, it is important to emphasize that these futures were settled in cash, rather than cryptocurrency. It is also worth noting that despite all the wild hype about pent-up demand and how this would send the Bitcoin price rocketing skyward, initial demand was more lacklustre than predicted, and instead of going moonwards, Bitcoin was soon in a bear market.

Whether or not these two facts were connected in any way, it is clear that this was at least partly what the SEC intended when they finally allowed futures to be sold. Former Chair of the US Commodity Futures Trading Commission Christopher Giancarlo went on the record to reveal that there had been concerns that without the normal safety valve of traders being easily able to short sell Bitcoin, the price would continue to rise in an unstable manner: 'I communicated with Treasury Secretary [Steven] Mnuchin and NEC Director Gary Cohn, and we believed that, should bitcoin futures go forward, it would allow institutional money to bring discipline to the value of the cash market' (Dale, 2019). (Short selling is the process of borrowing shares in order to sell them immediately, hoping that they will go down and then rebuying them to make a profit before returning them to the lender.)

Eighteen months later, and traders were once again talking about Bitcoin futures: this time it was the turn of Bakkt. A significant difference between the CME futures contracts and the Bakkt futures is that the latter are settled in Bitcoin, rather than cash. Again, Bitcoin aficionados presumed that the green light for the new product would ignite the price, which had been range-bound for some months before the Bakkt contracts were launched in September 2019, but again demand was low, and the predicted gains did not materialize.

Bitcoin ETFs

ETFs, or exchange-traded funds, are a vehicle that allows investors to benefit from trading an asset without having to buy or sell it directly. Often, ETFs contain a variety of different assets, such as stocks or bonds or even a mixture of asset types. For example, if you believe that the health sector is likely to be a growth area, but you do not feel you are knowledgeable enough about specific companies to sink your money into one particular stock, a healthcare ETF allows you to spread your risk. Or an ETF may track one particular asset: for example, only a small number of people want to take delivery of physical gold or silver, but a gold ETF ensures that if the price of gold rises, investors who hold the ETF will benefit in the same way as investors in physical gold.

While I am firmly of the opinion that anyone can learn the security procedures that are necessary in order to hold Bitcoin or any other cryptocurrency, many people do not feel they have the time or the expertise to try. Or they may simply want an asset that is both extremely liquid, and which can be traded easily online using existing exchanges and trading apps. It is probably – although we cannot be sure until one actually launches – that there is huge pent-up demand for a regulated Bitcoin ETF, particularly in the United States, and there have been repeated attempts made to get the SEC to permit this.

So far, all proposals have been rejected or placed on hold, on the basis that the Bitcoin market is still too volatile and subject to market manipulation, but most people believe that an ETF will be permitted at some point.

The pragmatic view is that, given the existing demand, permitting US investors to invest in a well-regulated ETF will provide more protection in the long run than driving them to buy into offshore funds whose regulation may not be so stringent. Another argument that has been made is that while there have been questions raised over manipulation of the Bitcoin price, the SEC has previously approved ETFs for commodities whose spot market is equally opaque.

While the wait for a regulated Bitcoin ETF continues, there is at least one product that is similar: a Bitcoin ETN (or exchange traded note) called Bitcoin Tracker One, which started trading on the Stockholm Nasdaq in 2015. While the product was originally available only in Swedish krona, in 2018 the product was made available in US dollars. Meanwhile, there are a handful of blockchain ETFs available around the world, which allow investors to buy into the success (or otherwise) of blockchain- and cryptocurrency-focused companies such as crypto-friendly payment operators, mining chip manufacturers and Bitcoin futures operator CME Group.

Security tokens

We touched on security tokens in Chapter 8, and it is important to recognize that not only are security token offerings (STOs) a new, frictionless and transparent way for companies to raise money, but are also a new way to organize the security value chain, from issuance to custody. Entities wishing to organize a funding round by selling security tokens are required to meet various regulatory requirements and, as noted previously, large fines have been levied for breaching these requirements. As we saw in Chapter 5, the importance of getting the tokenomics right is considerable. However, the benefits are also considerable, not only in terms of low-cost automated issuance, but also because it is possible to set certain conditions around the sale or purchase of tokens that can be governed by smart contract.

During the ICO boom, startups raising money via ICOs were keen to represent their tokens as something akin to a voucher, which could store future value in the sense of an advance payment for a service – usually, the ability of the individual to create and pay for transactions on a public blockchain. For example, if you bought tokens in VEChain or WanChain (VET and WAN respectively) these tokens could be used to pay for smart contracts to be executed on the network. In this sense, it is like buying a prepaid API key on a cloud service like Amazon Web Services (AWS), Microsoft's Azure or Google Cloud, allowing the token owner access to a certain amount of computing power on a network on which one might host decentralized applications. Unfortunately, during the ICO boom, many of these tokens increased in price far beyond any level that would be sustainable when used in this way, and the secondary function of their use as tradable tokens on cryptocurrency exchanges became their primary function in the eyes of investors. Many inexperienced crypto traders who entered the market in 2016 and 2017 did not realize, or maybe even care, that the tokens they had just bought entitled them to nothing at all except for the vague promise that they would be able to execute some unspecified transaction on a blockchain that did not exist, and that they would be left holding nothing at all if the notional value of the tokens on a crypto exchange did not continue to rise.

Security tokens were the result of an attempt to bring sanity and order to the world of cryptoassets, even if the original momentum behind them was driven by the fear of being criminalized by regulators for something that they had not done intentionally. While utility tokens undoubtedly are the key to many revolutionary new business models, they may not be the best choice for a startup's initial fundraising rounds. Security tokens, on the other hand, allow investors to purchase a stake in the company itself, just like a traditional share, and are regulated as a security. This may have both positive and negative side-effects – for example, purchases of security tokens within the United States are often restricted to accredited investors, with all the onerous conditions this involves.

Where security tokens improve on traditional company shares is that they can be programmable. In other words, shares may be automatically programmed to repay loans, to change hands or to be converted on a particular date, without the friction of someone having to do this manually. There is also the massive advantage over traditional securities, which tend to be launched on one exchange in a particular country, that the company looking to raise funds will have access to a huge, global liquidity pool instead of one that is geographically limited.

Real estate tokens

It is not just companies that can be tokenized. We saw in Chapter 6 how new business models involving tokens can create entirely new markets, rather than simply provide efficiencies in existing markets.

Let's use the example of property, as there are various companies, such as BrickBlock and Exporo in Germany, and Alliance Investments in the UK, which offer the chance to allow multiple people to own a property and gain an asset that can be traded. Traditionally, the property market is illiquid, as the owner becomes responsible for a bricks-and-mortar asset, which is tied to one geographic location and which is sometimes difficult to resell. Of course, fractional ownership of properties via a holding company has long been possible without the need for a blockchain. But the legal fees involved in such a structure can be high, the initial investment threshold is usually substantial and there is often no easy way for stakeholders to sell their share.

A property that is tokenized can be split into numerous, almost infinitely small pieces. Because these tokens can be traded, they bring liquidity to the market and enable people who would otherwise be excluded from the market to take a bet on rising property prices, while also providing a mechanism for shorting property assets that does not currently exist.

TOKENIZING COMMERCIAL REAL ESTATE

Exporo is a German company that does exactly that, allowing companies or individuals to invest small or large amounts in commercial real-estate ventures, such as a medical centre in Hamburg. While the company itself has been dealing in digitized real-estate crowdfunding since 2014, the process of issuing tokenized bonds on the Ethereum blockchain and allowing shareholders to trade their tokens on the Exporo exchange was done for the first time in 2019.

It is perhaps no surprise that this approach to crowdfunding originated in Germany, which has a rich history of property development by small cooperatives called Bauengruppe. However, the potential returns from commercial property without having to make a huge investment make this a compelling idea, which will surely have growth potential worldwide.

Tokenize yourself!

If a house can be tokenized, what of the people inside it? We have already seen how some tokens can monetize human attention – for example, the Brave browser's Basic Attention Token – but we have also seen the beginnings of people attempting to tokenize themselves and their future productivity.

American basketball player Spencer Dinwiddie hit not only the sporting headlines but the crypto and financial press in January 2020, despite the opposition of the National Basketball Association, with the issue of a bond representing his future performance. Via a platform named Dream Fan Shares, he made 90 so-called SD8 coins (named for his initials and his number) available to US accredited investors on the Ethereum blockchain. The initial coins were worth $150,000 each and were locked to prevent trading within the first year.

Dinwiddie reported strong interest from other athletes in doing the same thing, and he also received much support from the cryptocurrency industry, as he told *Forbes* (Sprung, 2019): 'It's been an outpouring of not only support, but interest', he said. 'There are a lot of people that want to be a part of this, not only that my offering is cool but also as a business and looking at what this asset class could be as a non-correlated market.'

Where celebrities lead, mere mortals often follow, and there has already been conversation around the probability of someone launching a platform that allows investors to buy tokens in poverty-stricken but talented individuals who are seeking funding for their education in exchange for a slice of their future earnings... in other words, a new form of indentured servitude.

Prediction markets

So far in this chapter, we have talked about products that represent assets, whether that is a cryptocurrency such as Bitcoin or a physical asset like a house or even a person. In all of these cases, the buyer is making a bet that the price will go up, and in some of these cases, there is even a return. They are all products that are issued by a third party and regulated in some way. But what if you could create your own market? Some are used to visiting betting sites where they are issued with a wide array of subjects on which they can gamble money, from sport and lottery numbers to politics and (if they live in the UK) the colour of the hat that the Queen will wear to a royal wedding. Other specialized websites offer the opportunity to bet on share prices and other financial assets. It sometimes seems that you can bet on everything under the sun, but this is an illusion. People may want to create their own bets on a particular set of events happening or surround an existing bet with conditions that narrow down the odds. Or some friends may wish to place their own bet on the likelihood of something happening, without the complication of having to put physical cash into a hat or PayPal each other a deposit as a sign of good faith.

Smart contracts on a public blockchain, when combined with a user interface and sufficient liquidity can allow ordinary people to create and configure their own betting markets. And these markets can be very useful not only as a form of entertainment but as a source of information, which is why we call them 'prediction markets'.

James Surowiecki's *The Wisdom of Crowds* was a seminal work, which posited that if you questioned enough people about the likelihood of a particular outcome, you would get a more accurate result than if you questioned one or two – even if the one or two happened to be experts in their field. Or, as he puts it succinctly: 'You could say it's as if we've been programmed to be collectively smart' (Surowiecki, 2004). And once you get people to put their money where their mouth is and stake cold hard cash on the odds of something happening, accuracy goes up again. Hence betting patterns can be a better predictor of political election results than pundits' opinions or opinion polls. Hence the idea of providing a platform where people could create their own prediction markets, and the valuable information in these markets monetized, is an attractive one.

The prediction platforms Augur and Gnosis, both early token issuers in pre-ICO days with their respective tokens REP and GNO, are examples of this. Both allow anyone to create a market in which others can participate and place bets, although the relative complexity and lack of market reach have so far resulted in a low-liquidity environment in which bets can languish with no counterparty to bet against the creator. Certain moral rules are observed, and no bets are allowed to be placed, for example, on the likely assassination of a particular individual. (Not only is this in poor taste and distressing for the individual, but it also carries the risk that someone would be motivated to carry out the assassination to cash in on their bet!) These platforms are trying to do something interesting and revolutionary – yet they are, as centralized entities, bound by the rules of the jurisdictions in which they reside. But what if you could trade or create whatever financial assets or markets you wanted? Decentralized exchanges and the broader area of DeFi offer just this tantalizing possibility.

DEXes and the DeFi movement

All the products mentioned so far in this chapter have one thing in common. While they may be issued on a decentralized network or –

in the case of Bitcoin futures and ETFs – based on a product that is decentralized, they are generally bought and sold through entities that are centralized: issued by corporations or traded on centralized exchanges where the cloud computing accounts that contain the trading data and the wallets where the tokens are stored remain under the central control of the person or company who runs the exchange. If we take Binance, since 2018 the world's largest crypto-currency exchange by volume as an example, while it deals in decentralized products, the tokens themselves are held in Binance's custody while the trades take place. Traders may see the balance in their exchange wallet increase or decrease, but these are purely inter-nal transactions and do not take place on the blockchains of whatever cryptocurrency is being moved: the tokens remain under the control of the exchange while these transactions take place.

Of course, one of the huge problems with cryptocurrency has been the depressing regularity with which exchanges have been hacked and resulted in lost funds for traders. While the mantra of 'Not your keys, not your money' is repeated multiple times, it remains the case that unless people are holding for the long term, many are likely to want to trade their Bitcoin, and this means using an exchange and trusting that someone else will have both the intention and the ability to guard their cryptocurrency as carefully as you would yourself. Even Binance has not been immune to thefts – in May 2019 a hacker stole 7,000 Bitcoin worth $40 million at the time in a single transac-tion. The exchange had sufficient funds to repay users who lost Bitcoin, but it was a sobering reminder that even the best-resourced and best-run exchanges are vulnerable.

So, what is the alternative if you want to trade but do not want to trust someone else's security, or if you want to make truly censorship-proof transactions where your real-world identity is not tied to your trading account? The latter preference does not have to mean that you are a money-launderer or a tax evader: one reason why people might not necessarily want other people to know how many Bitcoin they own is that it makes them a target for extortion or violent theft. With the Bitcoin price so volatile, and many Bitcoiners working on the optimistic assumption that the price will one day be 10 or 100 times what it is now, most people are aware of the need to obfuscate their current holdings. Hence it is not only to guard against theft that drives traders' desire for anonymity. The October 2019 leak of thousands of account holders' names in an astonishing breach of security by BitMEX, in which a marketing email was sent to thousands of account holders by using the cc rather than the bcc field (Parkin, 2019), was met with anger and disbelief. The details were soon published online for anyone to view, with the result that not only tax authorities but also potential criminals were alerted to Bitcoin ownership by the owners of those email addresses.

Decentralized exchanges (shortened to DEXes) aim to remediate many of the problems described above by removing the necessity for any single person or entity to act as an intermediary when two individuals want to trade tokens or other cryptoassets, and also allow people to transact without imposing KYC (Know Your Customer) protocols. Just as Bitcoin is a peer-to-peer electronic cash system that requires the user to take full responsibility for their own private keys or else risk losing their cash, DEXes match buy and sell orders between parties, who keep control of their own wallets throughout the process. Hence, while if you lose your password to Binance or Bittrex it is possible to ask the exchange to reset it and gain access to your cash, if you lose your wallet credentials while trading through a DEX, there is no way to recover them. While many organizations claim to be decentralized, the degree to which this is true can vary. Colin Platt, independent consultant in cryptocurrency and digital technology, refers to 'decentralization theatre': 'A lot of expense goes into making it look like it's something that is decentralized when in actual fact there are four or five monkeys that are pulling all the strings behind the curtains.' As we will see in the next chapter, which deals with regulation, this becomes an important legal distinction, as well as a philosophical one.

While DEXes are certainly gaining in popularity, they have yet to make great inroads into the trading flows of the centralized exchanges. Some of the better-known DEX names are Uniswap, Dydx, Shapeshift, Changelly, Kyber Network and Etherdelta. However, while interactions between traders may be carried out on an entirely peer-to-peer

FIGURE 10.2   DEX volume vs centralized exchanges

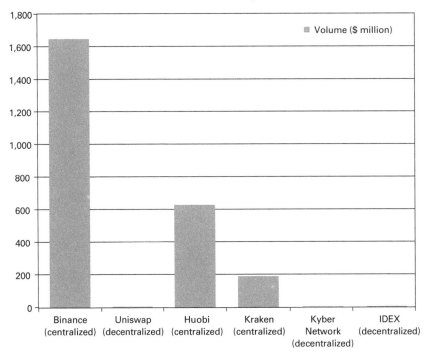

Figures are daily volume examples from January 2020.
DATA SOURCE Coinmarketcap.com (archived at https://perma.cc/CQJ9-WJ57)

basis, the services themselves have to be hosted somewhere, and the authorities in various countries have been fighting a rearguard action to force DEXes to comply with local regulations. We will look at this more closely in the chapter that deals with regulatory issues. There have also been questions raised over how decentralized various exchanges really are.

It is also worth noting that most of these exchanges offer crypto-to-crypto trading only, so the lack of fiat on-ramps has so far deterred many people, other than the most committed, from the extra steps that are needed to trade. Figure 10.2 shows the gap between the volume of trade on some popular DEXes compared with centralized exchanges.

Many people believe this will change, not least because DEXes are a critical piece in the jigsaw that makes up DeFi which, while it is in danger of becoming an overhyped and often incorrectly used buzzword, offers exciting possibilities for the future of finance. The abbreviation stands for 'decentralized finance', and its proponents believe that along with Open Finance (the unbundling of services from legacy banks and institutions, allowing challenger banks and fintech startups to offer new services to consumers), the DeFi ecosystem will make a whole range of financial products and possibilities available to ordinary people.

In their paper 'What is decentralized finance or DeFi?', Outlier Ventures describe DeFi as 'a peer-to-peer electronic financial instrument system' (John and Lundy-Bryan, 2019), and helpfully provide a list of five attributes that define whether a product or platform can really be considered as DeFi or not: censorship resistance, having programmable assets, pseudonymous, transparent and trustless and permissionless, going on to provide this definition: 'One could define a decentralized finance application as a censorship-resistant, transparent tool that enables the transfer, custody, and exchange of tokenized assets that may be fungible or non-fungible in a permissionless environment with almost no requirements for identity verification' (John and Lundy-Bryan, 2019).

Barney Mannerings, founder of Vega Protocol, who provide software infrastructure for creating and trading derivatives on a fully decentralized network, succinctly defines DeFi as: '... the idea of creating or recreating parts of the existing financial system and the products and services that exist today, and quite possibly creating new types of products and services on top of decentralized technology... a parallel financial system.'

So much for the theory, but what does DeFi mean in practical terms? Let's revisit the best-known DeFi product of 2019: MakerDAO and its collateralized debt positions (CDPs), issued in the form of smart contracts on the Ethereum blockchain. This product's popularity is not in doubt: by the end of 2019, nearly 500,000 Ether were locked up in nearly 2,000 CDPs. So, what is the big draw, and why are people so interested in this particular tool? We have already talked about stablecoins, and why Dai is so useful for those seeking a decentralized, censorship-proof currency that lacks the volatility of Bitcoin and Ether, but there are more advantages to minting Dai than simply producing a stablecoin. There is sometimes confusion about why someone would take out a loan in Dai and at the same time lock up an equivalent amount of Ether or other tokens to back the loan. Why does someone who already owns a certain amount of value need to tie that value up in order to take out a loan? Why do they not simply sell the Ether?

If we translate this into real-world terms, perhaps it starts to make more sense. Rather like taking out a second mortgage against your home, or leaving your watch at a pawn shop, collateralizing your Ether means you are effectively placing a bet against either your Ether or your Dai rising in value. The 1 per cent fee you pay for minting Dai is a small price to pay when compared with the possibility, for example, of taking the minted Dai and using leverage to take an Ether position on an exchange that could earn you many multiples of what you have collateralized. The new variant of Dai, which allows creators to lock up various other tokens, not just Ether, adds even more possibilities of this nature. Or you could take advantage of the algorithm built into Dai, which adjusts its value against the US dollar in order to keep it stable, and opt to trade the Dai itself.

Colin Platt talks about this in terms of moving value across time, rather than simply space:

> The two functions of finance are moving money across time and space and the first era of crypto was really about moving things from one point to the next – taking money, moving it as a payment from one account to the next. That's great and it's useful.
>
> But that's much more limited than what we'd expect from finance, which is moving money across time, thus making money that I don't have today available to me today in return for an interest payment... And then with that you have lots of second and third order risks that need to be monitored, including credit risk and all those things. The point of DeFi is really that second dimension, that time dimension, I think that's a very powerful notion.

Platt is enthusiastic about the possibilities of DeFi but warns that, as with all new domains, there can be downsides:

I love the fact that within 30 seconds if I have some Ether, I can log into a website that I've never been to before and invest money and earn interest on that. It's mind-blowing, the speed in which that can happen. Even with some of the best fintech innovations, and even in the UK, which has a very advanced fintech market, you still can't do anything like that in 30 seconds.

However, one of the issues we see with DeFi is that just because it is permissionless nobody really understands the risks themselves, even the creators. In many cases, even if they are very good technologists... there are a lot of risks and sometimes they don't disclose the ones that they are aware of in a way that is understandable.

Speed and innovation are two of the hallmarks of the DeFi movement. While Barney Mannerings personally prefers talking about a 'parallel financial system', rather than using the specific term 'DeFi', he is passionate about the idea of freeing up individuals to create and issue their own instruments. Protocols such as Vega will, in his opinion, '... remove friction and fees, and more importantly, allow creative ideas to flourish and fail outside the banking sector, freeing up talent from the sector to see their ideas realized without constraints'.

His vision is one of a level playing field on which anyone can create their own financial products without profiteering and interference by the privileged institutions that currently gatekeep the capital markets. Vega Protocol and other DeFi leaders envisage a framework for creating and customizing products that give everyone the freedom to build new financial instruments and markets. Incentives for market-making and innovation are a critical part of the decentralized finance landscape, seeking to reward the best and the brightest, rather than the privileged few.

What is the growth potential of this sector – and are there really enough people seeking to participate in this sometimes obscure marketplace? Barney Mannerings makes the bullish case that demand will be driven by consumers once they realize what is on offer, in the same way the internet underwent organic growth:

Where it will start getting really interesting is when people, entrepreneurs and businesses and people doing business in real life start to use it instead of the existing financial system.

For example, as the internet and email started to take off, I became less and less willing to engage with companies that insisted on communicating via the post rather than email. And now no one would dare set up a company that works that way. And I think we'll get to the same point with DeFi and this parallel financial system eventually, where it is so obviously much more functional, quicker and cheaper that people demand it.

You wouldn't open a bank account that wasn't connected [to the internet], and in a similar way, eventually companies won't seek funding unless you can represent the assets on a blockchain, and all of these things would just be kind of expected over time. That means that some of the old ways of regulating things as well as the old ways of doing things will have to change because they don't work, but the number of benefits that come with composability and interconnectedness will be really huge.

By July 2020, more than $3 billion was locked up in DeFi instruments, and several high-profile hacks involving flash loans and other complex financial contracts highlighted the fact that innovation often comes with its own risks. It also goes without saying that trying to shoehorn this explosion of exciting new ideas, liberated by technology, into existing legal frameworks is a challenge. Governments and regulators have largely been left on the back foot by the rapid advances in what technology has made possible. The tension between countries wishing to cooperate with each other to crack down on criminality, and their need to compete with each other in order to encourage inward investment and not stifle innovation is becoming stretched to breaking point. In the next chapter, we will look at regulatory challenges, and assess how different governments are seeking to tackle this.

References

Dale, B (2019) Trump administration popped 2017 Bitcoin bubble, ex-CFTC Chair says, *CoinDesk*, 22 October. Available from: https://www.coindesk.com/trump-administration-popped-2017-bitcoin-bubble-ex-cftc-chair-says (archived at https://perma.cc/FY74-XXQY)

John, J and Lundy-Bryan, L (2019) What is decentralized finance or DeFi? *Outlier Ventures*, June. Available from: https://outlierventures.io/research/mapping-decentralised-finance-defi/ (archived at https://perma.cc/58Z4-TS55)

Parkin, D (2019) Bitcoin: BitMEX just accidentally leaked THOUSANDS of private email addresses, *Daily Express*, 1 November. Available from: https://www.express.co.uk/finance/city/1198699/bitcoin-bitmex-private-email-addresses-leaked (archived at https://perma.cc/8X28-TENB)

Sprung, S (2019) Spencer Dinwiddie discusses digital tokenization plan, happening against the NBA's wishes, *Forbes*, 17 October. Available from: https://www.forbes.com/sites/shlomosprung/2019/10/17/spencer-dinwiddie-discusses-digital-tokenization-plan-happening-against-the-nbas-wishes/ (archived at https://perma.cc/2Y8C-75MV)

Surowiecki, J (2004) *The Wisdom of Crowds*, p 11, Doubleday Books

11

Regulation

Just as the internet meant that information could spread more or less freely around the world, the birth of Bitcoin means that value can be relayed around the world as easily as an email or a web page. This is what people mean when they talk about Bitcoin as censorship-proof money. There is no centralized server to be shut down, no premises that can be raided and no one who can be ordered to turn off the Bitcoin tap. If you have a Bitcoin wallet and you hold the 12-word mnemonic phrase in your head, which allows you to restore your wallet, there may be no physical proof that you have access to this unique store of value, and thus it is challenging for a government to find out who controls which assets. This lack of control is anathema to state authorities for many reasons: not only may assets not be subject to the appropriate taxes, and consumer protection laws may be flouted, but also, in a worst-case scenario, capital can easily flow from one country to another without governments' knowledge or permission, which is not only a regulatory nightmare for taxation, anti-money laundering and anti-terrorism finance, but furthermore questions the authority of states in regard to fiscal and monetary control.

While much of the negative publicity around Bitcoin in particular has focused on the risk of people using it for illegal activities, there is a flaw in this argument. Teana Baker-Taylor, Managing Director of Looking Glass Labs, a cryptoasset policy and regulatory affairs expert, explains:

Yes, people can use Bitcoin to buy drugs, but people also use US dollars to buy drugs. There are electronic holes in the wall of every street corner in the world where you can insert a card and withdraw cash to purchase drugs. But if you're a drug dealer and you're using Bitcoin, you're going to get caught. With blockchain analytics and transaction monitoring, tracing someone who's used Bitcoin for illicit purposes is easier than tracing someone who has used cash. Many policymakers don't fully understand a public blockchain can be audited and wallet addresses can be traced and monitored. So this is an education process, and it is up to the industry to champion and facilitate that education.

Of course, it is not simply limiting the flow of money for illegal drugs that has made governments want to regulate digital currencies.

Governments generally have three primary reasons for regulating the flow of money within their country by introducing laws that force businesses and individuals to comply with them: ensuring money comes from legal sources and not from illegal activities such as arms or drug sales; making sure financial transactions are transparent so that tax cannot be evaded; and finally, most governments believe they have a strong responsibility to provide protection for consumers. With regard to this last ambition, the hardest part is striking a balance between allowing people to make their own financial decisions and protecting naive investors who provide easy prey for scammers.

The unregulated ICO boom of 2016 and 2017 shows how easy it is for people to convince themselves that a company about which they know nothing, with no proven business models, is capable of returning multiples of their original investment. While some of these businesses were out-and-out scams, many were genuine ventures with founders who were simply inexperienced or naive themselves. Or in some cases, as evidenced by the tokens shown in Figure 11.1 below, the tokens were entirely genuine enterprises whose prices had been driven up by wild speculation.

Of the deliberate scams that have been perpetrated over the last few years, one in particular stands out: OneCoin was nothing more than a get-rich-quick pyramid scheme, which was sold as a bona fide cryptocurrency. Self-styled 'cryptoqueen' Dr Ruja Ignatova claimed that OneCoin was a 'Bitcoin killer' despite the tokens simply being stored as entries in a traditional database rather than being recorded in a blockchain or distributed ledger. The coins rose in value from a few cents to hundreds of dollars each and were promoted heavily through MLM (multi-level marketing) schemes all over the world. Many people, some in the poorest countries in the world, lost their life savings after being promised that one day they would be able to exchange this fast-rising currency for euros, pounds or dollars and were left distraught by the criminal investigation and collapse of the company. The $1 billion lost in the OneCoin fraud was the subject of an excellent BBC podcast series by Jamie Bartlett (Bartlett, 2019) and, sadly, will undoubtedly not be the last scheme of its kind.

In fact, the history of so-called 'boiler-room' scams over recent decades shows that such fraudulent enterprises are not limited to the world of cryptocurrencies. In 2018, a court heard the case of Michael Nascimento, who set up a call centre selling bogus property investments and defrauded 170 small investors out of sums totalling £2.8 million (Verity, 2018). It is an unfortunate truth that because returns on legitimate schemes are so low, as governments promote spending instead of saving to artificially stimulate their economies, ordinary people seeking a return on savings are easily driven into the arms of fraudsters, whether these criminals originate in the decentralized space or within traditional financial spheres.

When it comes to protecting the public, governments have an unenviable job. If they do nothing, people will complain that criminals are allowed to operate with impunity. But if they impose strict restrictions, this can have the reverse effect. If products with high returns are allowed to be bought only by a select group of investors who are considered sophisticated and intelligent enough to assess the risks, it drives the people who fall outside this group to seek risky high returns in less legitimate schemes. Not only can this have unintended consequences, but in a world where nation states desire to foster technical innovation in order that they can compete for investment and talent on the global stage, this kind of artificial limit on capital flow can be counterproductive. More than anything, businesses need certainty. It is difficult to establish a company, acquire

FIGURE 11.1   Value collapse in selected tokens

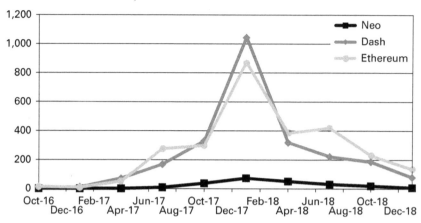

customers and hire staff if you have no certainty that your business will not be declared illegal next year, that your software will have to be rewritten at great expense to comply with new laws or even that you could be criminalized in future for actions you are taking now that are not currently illegal.

The Securities and Exchange Commission in the United States announced in 2019 that it was looking at overhauling the accredited investor rules. 'The current test for individual accredited investor status takes a binary approach to who does and does not qualify based only on a person's income or net worth,' said Chair Jay Clayton. 'Modernization of this approach is long overdue. The proposal would add additional means for individuals to qualify to participate in our private capital markets based on established, clear measures of financial sophistication' (SEC, 2019).

This initiative looks to be a sensible measure for more than one reason. Not only did the ICO boom illustrate the huge pent-up demand for access to higher-risk, higher-return investments, particularly among Millennials and Generation Z, but a quick glance at the disparity between returns on early-stage private tech company shares as compared to the shares that are available to the wider public on the Standard and Poor's Index illustrates why there is a growing frustration with the status quo. Instead of being grateful that the government is protecting them, those who are shut out of these opportunities feel that the highest rewards are being reserved for the elites.

Furthermore, the way accredited investors are categorized in the United States is something of a blunt instrument, based on wealth rather than acumen. This would theoretically mean that a 19-year-old heir or heiress with no financial experience would be judged as 'sophisticated' whereas a professional broker whose net worth did not yet meet this benchmark, yet who had extensive knowledge of investment products, would not meet the criteria. The new SEC proposals 'would allow more investors to participate in private offerings by adding new categories of natural persons that may qualify as accredited investors based on their professional knowledge, experience, or certifications' (SEC, 2019).

Congress versus Facebook

If one event illustrated the confusion of opposing political views on how to deal with the rapidly evolving innovation of digital currencies and money not issued by nation states, it was the hostile questioning of Mark Zuckerberg by many members of the US Congress, when he was called to testify on Facebook's plans for Libra on 23 October 2019. It is one of my personal bugbears that many people in government seem to have very little knowledge of – or interest in – technology. It is perhaps not reasonable to expect lawmakers to be programmers, but given that the digital world is so inextricably interwoven with our physical world, it is not unreasonable to expect them to educate themselves a little more, rather than repeatedly proving the aphorism that people tend to fear what they don't understand.

It is notable that unlike many issues that prompt a partisan response along party lines, strong views about digital currencies and the involvement of technology companies in something that is traditionally and uncritically viewed as 'government business' run across all shades of political thinking in the United States.

Some politicians are prepared to countenance the idea that the choice between allowing private innovation or consigning the United

States to a technological future in which it is left behind is a difficult one, including the Committee's lead Republican, North Carolina Rep Patrick McHenry, who warned that: 'American innovation is on trial today' (Kang, Isaac and Popper, 2019) and suggested that US lawmakers should be more concerned about China's growing influence than about US companies' expansion efforts.

'I have my qualms about Facebook and Libra, I do, and the shortcomings of Big Tech – there are many', said McHenry. 'But if history has taught us anything, it's better to be on the side of American innovation, competition and most importantly the freedom to build a better future for all of us' (Kang, Isaac and Popper, 2019).

Even the most die-hard Facebook critic would feel some sympathy for Zuckerberg as he faced a hostile committee, pointing out very reasonably that:

> If America doesn't innovate, our financial leadership is not guaranteed… As soon as we put forward the white paper around the Libra project, China immediately announced a public private partnership, working with companies… to extend the work that they've already done with Alipay into a digital Renminbi as part of the Belt and Road Initiative that they have, and they're planning on launching it in the next few months.
>
> (United States House of Representatives, 2019)

Instead of focusing on Libra, the hearing became mired in discussions about Facebook's politics, policing of speech and about the company's wider role in society, revealing a wider unease among politicians of all stripes about their inability to control new technologies. Zuckerberg suggested at one point that perhaps Facebook was not the ideal messenger for Libra, but the reality is that whoever had appeared before Congress with plans for private currency issuance would likely have been met with the same degree of suspicion.

Perhaps it is a sign of more restrictive regulation to come that Brad Sherman has been appointed new Chair of the subcommittee of the Financial Services Committee. Brad Sherman claimed that Libra may do more to damage the United States than the terror attacks of 9/11 (Price, 2019).

European challenges

Of course, the United States is far from unique in grappling with the treatment of cryptocurrency. Most large countries have been forced, albeit reluctantly in some circumstances, into releasing a statement defining how cryptocurrency is categorized not only to protect investors, but also to ensure that the correct rates of tax are applied. Whether cryptocurrency is classified as money, an asset or a commodity can have major impacts in terms of taxation, and crypto investors eye opportunities for this kind of tax arbitrage as carefully as regulatory arbitrage when deciding where to locate their companies. Table 11.1 shows how different and varied these approaches can be.

TABLE 11.1   Treatment of cryptoassets for regulatory purposes, by country

Country	Treatment of cryptoassets
Israel	taxed as asset
Bulgaria	taxed as financial asset
Switzerland	taxed as foreign currency
Argentina & Spain	subject to income tax
Denmark	subject to income tax and losses are deductible
United Kingdom	corporations pay corporate tax, unincorporated businesses pay income tax, individuals pay capital gains tax

SOURCE Library of Congress (2018)

Of course, the table above represents only a small part of a rapidly changing picture. Attitudes to new technologies and societal change can be transformed rapidly, and sometimes it only takes one influential person to voice their opinion before a dramatic shift in opinion takes place. The shifting stance of the ECB (European Central Bank) on digital currencies is a case in point. Outgoing ECB president Mario Draghi was openly critical of cryptocurrencies, denouncing them as 'not really currencies', adding: 'A euro is a euro – today, tomorrow, in a month – it's always a euro. And the ECB is behind the euro. Who is behind the cryptocurrencies? So they are very, very risky assets' (ECB, 2019).

In contrast, his successor Christine Lagarde has signalled a new openness to looking at the advantages digital currencies could bring. However, this does not mean that Lagarde, who has been openly critical of Bitcoin in the past, has undergone a Damascene conversion. On the contrary, she is looking at the evolution of corporate and banking coins such as Libra and JP Morgan's coin, and envisaging that they will take their place within a highly regulated system in which there may also circulate government cryptocurrencies. As managing director of the IMF (International Monetary Fund), she spoke at length about the pros and cons of state-issued digital currencies (Lagarde, 2018) but has also warned against unregulated currencies such as Bitcoin, arguing that they should not be allowed to 'shake the system'.

While some within the crypto community have welcomed Lagarde's appointment, viewing her as more open to innovative ideas than Draghi, the ECB has the unique problem that while it can introduce directives and potentially even develop its own currency, the individual countries within the eurozone are free to introduce their own legislation.

For example, while many European cryptocurrency and block-chain startups are based in Berlin, the German government has announced new legislation requiring any company involved in the custody of cryptoassets to hold a BaFin-issued banking licence. For more on the BaFin approach to virtual currencies, see BaFin (2019).

While this may sound uncontentious, and many companies have welcomed the regulatory certainty such a law will bring, it introduces potential complications around cases such as machine-to-machine digital wallets for utility tokens, of the type described in Chapter 3. If an auto manufacturer has to apply for a banking licence to allow token exchange in some future IoT business case, then this could potentially slow down innovation and drive smaller companies to friendlier jurisdictions.

In contrast, France's top financial regulator, the AMF, laid out new proposals in December 2019, which set out a licensing framework for companies offering digital asset custody. The new rules are very specific and – other than requiring participating crypto firms to provide certain information, such as their organization structure, a list of the cryptoassets which they intend to hold and a two-year business plan – lay down criteria such as multi-signature validation and a responsibility to compensate clients in the event of private keys being lost or misused. While the licence is not mandatory, France rules that all cryptocurrency firms operating within the country must be registered with the AMF to avoid money laundering.

A company called French ICO announced in December 2019 that it was going to take advantage of this voluntary licence arrangement in order to register to issue an ICO in 2020, which was an early test of the legislation (Cheng, 2019).

Colin Platt, who is based in France, is of the opinion that the French government's willingness to engage positively with digital asset companies is an indication of the opportunities they see for the technology, even if their enthusiasm is not necessarily matched by the enthusiasm of the incumbent financial companies:

> The French government has a much larger appetite to welcome crypto than French banks do. Part of that is for regulatory reasons, and part of that is just general business reasons. But the French government definitely sees an opportunity and wants to try to become very important in the ecosystem, which is great. Whether they'll be able to achieve it or not I don't know, but it's great to see them try.

The contrasting approaches of Germany and France, the two largest economies in the European Union, are an illustration that even within countries sharing a common currency, there can be significant cultural differences in their approach to digital assets. Besides there being different legal cultures in each country and region, there seem to be two general approaches to regulation: draw up new regulations for these new assets or build on top of the existing ones and work in an amend-only mode. The latter can often be faster as it is always easier in a political process to amend or reinterpret than to create new laws and regulations, as it is more difficult to create consensus for something new.

The UK regulatory approach

While there are countries that explicitly aim to appeal to crypto-currency entrepreneurs, as we will see later in this chapter, they usually tend to be smaller. Of the larger economies, the UK has been cautiously welcoming to the new technologies described in this book. Particularly in London, the Mayor's office has been supportive of blockchain conferences and initiatives.

Entrepreneur Helen Disney, founder of Unblocked Events and a prominent thinker in the blockchain space since 2014, welcomes the British government's approach thus far:

> In my view, it's the role of the government to create the right conditions or set the rules of the game. So, while I wouldn't necessarily want governments to be running their own blockchains, it's their role to make Britain a place where innovation is possible and where we can bring in new ideas and create new jobs. That will be a big role for the private sector, and I think the clear signal they can give in terms of the policy environment is that they want blockchain businesses or other frontier technology businesses to be in Britain, including potentially implementing public sector blockchain projects.
>
> One idea would be to create some kind of multi-disciplinary forum, not so much of a think tank but more of a 'do tank' where the government would say, 'Look, these are the kind of problems that we think need fixing. Are these possible with this technology? And if so can you give us some examples of how that could work?' Then the government can really understand what is possible with blockchain technology, and then potentially that could be public–private partnerships or private companies bidding for contracts or any other possible solutions to those problems.

This willingness to work in partnership with businesses rather than simply decreeing regulations from on high can be seen in the financial sector in the shape of the FCA regulatory sandbox. The FCA (Financial Conduct Authority) offers a scheme where one cohort of companies at a time are allowed to issue innovative products under supervision so they can test new ideas with the support of the authorities and without the fear of being prosecuted, for example, for offering unlicensed securities. The FCA explains the advantages of such an approach on their website: 'The sandbox provides access to regulatory expertise and a set of tools to facilitate testing. The tools include restricted authorization, individual guidance, informal steers, waivers and no enforcement action letters' (FCA, 2015).

Richard Crook, founder of LAB577 and former head of innovation engineering at Royal Bank of Scotland, also thinks that the regulators in the UK are getting it broadly right, especially in the area of settlements:

> They are very much on top of this. We learned very, very quickly in 2008 how much they know about the overall system. They may only know a little about a lot [of different things] but they certainly know the important pieces... we have always asked for better regulation later than bad regulation early, so in that respect it is exactly where they are sitting.
>
> What is important to recognize is that they are working towards their next-generation RTGS [real-time gross settlements system] and they [the Bank of England] have always said that as they go through developing this, they will bring in the new thinking around blockchain and distributed ledgers and tokens, and we expect that to be the case. So that is what we are watching.

Crook's point about 'better regulation later than bad regulation early' is a critical one. We have seen many times that it is uncertainty rather than regulations themselves that makes for a difficult operating environment. It is hard for companies to establish a headquarters, recruit staff and make future plans if they do not know whether they will be allowed under local laws to offer their current products in a year's time, or whether they will face problems with suppliers or banks because the latter fear falling on the wrong side of the law.

China and India: two different approaches

If the UK's regulatory approach is seen as a broadly helpful one, where there may not be quite as much freedom as some proponents of decentralized technologies would like, but where there is some certainty given, spare a thought for those companies operating in jurisdictions where the approach can range from welcoming to draconian – and can change with a single pronouncement from a leader.

In November 2019, few crypto observers can have failed to notice a temporary spike in the price of Bitcoin and notably, tokens with strong links to China, with VeChain (VET) and NEO posting strong 24-hour gains of 10 per cent and 13 per cent respectively. This followed an announcement by Chinese president Xi Jinping that he intended China to become a world leader in the field of blockchain. However, these gains swiftly reversed with further announcements clarifying that while China would push ahead with the use of block-chain technology to assist state record-keeping in areas such as fraud prevention and food safety and in launching a state-backed digital currency, to be known as DCEP, the government also fully intended to crack down on crypto exchanges. In late November the same year, at least five crypto exchanges were closed down, and investors were left scrambling to withdraw their assets to their personal wallets. The closing down of trading operations was accompanied by content bans on crypto-focused groups and discussions on social media platforms such as Weibo. Binance creator Changpeng Zhao's 2017 decision to move Binance out of China (Binance first relocated to Japan, and then announced a move to Malta) was a shrewd and prescient move.

If China's approach can be summed up, rather like that of the major banks back in 2015, as 'blockchain good, Bitcoin bad', then it is not the only big player among emerging economies to take this approach. The surge of interest in cryptocurrencies in India prompted the country's central bank, the Reserve Bank of India, to launch a draconian crackdown in 2018, when it banned banks from providing banking services to cryptocurrency businesses such as exchanges. 2019 saw a steady stream of exchanges leave the country, as there was now no longer a fiat on-ramp for customers. Indeed, a subsequent statement by a government panel in July 2019 brought further headaches for anyone in India involved in Bitcoin or other virtual currencies: the conclusion of the panel was not only that non-state currencies should be banned, but also that anyone found to be using or dealing in them should be subject to a jail sentence of up to 10 years. While these penalties have yet to be implemented, the legal uncertainty has meant that innovation in the country in this field has been stifled as entrepreneurs move to countries with more welcoming – or at least more certain – regulatory approaches.

Code as free speech

We saw in Chapter 10 how DeFi platforms and decentralized exchanges (DEXes) are pushing the boundaries of regulation simply because there is no geographically defined central entity for a jurisdiction to prosecute. When assets are traded on a network of computers that can be located in any country in the world, and there is no company in the traditional sense that operates these computers, it becomes challenging for governments to pin down exactly who is responsible for breaking financial services laws in a particular country. It is an often-cited argument that computer code is a form of speech and is thus, in the United States at least, protected by the First Amendment, which guarantees free speech. However, those who rely on this convenient get-out clause should be aware that the arm of the law is long, and governments can often find a way to chase down those who are responsible for activities they deem unacceptable.

Take, for example, the case of Zachary Coburn, who was fined $400,000 in 2018 by the Securities and Exchange Commission in the United States for running the EtherDelta website (SEC, 2018). While Coburn was not technically operating an exchange – EtherDelta was, in theory at least, a decentralized exchange operated by an Ethereum smart contract, rather than by humans – Coburn operated the EtherDelta website, which provided an interface for traders to exchange tokens via the EtherDelta smart contract, and was thus found to be responsible. Similarly, the controversial imprisonment of Ross Ulbricht in the United States for hosting a website, Silk Road, which was used to sell items for Bitcoin that are illegal in many countries, shows that there are limits to the legal defences that can be used when one writes code.

Because, unlike many tokenized enterprises, Bitcoin is truly decentralized, a government cannot close it down. Data can simply hop from one jurisdiction to another, or even into space. Some developers who believe in the importance of having a truly free, censorship-proof payment network have invested significant work in developing technologies that can help people send Bitcoin in areas where there is no internet, using a system called 'mesh networks', where small amounts of data hop from one person's device to another.

However, while the Bitcoin blockchain itself might not be under direct threat from individual governments, it is entirely possible in the future that governments might simply ignore the 'code as free speech' argument and seek to prosecute those who write code to enable others to interface freely with public blockchains, such as wallets, exchange software or privacy-enhancing software. This is a particularly dangerous road for governments to tread, as stifling innovations in privacy tech can also stifle innovations in security. The code that keeps governments out of individuals' private affairs also keeps out criminals who try to steal the same individuals' assets, and threatening software developers with penalties – or even prison time – for creating innovative technology seems to be a prime example of the law of unintended consequences.

The rules that Germany, in particular, is introducing in response to the Fifth Anti-Money Laundering Directive (AMLD5), reveals another possible unintended consequence of regulation. If your car, for example, contains a wallet that allows it to exchange mobility tokens with toll booths or other cars, or if you have a wallet on your mobile phone that allows you to transact with decentralized applications, or where the wallet is merely providing you with a gateway to assets held elsewhere, it may mean that the programmers of these wallets need to register for BaFin licences as financial custodians. Teana Baker-Taylor says:

> We're still waiting for some clarity around centralized dApps and wallet and providers of software – for example, you may have an app on your

phone that is a wallet that holds or secures your virtual assets, but you don't trade assets on the app and no one else has access to it, or has control of your keys. In this case, the company providing the app is simply a provider of software. What responsibilities do they have? It would be very difficult, if not impossible to regulate code.

Barney Mannerings, founder of decentralized trading software startup Vega Protocol, makes the point that regulatory authorities may find it more difficult than they think to strike the right balance:

The first thing people are going to learn is that these systems are very difficult to stop. It is human nature to want to engage in activities that are beneficial or interesting to them. And the second thing, which we seem to have to learn again and again, is the fact that cryptography is maths – and maths is extremely difficult to regulate. So, you can decide that you don't want everyone encrypting everything end to end but at the same time, you can't really stop them doing it.

And so, then you criminalize a whole set of activities, and you stifle innovation, and the result is that the money and the benefits of this innovation go elsewhere. So being successful at regulating in that way is actually probably a downside in the long run because it puts you behind everyone else.

I think different countries are coping better than others. The US has a real problem in that every regulator thinks they should regulate this stuff, but none of them regulate particularly well. I've heard interesting anecdotal stories of the Financial Crimes Enforcement Network in the US requesting that the SEC actually do a bit less regulation. Why? Well, the information that these agencies can get about cryptocurrency capital flows is actually very useful.

So even among regulators, they can disagree. Some of them think, 'Hey, I can see all these transactions – this is better than people using the US dollar', while others are thinking, 'Hey, look, these people are issuing unregulated securities and I hate this.' So even within the regulators, there is an inconsistent position.

Mannerings agrees that the UK position is broadly sensible:

The UK seems to be doing a little better than others in that they have been extremely slow to actually codify anything in law, which means that they are willing to tolerate some grey areas and lack of clarity now in the interest of getting things right in the long run. Of course, this comes with the cost that without that clarity there's a lot of uncertainty, which makes it riskier to build a business in this space in the UK.

Regulatory arbitrage

As we saw from Mark Zuckerberg's words to Congress, the dilemma for regulators arises from the conflict between the desire to prevent fraud and/or money laundering and losing competitive advantage. The risk of companies moving offshore or adopting less innovative business models depends on many factors, such as location and the ease with which entrepreneurs can move across national or state boundaries. For example, it is easier for a company to relocate from Idaho to Delaware or from Italy to Malta, than it is from China to Russia or India to Mexico. It is not just the specific laws that may affect a company's activities at a particular time: it is the whole philosophy of the government and their attitude to technical and financial innovation that can provide incentives or disincentives for relocation.

If an administration gives the impression that they do not know or care about technology, or that they are likely to behave in a manner that swings wildly between being supportive of new crypto ventures and ill-thought-out crackdowns, then this will see business moving elsewhere. While some crypto entrepreneurs of a libertarian mindset will simply choose the jurisdiction with the fewest laws and restrictions on what they can and cannot do, others will look for sympathetic legislation by policymakers who understand technology and economics and are focused on supporting growth while at the same time not overstepping international conventions, for example, concerning money-laundering.

While it is easy for governments to make welcoming noises and local regulatory authorities to draw up helpful frameworks, sometimes these are not enough in themselves. While Malta has been at the forefront of efforts to attract crypto businesses, companies that located there subsequently found difficulties in finding institutions who would provide them with banking services, and ended up having to open accounts with banks outside Malta. Similarly, in the UK, the intervention of the FCA has meant that it can still be difficult for crypto-associated companies to open business bank accounts. In contrast, the measured approach taken by Switzerland has paid off, making it a prime destination for companies dealing in digital assets.

While the importance of the financial sector to the Swiss economy has dropped slightly over the last few years – it was 9.1 per cent of the economy by value in 2018 (Swiss Info, 2019), a critical mass of traditional financial institutions and fintech startups, combined with an environment that encourages research and development, have resulted in a healthy ecosystem for crypto startups that goes well beyond regulating digital assets in a helpful manner. It is worth remembering that helpful legislation does not necessarily mean lax legislation. The latter can be problematic for companies, as it does not bring certainty. If overly loose regulation is later tightened dramatically, then it makes planning difficult. FINMA (the Swiss Financial Market Supervisory Authority) certainly wants to avoid any accusations that they are making life easy for scammers. In September 2017, FINMA closed down the issuers of the fake crypto-currency 'E-Coin' and liquidated the companies, for example.

Additionally, within Switzerland, the individual cantons (regions) have a great deal of flexibility to set their own taxes. This has meant that the municipalities with the lowest tax rates have been able to flourish and have created entrepreneurial microclimates where technology startups tend to cluster. The 800-year-old city of Zug, close to Zurich, has for this reason among various others become known as Europe's Crypto Valley, with such companies headquartered there as Bitmain, Dfinity, Bancor, Waves, Lisk, Aragon and Cardano.

What is notable about Switzerland's approach is that legislators are as open to Bitcoin as they are to cryptoassets issued by banks, or to smart-contract platforms. Visitors to Zurich can catch a tram emblazoned with the livery of Bitcoin Suisse and can purchase Bitcoin alongside their train tickets from automatic ticket machines in Swiss railway stations, while some districts such as Zug and Chiasso allow local residents to pay their municipal taxes in Bitcoin.

Individual cantons may have their own reasons and their own processes for welcoming cryptocurrency entrepreneurs, but one thing is for sure: Swiss legislators are not prepared to see this revolution pass them by, and in 2019 innovations came thick and fast, with SEBA, the cryptocurrency bank, being authorized to accept investor deposits, and FINMA allowing blockchain startups to apply for a FinTech licence that would let them handle deposits of up to $100 million (Beedham, 2019).

While it has been tempting for cryptocurrency businesses to shop around and opt to domicile themselves in the jurisdiction with the most permissive rules, this kind of regulatory arbitrage has become less appealing as countries bring their financial and money-laundering regulations into greater harmony with each other. The changes to German and French regulations mentioned above have been prompted by the EU's implementation of the AMLD5 (Anti Money-Laundering Directive), which was published in June 2018. One stated aim of the legislation was to bring EU countries into line with US laws, and while the detail of how each member state should implement the Directive is left to local lawmakers, it is expected to have major impact.

Obviously, not all countries are members of the EU or the Financial Action Task Force (FATF) but Teana Baker-Taylor makes the point that it is getting harder and harder to move outside the confines of regulation:

> Many jurisdictions are still assessing how to approach their digital asset regulatory frameworks. In other jurisdictions, frameworks don't easily harmonize with other jurisdictions. If national frameworks continue to differ, a regulatory arbitrage opportunity will remain. A classic example of this is when AMLD5 came into effect, there was a company based in the Netherlands who decided to move to Panama. Although Panama is not a FATF member country, it is part of a FATF working body in Latin America. And so at some point, unless Panama

wants to risk being added to the FATF Grey list, it's likely they too in time will enforce the FATF requirements for virtual assets. Eventually, the jurisdictions available to those who wish to operate outside the confines of regulation are going to start to become fewer and fewer. The more mainstream cryptoassets get, and the more money starts flowing through cross-border financial channels, the more scrutiny we're going to see applied.

Self-regulation and blockchain governance

Many people, especially within the subset of those who use Bitcoin for ideological reasons, would argue that the governments of nation states and their institutions have no business at all regulating truly decentralized currencies. If a currency is decentralized, goes their argument, then existing regulation should be sufficient to deal with it, but a decentralized proof-of-work blockchain is essentially self-regulating and its administration determined purely by market forces.

How true is this? In the case of Bitcoin, we have seen that it has proved remarkably resilient to takeover challenges, notably by those who advocate a move towards larger blocks in order to improve scaling on the main chain. The particular formula of incentives that were written into the original algorithms and reward miners for validating transactions has meant that the network has remained largely independent from the control of one individual or group of individuals, with its rewards for proof of work facilitating this independence.

Other incentive structures may – intentionally or otherwise – mean that this independence is moot, and that decisions about the future of a network may fall victim to the influence of particular interest groups. In these cases, it is extremely important to look at the human decisions that can influence how a blockchain works, and who may be the beneficiaries of the decision-making process that took place in the original design of the algorithms that make up the ledger's governance mechanisms.

Blockchain technology researcher and educator Citlali Mora Catlett points out that establishing the consensus mechanisms is crucial:

First of all, we have to find out who has determined the internal governance system. Of course, the first example I always present is Bitcoin, which is a pure peer-to-peer system in which everybody gets a say, everyone has a single voice. It is a democratic system in which everyone has the same amount of power.

And at the same time, you can also see blockchain networks arising like Tezos, for example, that has its own governance mechanism. What is very interesting to see is that not only is there the concept of the blockchain being peer-to-peer as a democratic system in which everybody gets to say something because of the consensus mechanism, but also seeing how democratic governance mechanisms are going to be established when it comes to updates and optimization of the network's protocol. Decisions around updates and optimization make up the internal governance of the project, and at the same time there is the external realm of governance, which involves actors from all different sectors and realms. So, you need a governance level that has to find policy and legal frameworks that will fit all of this technological innovation and possibilities for internal governance into a framework that works for everyone and doesn't end in a catastrophe.

Ian Grigg sees governance as a process that happens in a much wider context than in the blockchain layer alone:

> For example, exchanges are operating as financial institutions holding the value of the user and deploying it as per the user's instructions. That is a governance technique – it happens to be a very convenient way to bring together enough orders to allow mapping to occur efficiently, but fundamentally, exchange operators offer a governance layer for the mass of users out there that probably will have trouble managing a wallet on their phone or laptop... It's a recognition that there's no perfect system out there. There will always be governance to clean up the edges to take the system to a higher level.

The point about who has the power to define the governance of a blockchain or a currency when it comes to code updates or policy decisions is an important one. We have already seen how the decision to fork Ethereum following the DAO hack has caused controversy and dogged later developments and decisions about what and when to release to the Ethereum blockchain. Hence we can see that there are factors outside the control of national governments that can affect the development of the way a particular blockchain or crypto-currency evolves, and that decisions that are taken by software developers or entrepreneurs can conflict with decisions made by policy-makers at state or national government level years later.

Much of this chapter has painted a picture of government policy as a reactive force rather than a proactive force, acting retrospectively to contain and restrict these innovative activities. However, Teana Baker-Taylor paints a more positive picture, pointing to new opportunities to communicate information about transactions that are far more efficient than those currently used. She cites the example of Zcash, a privacy coin that we mentioned in Chapter 3:

> Zcash has a shielding capability so one can choose to shield their transaction. But actually, only 1 per cent of all Zcash transactions today have ever enabled the shielding functionality. It's a privacy coin because it has privacy features, but people just aren't using these. However, interestingly, the same capability that allows one to shield their transaction would also enable them to send all of the information required by FATF with their transaction. So there's a token out there that already has the building blocks of compliance within it.

She suggests that rather than being a regulatory problem, cryptoassets could end up being the conduit for huge improvements in the way governments track the flow of money around the world:

> We catch 1 per cent of laundered money – just 1 per cent of $1 trillion. Wouldn't it be great if we could take a step back and pragmatically take a look at the potential solutions that could be derived from this new technology, and work to see if there could be a better way to identify money laundering as opposed to just applying the same systems we have in place that, quite frankly, don't do a great job?

In this chapter, we have talked about governments putting in place structures to monitor and regulate what companies and individuals within their jurisdictions are doing with digital currencies. But many governments are going a step further and looking at launching their own virtual money. In the next chapter, we take a closer look at how these central bank digital currencies will work.

References

BaFin (2019) Virtual currency (VC). Available from: https://www.bafin.de/EN/ Aufsicht/FinTech/VirtualCurrency/virtual_currency_node_en.html (archived at https://perma.cc/LQT3-HNTH)

Bartlett, J (2019) Cryptoqueen: how this woman scammed the world, then vanished, *BBC News*, 24 November. Available from: https://www.bbc.co.uk/ news/stories-50435014 (archived at https://perma.cc/C8H7-QA5E)

Beedham, M (2019) Switzerland gets another 'Bitcoin bank' that holds cryptocurrency for customers, *The Next Web*, 13 November. Available from: https://thenextweb.com/hardfork/2019/11/13/bitcoin-swiss-bank-greenlight-regulators/ (archived at https://perma.cc/K9AC-F4DA)

Cheng, Y (2019) French regulator grants its first approval for an initial coin offering, *The Block*, 20 December. Available from: https://www.theblockcrypto. com/linked/51252/french-regulator-approves-utility-token-ico (archived at https://perma.cc/6WRN-EB32)

ECB (2019) European Central Bank, Twitter, 8 May. Available from: https://twitter.com/ecb/status/1126172693739577344 (archived at https://perma.cc/V859-WVRW)

FCA (2015) Regulatory sandbox, Financial Conduct Authority, 11 May. Available from: https://www.fca.org.uk/firms/innovation/regulatory-sandbox (archived at https://perma.cc/Y6EH-SQ6T)

Kang, C, Isaac, M and Popper, N (2019) Facebook's Libra charm offensive meets bombardment on Capitol Hill, *Irish Times*, 24 October. Available from: https://www.irishtimes.com/business/technology/facebook-s-libra-charm-offensive-meets-bombardment-on-capitol-hill-1.4061290 (archived at https://perma.cc/ZJ25-RSHE)

Lagarde, C (2018) Winds of change: the case for new digital currency, IMF, 14 November. Available from: https://www.imf.org/en/News/ Articles/2018/11/13/sp111418-winds-of-change-the-case-for-new-digital-currency (archived at https://perma.cc/59PS-55T9)

Library of Congress (2018) Regulation of Cryptocurrency Around the World, June. Available from: https://www.loc.gov/law/help/cryptocurrency/world-survey.php (archived at https://perma.cc/EJQ6-Y4YE)

Price, R (2019) US Congressman Brad Sherman says Facebook's Libra cryptocurrency 'may do more to endanger America' than 9/11, *Business Insider*, 17 July. Available from: https://www.businessinsider.com/representative-brad-sherman-facebook-libra-911-2019-7 (archived at https://perma.cc/8B3H-P4MR)

SEC (2018) Administrative Proceeding File No. 3-18888, 8 November. Available from: https://www.sec.gov/litigation/admin/2018/34-84553.pdf (archived at https://perma.cc/QX86-QYB5)

SEC (2019) SEC proposes to update accredited investor definition to increase access to investments, 18 December, Available from: https://www.sec.gov/news/press-release/2019-265 (archived at https://perma.cc/B3DS-42US)

Swiss Info (2019), Switzerland's financial sector losing importance, 1 April. Available from: https://www.swissinfo.ch/eng/gdp_switzerland-s-financial-sector-losing-importance/44865968 (archived at https://perma.cc/2JMP-SCAH)

United States House of Representatives (2019) Committee on Financial Services, 23 October. Available from: https://financialservices.house.gov/uploadedfiles/hhrg-116-ba00-wstate-zuckerbergm-20191023.pdf (archived at https://perma.cc/5HRC-PHJJ)

Verity, A (2018) Fraud ringleader jailed over 'boiler room' scam, *BBC News*, 14 September. Available from: https://www.bbc.com/news/business-45521235 (archived at https://perma.cc/JE8U-K8YR)

12

State-issued digital currencies

That the world is rapidly becoming a cashless society is no longer in doubt. From European and US economies where the majority of the population pays with either contactless bank cards or mobile phone apps, through China where it is simply not possible to spend cash in many cities without using WeChat, to East African countries where telecom-based payment systems like M-Pesa reign supreme, the world's population is putting its money where its mouth is and declaring that physical coins and notes are no longer sufficient for economic interactions in a post-internet age. Not only does physical cash no longer meet the needs of a mobile, networked population, but it is costly for governments to produce and track. In the UK alone, there was £69,841 million circulating in banknotes, and the cost of ensuring these notes are counterfeit-proof, replacing them when they are damaged and getting them into circulation is considerable. This is for banknotes alone: when the cost of minting and circulating coins is also taken into account, the cost rises still further.

Even though cashless payments are rising exponentially in popularity, many people still prefer to use cash. Taking the UK as an example, although the proportion of payments made in cash fell from more than 60 per cent in 2006 to 28 per cent in 2018, the ratio of cash payments is still 1:3. There are various reasons why people might prefer to use cash: some people find it easier to stick to a budget when faced with the reality of handing over notes and coins; others do not necessarily trust banks and prefer to keep their money in hard cash where possible, despite the risk of theft or loss; and perhaps most importantly, using cash confers privacy and means that your bank does not have to know that you are spending your own hard-earned money on something that may be legal but which, for whatever reason, you may feel reflects badly on you.

However many people might like using cash, it is likely that we will see its demise in modern economies within the next 10 to 20 years, and hygiene factors prompted by the Covid-19 pandemic have hastened this. Sweden is predicted to be the first country in which cash will no longer be used routinely. Jonas Hedman, Associate Professor at the Department of Digitalization at the Copenhagen Business School, predicts in his paper 'Going cashless' (Hedman, 2018) that by March 2023, although notes and coins will still exist, Swedes will no longer be able to use them for everyday purchases: 'We arrived at this date through our research in which we surveyed 750 Swedish retailers. We studied their cash management costs and the decline of cash in circulation in Sweden. We found that when cash transactions fall below 7 per cent of the total payment transactions, it becomes more costly to manage cash than the marginal profit on cash sales.'

While this may seem to run contrary to the principle that the krona is legal tender in Sweden, contract law takes precedence, and as long as the retailer displays a sign that cash is not accepted, the customer can be regarded as having entered into a contract with the retailer.

The prevalence of cashless payments in Sweden has made it an ideal testbed for a transition to a central bank digital currency (CBDC) but despite this, the central bank (Riksbank) is not rushing into this project without careful consideration. The Riksbank announced in December 2019 that it would partner with professional services company Accenture to pilot an initial technical platform for the e-krona, built on Corda, and a user interface that would encompass payments via cards, mobile phones and wearables. The initial contract was for a year, but the Riksbank is prepared to extend the project in its test environment for up to seven years, and cautions that this project does not represent a firm commitment that the e-krona will even be issued.

Another interesting CBDC project is the Central Bank of the Bahamas' 'Project Sand Dollar'. Analysts curious to see how the pilot works and what implications it may have for larger economies wishing to implement their own CBDC may be disappointed by the modest scope of the project. Initially proposed in order to promote financial inclusion across the whole Bahamian archipelago, the Sand Dollar is supposed to have spin-off benefits such as allowing residents to make digital payments, regardless of their banking status; reducing merchant fees for digital payments; and bringing the estimated $1 billion of hoarded cash back into the economy. However, Central Bank Governor John Rolle insists that the Sand Dollar is not a cryptocurrency or a stablecoin: it is purely a digital version of the existing paper currency, and residents will be limited to keeping a wallet balance of $500 (the Bahamian dollar is pegged one-to-one with the US dollar). Thailand and Cambodia are other countries with well advanced plans for CBDCs.

Bank of England Working Paper 605

Of course, the idea of state-issued digital currencies is not new. While other countries have been launching, or preparing to launch, their own CBDCs, the Bank of England has in some senses been ahead of the game. Back in mid-2016 the bank released a Working Paper (Barrdear and Kumhof, 2016), which laid out the possible macroeconomic effects of a CBDC in normal economic times. The authors, John Barrdear and Michael Kumhof, suggest that some degree of decentralization is desirable for the sake of resilience, but they are agnostic about how that should be achieved:

> In this paper we define 'digital currency' as any electronic form of money, or medium of exchange, that features a distributed ledger and a decentralized payment system... There are several ways in which such a decentralized system could be implemented. A central bank could maintain all of the copies of the ledger itself, several public institutions could maintain copies for each other, or private sector agents could be involved in collaboration with the central bank.

Among the benefits they ascribe to moving away from a traditional currency issuance model towards a CBDC are a reduction in monetary transaction costs, greater insight for policymakers into interconnectedness in the financial system and improved economic stability. Risks include those associated with the transition to a new and untested system, the possibility of a bank run in the transition period, and the potential effect on exchange rate dynamics.

This was not the first time a digital currency was discussed in the context of the UK: in February 2016, George Danezis and Sarah Meiklejohn from UCL published their paper 'Centrally banked cryptocurrencies' (Danezis and Meiklejohn, 2016), describing in some detail how a CBDC might work in practice. They dubbed their fictional currency RSCoin, and noted that:

> RSCoin... provides the benefit over existing (non-crypto) currencies of a transparent transaction ledger, a distributed system for maintaining it, and a globally visible monetary supply. This makes monetary policy transparent, allows direct access to payments and value transfers, supports pseudonymity, and benefits from innovative uses of blockchains and digital money.

Given that thinking around CBDCs has been taking place in the context of the UK for some years now, the fact that the Bank of England has not yet announced a transition to a digital currency system – or even a pilot study – should not be taken as a rejection of the ideas discussed in Working Paper 605. The publication of such a paper does not signal either a recommendation or a rejection of a particular idea. Rather, it is a detailed risk assessment of the pros and cons of such a system, if applied to any large economy.

Richard Crook, LAB577 founder, refutes any suggestion that the Bank of England is behind the curve when it comes to CBDCs, or indeed any similar innovations in the payments space:

> When the Bank of England published Working Paper 605 in 2016, it was advanced and ahead of its time. It certainly led the other central banks in thinking about these things, but just because they haven't

implemented this does not mean that they are lagging. They simply put out a working paper that says these are the macro benefits if we were to do this, but the benefits were countered by the risks to the stability of sterling... So, it's totally unfair to think that the UK regulator is in any way behind.

How a government cryptocurrency would work

While the mainstream media have been quick to compare government-issued virtual currencies with Bitcoin and similar crypto-currencies, it is important to point out that in the case of a national currency, the validating nodes would remain under the control of the government's monetary authority, and thus the money supply would remain at the discretion of policymakers rather than being a straight-forward function of supply and demand.

Any form of money issued by a state that is not backed by an asset such as gold or oil, but whose supply expands and contracts according to the calculations of economists, is a fiat currency, whether this is represented by notes and coins, or values in a ledger. The validating nodes that would govern the creation of money and the transactions to and from individuals' and businesses' digital wallets would need to agree with each other, but proof of work would not be necessary to prove the consensus between the nodes, as all the nodes would be under the control of the issuing authority. There would be no incentives for the nodes to participate, as this would not be a public network that anyone could join. Access to the network would be strictly limited to nodes owned and run by the government for this purpose, or potentially to trusted partners in the major banks.

In the case of supranational financial institutions such as the ECB, the responsibility for issuing digital currencies would lie with the central bank, rather than individual national governments. Under the leadership of Christine Lagarde, the ECB has indicated a readiness to accelerate preparation for a digital euro, and in December 2019 published a paper to address some of the privacy concerns that could be raised by individuals' use of such a currency.

China's Digital Currency Electronic Payment project

China has been working on its blockchain-powered digital currency for at least the last five years. Contrary to rumours that had been circulating earlier, the currency is not backed by gold, but is instead under the control of the Central Bank of China. The new currency has features that enable it to be exchanged by mobile phone (via NFC) even where there is no internet coverage, and will eventually be available to the entire population, even those without bank accounts. It has been rolled out as a pilot in Shenzhen, Xiongan and Chengdu, where it can be used for transportation, healthcare and other goods and services.

As the only digital currency to have the status of legal tender in China, its adoption is guaranteed, especially when combined with firstly, the readiness and enthusiasm of the Chinese population to use digital payments and secondly, the powers of compulsion that the Chinese government appears prepared to wield in order to ensure its success. In many areas of China, tourists were already finding by 2019 that it was impossible to use cash, and merchants were only prepared to use WeChat Pay or Alipay, so it seems that there is no cultural barrier to transitioning to a digital payment system.

The rollout of the new currency has been planned in two stages: during the first phase, DCEP (Digital Currency Electronic Payment) will be distributed to commercial banks affiliated with the central bank, in the same way that physical yuan is distributed. The second phase will be targeted towards the general public, with DCEP being rolled out to consumer payments companies Tencent (WeChat Pay) and Alipay, to be passed on to their retail customers. To ensure nationwide adoption, it has been mandated that all businesses that accept WeChat Pay or Alipay must be prepared to accept DCEP or lose their business licence.

Later in the chapter, we will explore the implications of state digital currencies for individuals' privacy, already being explored by the ECB as mentioned above. The type of data that will be available to the Chinese government as a consequence of moving from physical yuan to DCEP is enough to give any privacy advocate pause for thought.

Some analysts, however, remain upbeat about DCEP, seeing it as a harbinger of crypto acceptance worldwide. In an opinion piece for CoinDesk, 'Sovereign powers could be key to mass crypto adoption' (Zurrer, 2019), Dialect founder Ryan Zurrer states:

> While Western crypto purists continue to point to concerns over privacy and surveillance of the DCEP, this is an overly simplistic evaluation in my opinion. I am confident Chinese ingenuity will lead towards a myriad of relatively seamless bridges between high-privacy crypto-networks and the regulated DCEP. I estimate the DCEP most directly impacts Chinese demand for Tether and other stablecoins going forward.

Implications of state digital currencies for individuals

When one considers the potentially seismic consequences, for both governments and individuals, that would follow a move towards an entirely digital money supply whose generation was determined by a ledger, it is hardly surprising that progress has been slow. Once the genie is out of the bottle, this is a change that would be difficult – if not impossible – to roll back, and along with the undisputed benefits and efficiencies for governments and businesses, it brings with it the likelihood of a fundamental reassessment of money itself and of our relationship with it.

Let's first look at what it might mean for individuals. As we mentioned right at the beginning of this chapter, one of the primary benefits of using cash in the form of notes and coins is that we have anonymity. Perhaps this is not true anonymity, as in order to transact in person, one needs to meet in a physical location and in societies such as the UK where there is a high degree of surveillance in public places, it is unlikely that one could, for example, withdraw a large amount of cash from the bank and then drive, walk or take public transport to deliver this cash for criminal purposes without at some point being captured on a CCTV network. Criminal activity aside, for normal people going about their daily business, cash payments involve a trade-off between a convenient and instant payment method that they know will be accepted and the risk of losing the cash, either from carelessness or by theft.

Both governments and businesses would prefer individuals to use electronic payments rather than cash, as a cash payment is one that does not yield useful data. Businesses value electronic payments just as they prefer customers with loyalty cards to customers without, as it helps them gather data over time and target particular offers or behavioural incentives to induce us to spend more money with them. Most people have heard the distressing story of the teenager in the United States whose family discovered her unplanned pregnancy when the household began to be targeted with special offers for baby and pregnancy products, based on the purchases she had made in-store. Despite this story and others like it hitting the headlines on a regular basis, it seems individuals are happy to part with a large amount of their own data in exchange for convenience. Hence moving to a system where cash payments ceased to become an option would enable those who benefit from gathering data to ensure that no purchase remained unmonitored.

It is easy for governments to sell their populations the idea that this is a good thing. Take, for example, the principle of compliance with taxes. Those who abide by the laws of the state in which they reside and pay their taxes diligently resent those who do not. Many governments, including the UK, have attempted to highlight the case of self-employed workers who allow their customers to pay them with cash and then do not declare all they have earned, so they can avoid paying their full tax liability. Sometimes, such workers will offer a lower rate to the customer in exchange for a payment in cash, with the unspoken implication that by colluding in this way, both supplier and buyer will benefit from not having to pay tax. Recent campaigns have reminded householders, at least in the UK, that such collusion is illegal and that they can be found liable if they have helped the small-business owner evade tax. The aim of the campaign is to capitalize on people's disapproval of this behaviour, and to make such tax evasion as socially unacceptable as, for example, smoking in a small room full of young children. Hence it is easy to see how a government might sell a move to digital-only payments to its population on the basis of fairness.

Similarly, in countries that have welfare programmes to help people who are unemployed or otherwise unable to engage in gainful employment, governments often use the tactics of division and social disapproval in order to prevent fraudulent behaviour, sometimes running advertising campaigns to encourage neighbours to report those whom they suspect of working while claiming social benefits, for example. Populist newspapers and individuals posting on social media sites are also quick to criticize benefit recipients who are perceived to spend their payments on 'unworthy' or luxury items such as cigarettes, alcoholic drinks or television subscriptions. The US government issues food stamps, for example, to certain groups of recipients in order to enforce such behaviour.

This is where a move to digital currency becomes an issue of freedom and human rights, and enters an arena where governments should tread carefully. If the majority of the population agrees that desirable behaviour such as eating healthy food and avoiding alcohol and cigarettes is the moral responsibility of those in receipt of payments that have been raised by taxing their fellow citizens, then if a government offers a way to enforce this behaviour, it is likely to become a vote winner. Digital money that is registered on a block-chain-type network can easily be made programmable, and once the idea of programmable money exists, particular payments can be targeted for specific purposes. Thus, recipients of state funding could be coerced into healthier habits by issuing them with electronic money with particular properties, which could not be used for apparently undesirable purposes. This might be a popular move from a taxpayer's perspective, but it would strike at the heart of individual freedoms and would open the door to even more intrusive measures, as well as presumably leading to a healthy black market as welfare recipients tried to barter goods or use non-state cryptocurrencies to buy what they really need.

While targeting benefit recipients is an easy populist win for any government seeking to divide and rule its population, people who vote for such measures should be aware that they are not immune to similar coercion. The field of behavioural economics that relies on 'nudges' rather than legislation to encourage people to behave in a socially desirable way may no longer rely on such prompts when a blunt instrument such as programmable money is at their disposal. What could possible examples of this be? All governments that have any kind of public health system would like to reduce the costs of medical care, and one of the most efficient ways to do this is to encourage one's population to follow healthier habits, such as smoking and drinking less, eating less processed food and taking more exercise. The private sector already encourages such behaviour via programmes offered by insurers where customers can receive a fitness tracking wearable and win incentives such as cheaper gym membership if they meet certain activity targets.

While some consumers are already uneasy about the intrusion into their private lives, others enthusiastically embrace the opportunity to save money. So far, so good, as these are voluntary schemes.

What would be the implications if governments began to target their populations in the same way, only not on a voluntary basis? Imagine a regime where your digital pound or dollar or euro bought you a certain quantity of alcohol at the normal price but once you had exceeded the weekly, monthly or annual threshold that government medics deemed to be healthily acceptable, the price per unit of alcohol increased in order to influence your behaviour? This sounds far-fetched now, but it is hard to imagine policymakers turning down the opportunity to meddle in this way once technology makes it possible.

Consider, too, the dystopian potential when a social credit system of the sort that is currently being rolled out in China is combined with an overarching state digital currency with no cash alternative. If you have been engaged in activities, whether criminal or political, that mean you fall short of the ideal behavioural standards demanded by a state of its citizens, it would be easy for the government to limit your activities by restricting your ability to buy airline or even train tickets, while leaving your ability to buy food and other essentials untouched. Much of the talk of the benefits of government digital currencies has focused on financial inclusion and ensuring that even those who are too poor to be profitable bank customers are not excluded from modern life, but it is also crucial to bear in mind that having a financial system that enables cheap and easy targeting of particular policies towards particular individuals could be invasive to the point where it is positively harmful.

Macroeconomics and global affairs

As we have seen throughout this chapter, while CBDCs share some attributes with public cryptocurrencies such as Bitcoin, such as the ability of the holder to sign transactions with a cryptographic key, and with all records being written to one ledger that may be distributed over multiple nodes, there are many differences. Probably the main difference is that while a cryptocurrency such as Bitcoin has a value that is determined entirely by supply and demand and the cost of the effort miners are prepared to expend in order to generate new Bitcoins, a currency issued by a government is issued on the same basis – by fiat – as the notes and coins we are used to seeing today. This means that the supply of a government currency is entirely at the discretion of the government that issues it, just as it is today.

Macroeconomic models allow economists and policymakers to decide when and how they should release additional cash into the economy in order to stimulate and dampen demand. Money supply is one way, along with interest rates and various tools, of influencing how the economy behaves. The decisions governments take are far more than theoretical: they have a direct impact on the way people live their lives, as seen by the trend over recent decades to reduce interest rates on savings – even to the extent of leveraging negative rates – in order to dissuade people from hoarding money and encourage them to spend and borrow instead. This has led to much misery for people who are dependent on fixed incomes, such as pensioners, and has also encouraged other individuals to take on more debt than is sustainable or sensible. As we saw in Chapter 1, if governments get this delicately balanced formula wrong, it can lead to outright disaster such as the hyperinflation seen in Germany in the 1930s or more recently in Zimbabwe and Argentina.

While state digital currencies might be extremely helpful to policy-makers by providing much more detailed data from a single source than they currently have access to, and by providing real-time statistics rather than having to wait for retail associations and banks to collate their data over a period of months, it is also easy to see how having such powerful tools at their disposal could lead them into a false sense of security and lead them to make harmful decisions, or those that limit the freedom of their populations to make sound economic choices. Let's look at the case of Japan as an example.

Since the 1990s, Japan has been locked in a deflationary spiral that means wages have been falling, consumers are unwilling to spend and companies are reluctant to raise prices. However aggressively the government has tried to kickstart the economy with successive rounds of quantitative easing and tax cuts, all attempts have failed. A combination of demographics and a pro-savings, anti-borrowing mindset has meant that any attempt to put money directly into the wallets of individuals has resulted in that money being saved rather than spent. Japan has one of the world's most rapidly ageing populations, which means that people tend to be more resistant to fintech innovation and the idea of taking on debt, and the idea of saving money instead of spending it has become a national obsession to the point of television programmes being based around thrifty practices. Once a way of thinking like this becomes part of a country's culture and identity, it is very difficult to change people's minds. Even a move to negative interest rates would be unlikely to get a population out of the savings habit – the net result would undoubtedly be an increasing proportion of the country's banknotes being stored under mattresses.

A state digital currency would potentially solve this problem, albeit at the cost of removing people's freedom to do what they wanted with their money. Imagine if you airdropped what is popularly called 'helicopter money' to the population, not in the shape of a tax cut, which means that any surplus cash could be squirrelled away in savings accounts or under the aforementioned mattresses, but in the shape of a credit to people's digital wallets. Add a programmable element to these payments and it would be possible to ensure that the government's largesse could only be spent in a particular way: for example, for the purchase of domestically produced consumer goods that would reflate a particular part of the economy.

Of course, most free-market economists would argue that while such tinkering might make the eyes of interventionist policymakers light up, it could have catastrophic unforeseen consequences – and not just for the economy whose leaders were prepared to go down this path. Notice in the paragraph above, the phrase 'domestically produced'. There is nothing more helpful to a government, particularly one seeking re-election, than a boost to local producers – whether these are farmers or manufacturers – from a surge of new orders. The dramatic rise in global standards of living that has happened over the last few decades has happened at least in part because of global trade flowing more or less freely, as a result of various free trade agreements being negotiated, and the creation of various trading blocs around the world. Protectionism poses a huge threat to these living standards, though it may not feel that way if you are one of the workers in a developed country who has experienced losing their job to cheaper manufacturing processes overseas. While individuals have undoubtedly suffered hardship from global competition, overall economies are stronger for it, and the recent trade war of words between China and the United States has threatened to cast a pall over this prosperity.

Economists generally regard consumers as making rational choices overall, and while appeals to patriotism – 'Buy British', for example – can influence behaviour to a limited degree, once the disparity in price or quality becomes too great, most consumers will disregard emotion and default to rational behaviour. If politicians want to boost demand for local produce, there is only so much they can do by appealing to the population's hearts rather than their heads.

Now imagine a scenario where, just as in our hypothetical example about helicopter money being targeted towards lagging sectors of the economy, digital payments could be targeted towards domestic production in certain areas of the country that happened to be marginal voting areas.

While digital fiat money can offer policymakers and government economists unparalleled access to information and tools for tinkering with the economy in a highly targeted way, anyone who is concerned about individual freedoms and the smooth functioning of the world financial system should keep a weather eye on how governments intend to use their new superpowers.

It is not just protectionism that is a concern in this brave new world of state virtual money. While we are used to the idea that war bubbles away under the surface of the world, ready to emerge at any moment, the real war is happening in the fields of technology and economics. As we saw Mark Zuckerberg warn in his testimony to Congress about Libra, the United States faces a significant risk if it decides to close down avenues of innovation and let countries such as China steal a march in the field of digital currencies. The US dollar is one of the most powerful tools in the history of the world for influencing global politics. Over decades, the use of financial sanctions against countries perceived as rogue states has brought about regime change and, with varying degrees of success, influenced the behaviour of other world leaders who the US leadership sees as threats. With the dollar having been the world's de facto reserve currency for the duration of the last century, this is a powerful tool that the United States would undoubtedly not want to lose.

Yet, as Kenneth Rogoff points out in his fascinating article 'The high stakes of the coming digital currency war' (Rogoff, 2019):

> Just as technology has disrupted media, politics, and business, it is on the verge of disrupting America's ability to leverage faith in its currency to pursue its broader national interests. The real challenge for the United States isn't Facebook's proposed Libra; it's government-backed digital currencies like the one planned by China... a widely used, state-backed Chinese digital currency could certainly have an impact, especially in areas where China's interests do not coincide with those of the West.

It is not simply China whose plans for a digital currency have rattled cages in the United States. Mark Carney, former governor of the Bank of England, has spoken several times of the advantages of having digital currencies that are not specifically tied to the US dollar, and this prompted a prominent former Fed official to speak out against Carney's comments. 'Not having one currency that you can basically price things and have a deep market in, that makes life much harder for the global economy', said Simon Potter, the former executive vice-president and head of the markets group at the Federal Reserve Bank of New York (Greifeld, 2019).

Some within the United States see a fully digitized dollar as the way to prevent other virtual currencies from taking over. J Christopher Giancarlo, former Chair of the Commodity Futures Trading Commission, who hit the headlines in 2018 for his positive remarks about Bitcoin, has partnered with Accenture and cryptoassets to create the nonprofit Digital Dollar Foundation, which will conduct research into converting the dollar into a fully electronic currency based on blockchain technology. And at the World Economic Forum in Davos in January 2020, a group of central banks from countries including the UK, Japan, eurozone members, Sweden and Switzerland announced a new working group, co-chaired by ECB board member Benoît Cœuré and Bank of England Deputy Governor Jon Cunliffe, to investigate use cases for CBDCs.

However, Ian Grigg stresses that central bank digital currencies may not make sense for countries where payment systems are already efficient and cheap, and points out that from some central banks' point of view, the risks may well outweigh the benefits. 'The problem is that actually CBDCs are not competitive to existing payment rails… SEPA is very efficient if you're in mainland Europe, for example. We already have a good, fast payment system.'

If there is little advantage to be gained, there may be a considerable downside risk if an alternative payment system emerges that has the potential to divert money from the existing banking system, he explains:

> If you take payments away from the bank and you show people a better alternative, what that means is people will take out their deposits from the bank and put them into these payment systems. But this reduces the deposit base of the banks, which naturally shrinks the banks and means

that the issuance of loans and so forth also has to shrink. Every central bank that has analyzed this realizes if it allows an independent system to challenge the banks, that is actually going to shrink the economy because the banks are the ones who put the loans out there which finance the economy.

However, Grigg uses the example of Kenya to demonstrate that central banks are more than willing to support innovation and new payment systems in the right circumstances, for example where payment systems are less well established:

> The great success of M-Pesa [the mobile-phone payment network] was that you didn't need a bank – you just needed a phone... the central bank in Kenya ran a very strong interference campaign to stop the banks killing M-Pesa and to stop the Western OECD-led AML-KYC system from coming in and killing M-Pesa. So consequently M-Pesa was able to reach an entire country before those huge barriers were loaded against it. And this was a deliberate policy of Kenya's central bank.

Hence we see that while the decision of any particular country to issue its own CBDC is an internal one and should be weighed up carefully in terms of macroeconomic risk, the overarching dangers of being too late to the party are also considerable in our financially interconnected world.

While CBDCs are undoubtedly a huge part of our financial future, one would need a crystal ball to attempt to predict where the revolution in digital currencies will take us over the next 10 years and beyond. In our final chapter, let's take a speculative look at what may possibly be in store for the future of digital currencies.

References

Barrdear, J and Kumhof, M (2016) The macroeconomics of central bank issued digital currencies, Bank of England, 18 July. Available from: https://www.bankofengland.co.uk/working-paper/2016/the-macroeconomics-of-central-bank-issued-digital-currencies (archived at https://perma.cc/7ZJR-PG4M)

Danezis, G and Meiklejohn, S (2016) Centrally banked cryptocurrencies. Available from: http://www0.cs.ucl.ac.uk/staff/G.Danezis/papers/ndss16currencies.pdf (archived at https://perma.cc/XR84-QN3D)

Greifeld, K (2019) Ex-Fed official takes aim at Bank of England's crypto proposal, *Bloomberg*, 25 September. Available from: https://www.bloomberg.com/news/articles/2019-09-25/ex-fed-official-takes-aim-at-bank-of-england-s-crypto-proposal (archived at https://perma.cc/KHT3-XZ6G)

Hedman, J (2018) Going cashless: what can we learn from Sweden's experience? *Knowledge@Wharton*, 31 August. Available at: https://knowledge.wharton.upenn.edu/article/going-cashless-can-learn-swedens-experience/ (archived at https://perma.cc/5MLD-3MSX)

Rogoff, K (2019) The high stakes of the coming digital currency war, *Project Syndicate*,11 November. Available from: https://www.project-syndicate.org/commentary/global-battle-for-digital-currency-supremacy-by-kenneth-rogoff-2019-11 (archived at https://perma.cc/28JW-NHGG)

Zurrer, R (2019) Sovereign powers could be key to mass crypto adoption, *CoinDesk*, 30 December. Available from: https://www.coindesk.com/sovereign-powers-could-be-key-to-mass-crypto-adoption (archived at https://perma.cc/3UDX-6KK6)

13

Future digital currency trends

Since the Bitcoin white paper was published in late 2008, it is astonishing how quickly innovation in the cryptocurrency and alternative finance sector has progressed – and also how quickly ideas that once seemed revolutionary have been assimilated into the mainstream. Perhaps it is useful to wrap up the book by considering what the financial landscape might look like in the short to medium term and picking out some of the macro themes that currently hint at what may lie ahead.

For the Bitcoin network itself, one of the most-awaited software upgrades is an improvement proposal called Taproot, which will add smart contract-like functionality to Bitcoin transactions and also allow for multiple signatories, while keeping the details of such transactions private (Van Wirdum, 2020).

As Bitcoin itself becomes more mainstream, while those who value truly censorship-proof money will still continue to manage their own security and hold their own private keys, we should expect to see the parallel growth of custodian services for those who would rather pay others to take the risk, especially at an institutional level. Insurance schemes such as that offered by the Winklevoss twins' Gemini exchange will undoubtedly become the norm, especially if more institutional money is to flow in.

The Lightning network and other second-layer solutions

We discussed earlier the trade-off between the volume of transactions on a network and the security of the network, noting that the Bitcoin and Ethereum blockchains are not capable of processing anywhere near the number of transactions that a traditional payment system such as Visa can process. Despite various people having argued for bigger block sizes to accommodate more transactions, this is not necessarily seen as the only or best solution – as we discussed in Chapter 7.

Instead, there has been much development work done recently on projects that do not write every single transaction directly on a public blockchain itself, but which allow transactions to happen away from the main chain and only write the end result to the main blockchain.

The Lightning network, which is active on Bitcoin, is a great example of this, and allows for cheap and almost instantaneous payments, hence its name. It works by allowing individuals to set up a private channel to which they allocate sufficient Bitcoin to cover payments between the two participants, which are recorded in the channel only, rather than the blockchain itself. The channels have an unlimited lifespan, and are only closed when at least one participant initiates a closing transaction. At this point, the transaction is written to the blockchain and the funds that were deposited to open the channel are returned to the users. While users are warned to send only small amounts of cryptocurrency using Lightning channels, many are hopeful that the principles underlying so-called second-layer solutions like Lightning will be a way forward, enabling many more transactions to happen on the Bitcoin network.

It is also possible to use Lightning payments on the Litecoin blockchain, while Ethereum has its own second-layer solutions in development. An innovation called Optimistic Rollup allows large numbers of transactions to be aggregated, included in a 'rollup block' and published to a smart contract on the main Ethereum network, thus vastly increasing throughput.

Ethereum 2.0 and the DeFi explosion

Ethereum's ambitious roadmap, which is intended to move the network away from an energy-intensive proof-of-work incentive system towards proof of stake, will continue to be controversial, with more questions over governance and who makes critical decisions that will determine the future of the network. Will Ethereum really reach its potential as the world computer its creator, Vitalik Buterin, envisaged it to be, or will other competitors emerge to take its place?

Much depends on what the Ethereum network is ultimately used by, and who has a financial interest in it. Ethereum is now several years on from the days when it was primarily used for games such as CryptoKitties and minting tokens for ICOs. If the DeFi ecosystem lives up to its early promise, then we can expect to see an explosion of new financial products, while its huge dependency on Ethereum as the primary DeFi platform, potentially hosting billions of dollars' worth of value in synthetic assets and derivatives, becomes ever more of a risk.

Expect, too, to see other blockchains used for DeFi purposes, and for open-source software to allow individuals to create constellations of novel financial products, untrammelled by the conventional thinking of slow-moving corporates. Progress is moving at a dizzying pace, and 'yield farming' is the new buzz word as speculators seek higher and higher returns. Governments will have to be careful about over-regulation, but the more forward-thinking will focus on how to harness this great creative energy in a positive direction.

The Convergence Stack

Whatever promises cryptoassets hold for the future, one thing that is guaranteed is that they will not operate in isolation. This book has already described use cases in the automotive and energy sectors, as well as media, gaming and art, and the use of digital currency as the native money of the internet means that this technology will fit into a whole plethora of complementary innovations, such as artificial intelligence, virtual reality and that overused term, big data. From an investor's point of view, it can be helpful to think in terms of what Outlier Ventures call the 'Convergence Stack', which they characterize as: 'a set of privacy-protecting, peer-to-peer, and open-source technologies that will decentralize the cloud and unbundle the internet platforms'.

In other words, in order for many other revolutionary technologies to reach their full potential and transport us into a world of connected devices and unprecedented opportunity and networking, digital currencies will need to be a critical part of this jigsaw.

If the future really is to be decentralized, expect there to be resistance from the incumbents – at least until they can figure out how their own revenue models will work. December 2019 saw an outcry from the Ethereum community when Google's PlayStore suddenly and without warning banned the popular MetaMask tool, a Chrome extension that allows users to interact with Ethereum decentralized applications in the browser and incorporates a wallet for payments. Google initially stood firm on their decision, citing their ban on tools that mined cryptocurrency, even after an appeal pointed out that MetaMask does not actually mine anything. After a week, MetaMask was reinstated, but analysts were quick to point out this centralization as a point of weakness and to call for decentralized alternatives. In the same week, YouTube (also owned by Google) removed a swathe of cryptocurrency videos, many of them simply educational. Again, some were reinstated later.

As the big tech companies continue to develop their own tokenized economies and digital currencies, expect to see more of this type of pushback, either initiated by the corporations themselves or driven by governments who want their own digital currencies to be the only game in town. It is at this point that the existence of truly censorship-proof technologies such as Bitcoin will be crucial.

Interoperability and sidechains

Governments may want their own digital currencies to be the only money circulating within their state borders, but when Bitcoin's genesis block was mined, a Rubicon was crossed. A technology now exists that allows us to make verifiable payments without the intervention of trusted third parties, and in a world where consumer choice is everything, we should expect to see bridges between networks and other innovations that make it possible for consumers to move funds seamlessly between different types of money, whether these are CBDCs, corporate tokens issued by banks or large tech companies, or genuine cryptocurrencies.

Development also continues on sidechain-based networks such as Liquid, developed by Blockstream, which allows for the fast, secure movement of funds and for the issuance of new digital assets. Major exchanges and wallets such as BitMEX, Huobi, Xapo, OKCoin and Bitfinex already use Liquid, which acts as a secondary blockchain on which corresponding value exchanges can occur without every single transaction being recorded to the main Bitcoin blockchain. While these networks allow for fast and cheap transactions, it is important to remember that in the case of Liquid, it is a private network based on trusted entities, rather than a fully decentralized platform like the Bitcoin network itself.

However, with the potential for cross-chain swaps of assets such as Tether, expect to see more sidechain action in the future.

Redefinition of money

Above all, as these digital currencies proliferate among the general population, we should expect to see a new understanding of money emerging. We will see a realization dawning that the old system of notes and coins issued by governments is not only a poor fit for our modern, digital world, but that it was a one-dimensional blunt instrument that was unable to reward us for our efforts, labour and attention in an accurate and targeted manner.

After all, money is simply something that allows us, like some kind of magical machine, to move value across space and time. At first, we created this magic with notes and coins, and then some kind of clumsy digital representation of these notes and coins. As we power through the 21st century towards a future where humans talk about establishing colonies on Mars, where vehicles become autonomous and where medical treatment is tailored to our genes, it is likely that many babies born today will never have the need to use a banknote or a coin. We are moving inexorably towards a tokenized future, and to navigate this fundamental shift in our understanding of how we transfer value, we need to have the knowledge and tools to ensure that we make the right choices about the sort of future we want to live in.

References

Van Wirdum, A (2020) 2020 and beyond: Bitcoin's potential protocol upgrades, *Bitcoin Magazine*, 6 January. Available from: https://bitcoinmagazine.com/articles/2020-and-beyond-bitcoins-potential-protocol-upgrades (archived at https://perma.cc/V6QX-HD3H)

INDEX

CPSIA information can be obtained
at www.ICGtesting.com
Printed in the USA
JSHW011118130422
24891JS00011B/432